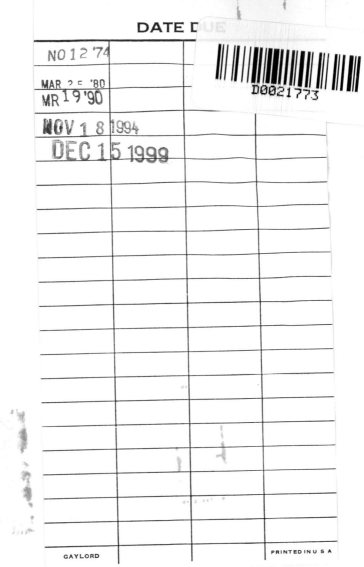

AFFIDAVITS OF GENIUS

KENNIKAT PRESS

NATIONAL UNIVERSITY PUBLICATIONS

SERIES ON LITERARY CRITICISM

General Editor

EUGENE GOODHEART

Professor of Literature, Massachusetts Institute of Technology

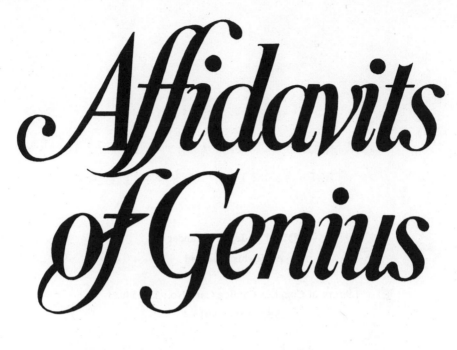

Affidavits of Genius

EDGAR ALLAN POE AND THE FRENCH CRITICS, 1847·1924

JEAN ALEXANDER

1971

NATIONAL UNIVERSITY PUBLICATIONS
KENNIKAT PRESS • PORT WASHINGTON, N.Y. • LONDON

Library of Congress Catalog Card No.: 79-154033

ISBN 0-8046-9015-4

Published by

Kennikat Press, Inc.

Port Washington, N.Y./London

PREFACE

Edgar Allan Poe is the most difficult of American poets to assess and place in historical perspective, for he can be evaluated in two literary orders, American literature and world literature. In American literature, Poe is eclipsed by his contemporaries, Thoreau, Emerson, Whitman, Hawthorne and Melville, and is studied largely for his historical importance in the creation of the modern short story. His international reputation, however, rests less on the short story than on poetry; this international life began at almost the time that his American life ended. At the same time that the American legend of the drunkard and the talented weakling was being formed, another more heroic legend was germinating in France. The result, for the modern student, is a bewildering, contradictory double identity for Edgar Allan Poe.

This duality has fascinated scholars and critics in both Europe and America, and it has been all the more compelling because three of the men who prolonged Poe's life were major French poets. Students of Baudelaire, Mallarmé and Valéry— as well as literary historians—have asked why French literature in the nineteenth century was influenced so long and so deeply by a writer whom American critics disdain. Much valuable research has been done by French scholars, particularly by Léon Lemonnier, Emile Lauvrière and Célestin Pierre Cambiaire, and illuminating critical studies have been written on Poe's esthetic theories in relation to those of Baudelaire and Mallarmé.

The historical facts are ascertained without much difficulty. Poe was introduced to France by two separate plagiarisms of his

The Murders in the Rue Morgue, which resulted in a lawsuit involving the two newspapers in which the plagiarisms were printed. The notoriety caused by the lawsuit not only led one of the journalists involved in the plagiarism to write an introductory essay on Poe, but also brought Poe to the attention of other translators and probably to the attention of Charles Baudelaire. From 1852 until his paralysis, Baudelaire identified himself with the American, studied his work intensely, translated his stories, adopted his poetic theory, and played the role of John the Baptist in his own literary circles. He tried to force Poe on the French literary public as a saint, a martyr in the cause of art. His challenge was accepted in a way lively enough to make the cause notorious and to fix Poe in the symbolic role Baudelaire had designed. After the death of Baudelaire there was a temporary lull in public interest, for the Parnassians who liked Poe were not disciples but simply quiet admirers, as poets usually are, with no reason to engage in combat for him. But the Symbolists, looking back to Baudelaire as well as forward to their own literary revolution, returned Poe to the prominence Baudelaire had given him. With the end of Symbolism, Poe's power in French literature diminished and he became what he had long been in America—a writer to be placed in proper historic perspective.

There is no dispute about the facts, but there is less agreement in interpreting them. The American critic asks himself why the French poets, whom he admires, were devoted followers of an American poet whom he cannot admire. If, like Patrick Quinn or T. S. Eliot, he considers the possibility that his own evaluation may be at fault, he may look for the virtue that the French poets have found. T. S. Eliot, re-evaluating, came to the conclusion that the French poets did not know English adequately, and that they were responding to myths of their own, creating Poes who were significant for them individually. Thus Baudelaire created Poe as the ill-starred poet; Mallarmé created Poe as the supremely subtle artist in language; Valéry created Poe as a theoretician. Eliot implies that the American Edgar Allan Poe did not deserve the good fortune to be recreated by French poets.

If there is accord among contemporary English and American critics, it is on this basis, and many of the new French studies of Poe (those of Marion, Arnavon, and Boussoulas, for example) are intent upon shattering the nineteenth-century myth and deflating Poe's French reputation. Because the French are taking the American attitude before America has quite digested the previous interpretation of French writers, another review of Poe's reputation seems advisable.

This study was undertaken with a double purpose: first, to present the evidence, and second, to consider it reciprocally, reevaluating Poe by the French commentary and the French commentary by Poe's work as understood by an American. Since most of the documents showing Poe's reception in France and his status in the nineteenth century are not available to American students, a judicious selection of essays enables them to weigh various critical interpretations against the evidence itself. For several reasons the collection is not exhaustive. Commentary on Poe often occurs in essays on other writers; some statements are too brief or too uninformed to warrant inclusion; some repeat the evaluation of authors who write better or carry more weight, and can represent an entire school of thought. The collection is, therefore, a carefully chosen one; selections were made on a double basis: first, to represent all the attitudes toward Poe from his introduction in France in 1846 to Valéry's 1924 essay, and second, to represent the writers who are most significant either in their own right or for their part in establishing Poe's reputation.

The ordinary study of a reputation is concerned with fluctuations in attitude toward a given writer; such a study is its own justification and is self-contained in that it usually does not claim to add to our understanding of that writer's work or the work of other writers. In exploring his field, the researcher is most interested in the statements of critics. However, Poe's reputation in France poses a different kind of problem. The criticis reluctantly concerned themselves with Poe because the poets persistently forced him into the literary magazines. Instead of finding a trend of criticism, we find trends of literary discipleship. For this reason, the collection is largely composed of essays by literary men. All but Forgues, Pontmartin, Delacroix, and Etienne were novelists or poets. I have deliberately imposed this limitation because one of the hypotheses of my study is that the professional critical mind necessarily begins to perceive literary patterns later (sometimes a hundred years later) than the creative mind. The critics who were the contemporaries of Baudelaire and the Symbolists did not perceive the tendencies and aims of literature as clearly as did the poets who were writing it, giving poetry new forms and direction; similarly, the critics failed to understand Poe's importance. The present rapidly growing list of books and articles indicate that critics and scholars are still deliberating Poe and his relation to nineteenth-century French literature. Therefore, the professional critics of the nineteenth century are represented only enough to reveal their basic attitude, which varied more in moral persuasion than in literary interpretation, and to show the grounds of their conflict with the creative writers.

While the French essays have been selected to give the full scope of criticism from 1846 to 1924, this study has a narrower range. It will not attempt to recapitulate the work of Célestin Pierre Cambiaire or Léon Lemonnier, whose formidable documentation provided a point of departure for my study. For an outline of Poe's influence on detective fiction, and the short story in general, the works of those two scholars should be consulted. Cambiaire's principal purpose is to trace Poe's influence in French literature, pointing out themes, plots and techniques for which Poe is the source. Lemonnier's major work (*Edgar Poe et la critique francaise de 1845 à 1875*) is largely a study of Poe's reputation. The more recent study by Patrick F. Quinn (*The French Face of Edgar Poe*) is less documentary; it is more concerned with critical than with creative reactions to Poe, and his final purpose is limited almost entirely to re-evaluation of Poe's stories.

The discussion introductory to this collection, on the other hand, attempts to clarify some of the basic motives and conflicts revealed in the early French essays, and in doing so it must introduce issues that are tangential to a purely literary discussion and alien to the art for art's sake tag attached to Poe by some critics. In fact, a sense of a highly refined esthetic thinker in the man Poe is readily combined, by a number of French readers, with a sense of highly dangerous social, economic, and philosophic issues associated with both Poe and America. That unlikely combination of intellectual challenges continues through the period of Symbolism. Thus the essential image of Poe as the ill-starred poet was far from being a sentimental icon; it contains the modern problems of cultural decadence, national character and philosophic revolt.

CONTENTS

AFFIDAVITS OF GENIUS

INTRODUCTION

THE OUTLAW

From our present perspective, as we review the life of Edgar Allan Poe, we may pass severe judgment and condemn him for weakness, for neurosis, for egotism; or we may pity his misfortune or his incomplete genius. An American tends to form one of these emotional images. If Charles Baudelaire had not decided to recast the destiny of the American poet, French opinion might have been similar. But Baudelaire did not see Poe as a deviant, defeated individual to be pitied for his weakness. Paradoxically, he cast him in the role of outlaw and saint, and he insisted on quarreling publicly about it. He tried to make an important niche for Poe in literature, and he succeeded. In order to understand the first phase of Poe's French reputation, we must examine Baudelaire's motives and his purpose.

According to his friend Asselineau, Baudelaire became acquainted with Poe's work in 1847, through the translations of Mme Meunier.[1] But not until nine years later did he finally make Poe the center of a bitter literary quarrel. Before 1852 there had been scattered references to Poe, but aside from the essays of Baudelaire and Forgues they were very brief and superficial; Poe was an interesting oddity. Suddenly, in 1852, Baudelaire launched a campaign to force the literary world to accept Poe on Baudelaire's terms.

Attracted by the originality of Poe's mind, Baudelaire had been desultorily translating Poe's tales for publication in the magazines, but there is a marked difference between his intellectual

5

interest during the late 1840s and his fervor during the 1850s. Although he stated more than once that he translated and defended Poe so persistently because Poe resembled him, imitating his own thoughts twenty years before they occurred,[2] Baudelaire developed none of the passionate intensity of his famous Poe essays until after he had seen the 1850 edition of Poe's works and knew something of Poe's life and death. In short, his partisanship was aroused not exclusively by the artist, but by the man and his destiny.

If we compare the preface he wrote in 1848 for his translation of the "Mesmeric Revelation" with the essays and prefaces he began writing in 1852, we find a revealing change. In the laconic preface to "Mesmeric Revelation," almost insolent in its brusqueness, Baudelaire limits himself entirely to a discussion of the originality and philosophic inclination of great novelists. Poe is one of several authors mentioned, but the particular qualities of his techniques and ideas are not analyzed. He receives scarcely more attention than Diderot and Balzac; all of these men illustrate the tendency of great writers to recognize and exploit their own natures and to fly free of accepted philosophic opinions.[3]

In contrast, the 1852 preface to "Berenice" claims that Poe will eternally be praised for "his preoccupation with all the really important subjects, those which are *alone* worthy of the attention of an intelligent man: probabilities, disorders of mind, conjectural sciences, hopes and calculations concerning the subsequent life, analysis of the eccentrics and the pariahs of this sublunary life, definitely symbolic buffooneries."[4] In the same year, the first version of "Edgar Allan Poe, sa vie et ses ouvrages" appeared in the *Revue de Paris* with this closing paragraph:

> I would gladly say of him and of a particular class of men what the catechism says of our Lord; "He has suffered much for us." . . . We could write on his tomb: "All you who have ardently sought to discover the laws of your being, who have aspired to infinity, you whose rebuffed feelings have sought a frightful relief in the wine of debauchery, pray for him. His corporeal being, now purified, floats among the beings whose existence he glimpsed; pray for him who sees and knows: he will intercede for you."[5]

The sharp contrast in tone between the 1848 preface and

those of 1852 is enough to send the reader in search of causes. Between 1848 and 1852 Baudelaire had studied Poe thoroughly, and he had also undergone a personal disillusionment. Although in the end he was to say, "When I have inspired universal disgust and horror, I will have conquered solitude,"[6] in 1848 he still hoped for the world's recognition as an intellectual leader. It must be admitted that, because of his irony, Baudelaire's intentions are not always self-evident. However, the famous episode on the barricades of 1848[7] can be cited to support the contention that he was in earnest when he dedicated his preface to the *Salon de 1845* to the bourgeois. He accepts the commercial middle class as the great political power and addresses it as a benevolent guide:

> You are the majority—by number and intelligence;— thus you are power—which is just.
>
> Some are learned, some are proprietors; a shining day will come when the learned will be proprietors, and the proprietors learned. Then your power will be complete, and none will dispute it.[8]

Even when his attempts proved ineffectual and his pride was offended by public and official indifference, Baudelaire retained his idea of government by intellectual aristocracy, but his attitude became less benevolent. Describing the pleasure he took in seeing a republican cudgeled by a policeman, he commented: "Thus philosophers and critics should mercilessly scourge the artistic apes, the emancipated workers, who hate the power and sovereignty of genius."[9]

In his journal, Baudelaire speaks of thwarted ambitions, and in his 1852 essay on Poe he speaks of thwarted sensibility. Neither his ambition nor the specific thwarting agent can be known with certainty, but references in his journal and elsewhere lead us to assume that, having been prevented from playing the part he saw as legitimately his (that of intellectual legislator) Baudelaire intended to make himself otherwise known as a power. He reversed his tactics and chose to campaign by radical defiance. The previously quoted list of subjects proper for an intelligent man could not have been more completely opposed to a traditional list of literary subjects or to bourgeois values. In short, Baudelaire was not content to be obscurely eccentric or quietly original like the men he had listed in his preface to the "Mesmeric Revelation"; he declared his own eccentricity as a universal law.

Personal disappointment and bitterness led Baudelaire to construct a perverse theory concerning the relationship between the superior individual and his society, and he sought a symbol to embody his ideas. Out of his social nihilism and his stubborn estheticism he had already created one symbolic figure to resist society before he encountered Poe. The dandy was his first idol. The dandy was English in origin; he combined aristocracy, cold beauty and elegance, intellectual control, and complete alienation from society. He was stoic, enduring whatever the world meted out to him, triumphing by his refusal to be moved. His motivation was not entirely esthetic; it was also moral. "Whether these men are called fops, beaux, lions, or dandies, all come from the same source; all share the same nature of opposition and revolt; all are representatives of what is best in human pride, the need . . . to combat and destroy triviality."[10] If Baudelaire's description had stopped here, the dandy would have been reasonably harmless, but Baudelaire makes it clear that the dandy is also criminal. The dandy is the "final burst of heroism in an age of decadence," and Baudelaire's list of heroes concludes with Balzac's immoralists and criminals, Vautrin, Rastignac, Birotteau.[11] "One could found glorious empires on crime," Baudelaire suggests in his journal.[12] The dandy was Baudelaire's persona: an elegant, mysterious, self-possessed enemy of society.

Yet when Poe became known, Baudelaire turned all his will to the exaltation of the new hero. Although Poe displaced the dandy, the two were not totally dissimilar. On the most superficial level, Poe was the epitome of dandyism because he could preserve his elegance in the midst of sickness, poverty, persecution, and death. In tracing Poe's background, Baudelaire made aristocrats of his ancestors; in describing Poe's appearance, Baudelaire emphasized his good looks, his intelligence, his distinguished bearing. Most of all, Poe's superior spirit and the consequent audacity of his independence from the patterns of society provide a thematic pattern running through all of Baudelaire's narrative, description and analysis.

Both Poe and Baudelaire, however, were men of imagination and intelligence, not criminals, and Baudelaire found that Poe represented his intentions and desires more fully than the dandy could. Poe was Baudelaire's double, for Poe was a poet, he lived in misery, he fought an inexorable vice, he was persecuted and betrayed by his literary world, he was a lone spirit and he was an original and astonishing experimenter. When Baudelaire thrust Poe into every conversation or quoted "The Raven" or "The Black Cat" it was as efficacious for him as a campaign for the recognition of his own genius. His power was strengthened by another and more productive brain.

These two factors determined the intensity and fidelity of Baudelaire's discipleship, and they provide what appear to be very personal and limited motives. No other poet has made a fetish of dandyism in the sense that Baudelaire used the term, and no other poet has had such fraternal resemblance to Poe. However, Baudelaire intended to immortalize Poe, and he did so by making Poe represent the poet—that is, the artist in general—as Baudelaire understood him from his own fate and from his interpretation of the literature and the society of the nineteenth century.

In the history of literature and literary criticism there is much analysis and elaboration of the nature of poetry, its function, its use, its limits, and its techniques. But not until the flowering of Romanticism is there any question about the nature and function of the poet. The Romantic hero was a poet, literally or figuratively, and frequently the poet was his own hero. These heroes were solitary, emotional and misunderstood, soaring above the comprehension of the society in which they existed. They were often rebels—politically, socially and morally: Byron, for a time, represented the poet. Not all Romantic poets, of course, were at odds with society; Wordsworth and Hugo were very respectable giants in their maturity. Yet by 1856 a pattern of alienation and grievance had been sufficiently established to make it a concern of literary journalists. In the year before Baudelaire's preface to the *Histoires extraordinaires* appeared, for example, Armand de Pontmartin castigated French novelists and held up English and American novelists (including Poe) as models. These writers were admired not for their dogmatic attitude, which the critic deplored, but for their loyalty to the life of their society:

> The thing that is desirable is that our novelists, instead of forming a separate caste and an object of uneasy curiosity for the average man, and instead of finding themselves constantly forced either to portray their own world, which is not the true or good one, or to travesty real society, which they do not know, should become, as in England and America,

the habitues and confidants of the family, the authorized
painters of acceptable manners, feelings and characters; and
that they should live on equal footing with their public, their
originals, and their models.[13]

While Pontmartin was obviously mistaken in his judgment of Poe,
he indicated fairly clearly that the place of the writer in society,
and his attitude toward it, constituted a cultural problem. From
the point of view of society, the writer was becoming delinquent.

From the point of view of the writer, society was ignorant
and tyrannical. In his 1852 essay Baudelaire cites the bitter statement of Alfred de Vigny that the poet has no place in any kind
of republic or monarchy. De Vigny had pleaded the case of the
artist even more vividly and explicitly than that. "But the case,
great heaven! the case pending in your court," he had protested
in his 1834 preface to *Chatterton,* "is the perpetual martyrdom
and the perpetual immolation of the Poet."[14] This statement, and
even its vocabulary, prefigure the theme of Baudelaire's essay,
"Edgar Allan Poe, sa vie et ses ouvrages."

A modern student is unlikely to read any of Baudelaire's
essays on Poe unless he has more than a casual knowledge of
Baudelaire. His first and perhaps only reaction is one of baffle-
ment. These essays are unlike any of Baudelaire's other literary
criticism and unlike any literary essay written by a man with
Baudelaire's reputation as a critic. One has only to examine Baudelaire's essays on Hugo, Banville, Gautier, Leconte de Lisle,
Petrus Borel, Marceline Desbordes-Valmore, in order to find the
littérateur, the self-possessed man of letters who judged urbanely,
beyond the reach of his own passion. Although he sometimes in-
dulged in anecdote, as in the essay on Gautier, or personality, as
in the essay on Desbordes-Valmore, these techniques were reasonable and relevant to the literary work. In one passing reference to
Poe in the essay on Banville, Baudelaire approached dispassionate evaluation of Poe more nearly than in either of the two important essays devoted entirely to him. "Byron in poetry, Poe in
poetry and the analytic novel—one, in spite of his prolixity and
verbiage . . . the other, in spite of his irritating conciseness—have
admirably expressed the blasphemous aspect of passion. . . ."[15]

The first installment of "Edgar Allan Poe, sa vie et ses ouvrages" in the *Revue de Paris,* and half of the second installment,
are devoted entirely to Poe's life and environment. It is an ardent
tract, with much of the energy and excess of the pamphleteer.

While it is permeated with violent sympathy, it is loosely organized and diffuse. The material is an uneven patchwork of various bits of information and misinformation on Poe[16] and of Baudelaire's own conceptions of the role of the artist in society. A long eulogy of Balzac distracts attention from the central idea. Baudelaire has presented Poe as a martyr, and has specified that he represents the poet in his eternal sacrifice to society; he has accused society of perverting the poet and then punishing him for the perversion; he has made Poe as tragic as Orestes pursued by the Furies; finally, he has made him a sanctified intercessor for the pariah. There is something wild and raw and unreasoned in this essay, yet it is moving as the poem "Benediction" is moving.

Whether because of its exaltation or its incoherence, Baudelaire acknowledged the article's weakness in a letter to Poulet-Malassis: "I've had a long article on a great American writer published in the *Revue de Paris*. But I'm really afraid the first time will be the last. My article is a disgrace."[17]

The second essay entitled "Edgar Allan Poe, sa vie et ses ouvrages," which serves as preface to the *Histoires extraordinaires,* makes it clear that the implied apology in the letter to Poulet-Malassis was not an apology for the content or the theme of the 1852 essay, but rather for its manner of presentation. The second essay is much more skillfully written; its organization is tighter and its details all serve a single powerful intent, but the original thesis has not been abandoned. Again he insists that society is the enemy of genius and the conflict is irreconcilable because art emerges from the very elements and configurations of life that society considers dangerous or unwholesome.

Three specific points would inevitably antagonize a conventional reader: (1) the conception of the artist as martyr; (2) the justification of vice by its artistic product; (3) the glorification of the abnormal (what Baudelaire underscores as the *exceptional in the moral order*). Not only does this program undermine society by rejecting traditional morality and by the blasphemous raising of idols—propositions so outrageous that a public might be inclined to discount them—but it also places society in an untenable position in more trivial and specific ways. Naturally, it was the gadfly attack that hurt (for example, "the rude apprenticeship of genius in this base world," and the suggestion, in the word *jongleur,* that the poet *plays with* the world). The latter idea, with

all its overtones of superiority, detachment and exploitation, was
to rankle critics for years.

Clearly, in this preface Baudelaire was not trying to make
Poe respectable or acceptable. He was exalting Poe by methodically denying all the conventional and public values. While the
1852 essay passed with virtually no comment, the 1856 essay
aroused immediate and sometimes violent opposition. In a review
of the *Histoires extraordinaires* in *L'Assemblée nationale,* Armand
de Pontmartin mingled qualified appreciation of Poe's stories and
rebuttal of Baudelaire's contention that the poet is the victim of
his society. In effect, although he put on an air of impartiality,
Pontmartin countered Baudelaire's argument of society's indifference with his own argument of individual responsibility, and opposed good sense to imagination. The review is reasonably good-
humored, but it falls into Baudelaire's trap by stating society's
case against the artist.[18]

Barbey d'Aurevilly's reply was not so mild. He began by
calling Poe's tales the only kind of originality possible in the decadence of a society, and went on to associate America with all
things decadent, incidentally aiming occasional thrusts at Baudelaire. He attacked Poe for "moral mutism," "satanism," "manic
notion of God" (especially Poe's pantheism, his replacing soul by
sensation, and his white and black magic). Baudelaire was attacked for his "criminal apology for suicide" and his tacit acceptance of the satanic and sensational in Poe.[19] Since Poe's tales had
been appearing for two years in the magazine Barbey d'Aurevilly
wrote for, one inevitably questions that the tales themselves appeared dangerous, decadent, or satanic before he read Baudelaire's
preface. But his review of the *Histoires extraordinaire*s was intended primarily as a rebuttal of Baudelaire's argument; therefore, he opposed Baudelaire's martyr with his own symbols—
America and Bohemia. From the first, there is no question that
Baudelaire is being censured. "Although it is always dangerous
to say to the imagination, 'Listen to me. I am going to amaze
you' . . ." is a direct reference to Baudelaire's first critical comment
on Poe; moreover, Baudelaire's penchant for astonishing people
was well known.[20] When he quotes the famous impressionistic passage in Baudelaire's preface ("No man has recounted more ma-
gically the exceptional in human life and in nature—the burning
curiosity of convalescence; the season's end, full of unnerving
splendor . . ."), then brands the sum of impressions as *material-*

istic, there is no doubt that Barbey d'Aurevilly was striking out at a type of literature, and its French exponent, through Poe.

This detailed summary of Barbey d'Aurevilly's response is presented in order to show more clearly what Baudelaire was trying to do and to what extent he succeeded. Although Barbey d'Aurevilly tends toward vituperation in his journalism and is not notable for kindness or broadmindedness, he is by no means stupid, unimaginative or timid. Bold and colorful in exposing the underlying issues, he is an opponent worthy of Baudelaire. In reply to the challenge of pariah poet, he countered with the accusation of decadence. While Baudelaire was occupied in trying to create a hagiolatry in art, Barbey d'Aurevilly saw the social and political implications clearly and expressed his opinion with his customary flourish:

> We who do not believe that Art is the principal end of life nor that esthetics should one day rule the world do not think the loss of a man of genius a great deprivation. On the other hand, no man is excused from being a useful moral being. . . .

In spite of Barbey d'Aurevilly's powers of invective, Baudelaire was the victor in that literary encounter, for his opponent intensified and strengthened Baudelaire's own strategy. His first essay had been calculated to shock society,[21] to present de Vigny's rather flaccid martyr more graphically and more powerfully. Baudelaire had greater psychological insight than de Vigny—or perhaps only greater insight into the conscience and the unconscious —and he showed the poet's immolation to be spiritual as well as physical. The Poe that Baudelaire described was the union of the poet and the criminal. Society was to blame for the criminal element; if society insisted on vitiating its superior specimens, then they would take their rationale and their art from the very vice or disease society had given them. Since Baudelaire himself had deliberately placed the modern poet among eccentrics and pariahs, declaring the domain of the abnormal to be his creative world, accusations of satanism, depravity and religious and social heresy could only make Baudelaire's point more forcibly. Not only did Barbey d'Aurevilly intensify the conflict between the individual and society and between art and morality, but he also removed the question to a level on which it took on vast importance. By posing the question of cultural decadence, stating that Poe was the only kind of writer possible in a decadent civilization, he magnified Poe's stature as a symbolic figure.

What Baudelaire has done to the Poet is now evident. From his Romantic predecessors in England and France he inherited a lofty vision of the superior constitution and destiny of the poet; he inherited a tragic vision of the poet's defeat through society's vulgarity, indifference and malignancy. However, the poets who were heroes of Romanticism did not satisfy Baudelaire. Poe is both similar to and different from the other heroes cited by one of Baudelaire's opponents: Chatterton, Hégésippe Moreau, Gérard de Nerval. Since the fictional Chatterton created by Alfred de Vigny had come to represent the poet, it is informative to compare him to Poe; Chatterton was a highminded young man, but decidedly meek, gentle and pure. If de Vigny's drama reveals hostility between the artist and the bourgeois class, it was almost totally one-sided and it was more contemptuous than fearful. Society crushed the poet almost without bothering to look. The cases of Nerval and Moreau are similar: Moreau was a reclusive, melancholy dreamer, and Nerval was a visionary innocent. But Poe was not a meek cliché, either in reality or in Baudelaire's imagination. Baudelaire could not endure to be the object of the kindred feelings of pity and contempt, and he was not content that the poet should suffer quietly without disturbing society. In one of his prose poems he compares his Demon with that of Socrates, which was a prohibiting Demon: "Mine is a great affirmer, mine is a Demon of action or a Demon of Combat."[22] Furthermore, he states twice in his journals that "Nations have great men only in spite of themselves. Thus the great man is the conqueror of his entire country."[23] Since it was not Baudelaire's nature to wheedle or temporize, he determined to take the world by storm; a gentle, virtuous Chatterton could never represent the combative, spiritually tormented Baudelaire. If there was no place for him in society, then society was wrong and Baudelaire would build a place. In Baudelaire's theory, the intellectual, who should be the ruler of the masses, is not guided by mass morality but by the principles of the dandy, who achieves the sublime by living in front of a mirror. In short, a Baudelaire or a Poe is above the judgment of society. The relation between poet and world is war, and the way of the dandy is the way to paradoxical conquest of a nation—if not by actively ruling, then by esthetic and moral subversion of the hostile crowd and by the brotherhood of the elect.

Poe, therefore, may ultimately have succumbed to society, but in Baudelaire's terms it is a gallant defeat for him and no victory for society. Because he is a poet, he can turn the acts of society back upon it. He is a sinner and a rebel, and he speaks for all sinners and rebels. Whereas de Vigny, in *Chatterton,* was a lobbyist demanding social reform, Baudelaire and Poe prepare for a long-range underground movement. Instead of clamoring futilely at the door of society, they disdain it and destroy its foundations. If there had been no subsequent history of the in-dividual at odds with his society, one might say that this one-man war is only an eccentric example of symbolic rechanneling of the power impulse. From our present perspective, however, it emerges as one of the dominant literary tendencies in modern literature.

With Baudelaire's 1856 essay and the opposition it aroused, Poe received enough special notoriety to prevent him from slipping back into the flux of ephemeral literary figures. However, Barbey d'Aurevilly had suggested another way for Baudelaire to exploit his first theme and to include more of his own theories. Baude-laire incorporated his reply to the charge of decadence into the preface of the second volume of Poe's tales, *Nouvelles histoires extraordinaires,* published in 1857.

While affirming Poe's superiority to the young positivist cul-ture in which he developed, Baudelaire takes the opportunity to develop his thesis that nature itself is depraved and the concept of progress is a fiction. Such an argument undermines the position of Barbey d'Aurevilly and all those who desired morally whole-some art for the uplifting of mankind. Baudelaire's pessimism was so profound, in metaphysics as in sociology, that all attempts at progress seemed puerile to him, and the only alternative he saw to an intellectual aristocracy was the end of the world. His nihilistic vision, with the dandy fine and self-possessed in the midst of disintegrating society, occasionally presented visions as gro-tesque as Goya's Caprichos, but in this preface the vision is tragic.

He accepts the epithet *decadent* given to Poe by Barbey d'Aurevilly, but as a condition of civilization, and affirms the heroism of the artist who has the courage and the genius to give voice to the essential and necessary response of a lofty mind and imagination in the world as it is. In effect, he has subtly reversed his opposition of artist and society, and has drawn a parallel un-welcome to his opponents. Whatever the qualities of the "deca-dent" art may be—and it is assumed that he still has the intel-

lectually deviant and the sensuously subtle in mind—they are the
essential characteristics of a modern sensibility, and all protests
are blind or hypocritical. The refined taste of an advanced culture
necessarily includes a taste for eccentric literature.

Barbey d'Aurevilly's response was to hold to the soundness
of French society and to make Poe the epitome of the Bohemian,
"the man who lives intellectually at the whim of his idea, his sensations, or his dreams"; he progressively saw Poe as more and
more thoroughly American, a man of sensation rather than soul,
an individualist.[24] The last may seem a strange argument to use
against a man or an artist, but its relevance to this verbal battle
between the two French writers is clear when we remember that
one of Baudelaire's premises had to be that an advanced civilization contains such a multiplicity of responses, actions, ways of
life, that a great variety of individuals is possible and *thus* a
literature of eccentricity becomes inevitable. D'Aurevilly, then,
would reject individualism in society.

In this argument Barbey d'Aurevilly put himself in an exposed position and he would have been disconcerted to know
who his neighbors would be a little later in the century. He
fastened a label to Poe that later writers would not be unwilling
to accept; he separated himself from the still-undefined cultural
trend of his century. Baudelaire's other opponents did not state
their position so extremely; they merely took the position that the
storywriter should celebrate the moral code of his society (assum-
ing that the society was not American but French). One critic
even suggested that he must accomplish this by writing historical
novels, and he volunteered sound topics from French history.[25]
Barbey d'Aurevilly and *Le Réveil* were Poe's only formidable
opponents. *Le Réveil* began publication in 1858 and launched
a series of literary attacks on Bohemianism. Poe was one victim
of the campaign, but the editor began the attack on the first page
of the first issue with an article on *Chatterton*, which spoke of
"these false, ungrateful, impious doctrines that teach people to
despise society, to hate and destroy it."[26] Two weeks later he continued the offensive with an article on *Madame Bovary*. Poe was
in illustrious company, but Baudelaire had succeeded in making
him dominant, for Barbey d'Aurevilly's article gave him the title
of King of the Bohemians.

At this point, with the prosecution of Baudelaire following
the publication of the *Fleurs du mal*, the destinies of the two poets

had become thoroughly intertwined. Baudelaire was attacked because of Poe, and Poe was attacked because of Baudelaire. Although Baudelaire had been branded as satanic and immoral, the flurry of controversy produced the result that he was apparently striving for: Poe-Baudelaire-pariah was taken seriously as a moral force.

In the interval between Baudelaire's death in 1867 and the ascendancy of the Symbolists, Poe fell into the background and new Poet-Heroes were imminent. Some references were made to Poe, but their number had diminished and their temper had changed. Most of the notices were reminiscences, the words of Baudelaire's contemporaries, looking back into the past, repeating the same judgments without any of the heat of the 1850s. The furor of surprise and shock had died, the great mid-century moment of poetry was past, and new literary men and periodicals were seeking their own discoveries. Poe was dismissed as a momentary curiosity.

The foreshadowing of a new hero with an almost unrecognizably pallid element of Poe came in a new review, the *Revue internationale,* which was begun in 1859. It was a "one-world" periodical, and the author of the opening article speaks of the master whom nineteenth-century youth (he does not speak of French youth) is seeking. The new era—restive, alive with optimistic humanism—is looking for the Master, who is unknown and perhaps disdained, without dog, wife or friend; he is pale and ironic; he reads and watches. Youth also seeks a master-idea. Among those who "foretold sublime, unknown destines for man," the author lists Plato, Goethe, Shakespeare, Poe, Dante, Raphael, Cavour, Diderot and Rousseau.[27] The writer's attitude is international in imagining an alliance of the elect across national boundaries, and his list of heroes represents an eclectic mingling of politics and art. He is a herald of Symbolism, but he has only the transcendental impulse of a Symbolist, without the clarity of design. Similarly, the hazy halo he gives Poe does not quite fit.

In 1872 *la Renaissance littéraire et artistique* introduced a new American genius to represent the time—Walt Whitman, "the founder of the poetry of the future." At the same time it dismissed Poe, along with Longfellow and Bryant, as more faithful to the old culture than to the American democracy.[28] This seems to be the inevitable tendency, particularly since many of the small periodicals that formed and collapsed overnight in the period

1870-1890 were politically radical, pro-worker, materialist or positivist. Whitman's place in such a pattern is immediately evident, while Poe's is not. The significance of this philosophic distinction will become more apparent as the following chapter traces some of the aspects of moral philosophy involved in the Poe myth. For the moment it is sufficient to say that an anti-intellectual, socialistic literary movement coexisted with Symbolism and mingled with it in the early days before Symbolism defined its metaphysics and withdrew from the uneasy coalition with the other great pariahs, the Poor.

The Symbolists published in a variety of radical reviews rather than in the long-established periodicals. *La Vogue,* a magazine that published almost exclusively the Symbolists—Verlaine, Mallarmé, Rimbaud, Villiers de l'Isle-Adam, Kahn, Adam, Ghil and Laforgue—was evolutionist, anti-clerical, capitalistic, international. Its political platform was not well-defined, but it was a revolutionary fellow-traveler:

> The social revolution will take place: all coalitions will only serve to hasten it. It is urgent that it occur consciously and intelligently, in contrast to the political revolutions of the eighteenth century, and that all lofty and liberal minds unite to study the problems without prejudice or bias, taking inspiration from the most rigorous methods of Science and the principle of universal Solidarity.[29]

Its ideological foundation was shared by the new school of poetry, at least in three of its aspects: several poets were evolutionists and the movement as a whole was interested in science and was international. There were affinities, then, between the new political movement and the new literary movement. One very serious divergence, however, eventually made them incompatible. Most of the political tendencies were collectivist, and although Carlyle's suggestion that only the worker and the artist are venerable provided one motif[30]—there was a revulsion against the mass-mind. The American-born Francis Vielé-Griffin, one of the most articulately political of the Symbolists, was the literary spokesman for *Entretiens politiques et littéraires.* He lashed out sarcastically at the new concepts which he thought inimical to art and intellect:

> What intelligence, too, among those that are outraged by the symbolist renaissance! Certainly we will not seek the cause of that exasperation in literary jealousy, for those who

attack this movement have testified by their writing that
literature was not their concern; they obeyed, we believe,
a very legitimate impulse of impatience; imagine, then, after
the entire nation, with banners flying, music playing, in a
rush of unanimous joy under a glorious June sun, had buried
Poetry forever under the pseudonym of Victor Hugo; now
a band of maniacs tries to revive the great Dead and poison
enlightened imaginations with a noxious lyricism. In the
face of the final triumph of matter and materialism, an
Orphic chorus dares to raise its sonorous voices in prayers
to the Ideal! Among the torpid youth of both banks some
have threatened to affirm personality, that sore of com-
munes persisting although the University cauterizes it every
day. Humanity, cure yourself of individuals![31]

In the face of Marxist opposition, the individualism that Barbey
d'Aurevilly had condemned in Poe again became significant. The
Symbolist poets resumed the identification of artist with individual,
and individual with outcast.

In a social struggle between idealists and materialists in an
era when the young felt revolution in the air, this is the logical
defense of idealists confronting a possibly collectivist outcome. If
Poe was to have any importance for this generation of French
writers in anything but esthetics, it had to be in his role of individualist or rebel. Other articles indicate that he continued to have
some of the rallying power he had had in the era of Baudelaire,
and for almost the same reason. If we substitute proletariat for
bourgeoisie, the opponents continued to be the conformist major-
ity. Theoretically, the art of the worker was strong, healthy and
without individuality. Vielé-Griffin answered charges that art was
too closely allied to philosophy (the extreme leftist magazines
were interested in experience rather than thought) and that it was
unhealthy:

People demand a *healthy inspiration*. Edgar Poe, for
example, is "of a disordered imagination" according to
Larousse; let us admit, for greater clarity, that François
Coppée has a sound lyricism—yet we come quickly to the
conclusion that *art is sickly,* don't we?
SICKLY, there is the word which can put us in accord.
In fact, what is a sick man? A being who no longer has the
normal balance, since the hypertrophic activity of one organ
is nourished at the expense of other organs. Aside from a
human brute, then, there are only sick men in humanity; the

artist, *a fortiori,* is a monomaniac and an eccentric; thought must be a sin against nature, and genius a madness—that, moreover, is the opinion of Lombroso and H. Taine.[32]

For the artists who were actively concerned in the course of contemporary events, Poe represented a complex of attitudes—idealism, individualism, intellectuality—in a complete human situation in which the esthetic could not easily be separated from the political or social. In the poets' rebellion against the standardization of humanity, partly or largely due to industrialization and the rule of the mass man, Poe was as valuable as he had been to Baudelaire. Again he was a talisman of defiance: in his name Vielé-Griffin accepted the epithet *maladif* as Baudelaire had accepted *décadent.* In a sense, the references to Poe follow the design created by Baudelaire; they merely elaborate on the legend he created. However, within Symbolism there is a great deal of temperamental and poetic variety, and there is also variety in attitudes toward the Poe myth. Verlaine and Mallarmé venerated Poe as hero more than Kahn did, for example, if we can judge by the type of commentary and the tone of it. At this point we encounter a less explicit definition of Poe's role, for Baudelaire had established the outlaw so throughly that there was no need for aggressive assertion of his identity. Consequently, most of the argument in the latter part of the century was more concerned with poetics than with heroics. Mallarmé's comments on Poe, for example, are almost entirely impressions or interpretations of specific poems or techniques. The only direct evidence of his attitude toward Poe as a symbolic figure is the sonnet preface to his translation of Poe's poems:

> Tel qu'en Lui-même enfin l'éternité le change,
> Le Poëte suscite avec un glaive nu
> Son siècle epouvante de n'avoir pas connu
> Que la Mort triomphait dans cette voix étrange!

Although this sonnet falls into the category of *tombeaux,* in which Mallarmé often used portentous capital letters, the upper case in *Lui-même* does more than add solemnity. It recalls the fact that Baudelaire has made Him a holy martyr. Poe is no mere poet, but rather the revealed Poet. Mallarmé insists on the religious imagery with the stone of the tomb and with the reminder of blasphemy. Two other elements of the original controversy are also evident: the baseness of society, the poet as gladiator. In this sonnet, however, Mallarmé has given Poe his apotheosis, and it could provide a motif for all of Mallarmé's commentary on the role of poets.

Unlike Baudelaire, Mallarmé is not combative, but his statements are sufficient to show why Poe could serve again as a symbolic man as well as a poetic precursor. Although Mallarmé was quiet, respectable and apolitical, he thought the role of pariah the proper one for a poet in his time. In 1891, when he was the acknowledged leader of the Symbolists, he gave an impromptu definition of the poet's place in society:

> I believe that poetry is made for the supreme pageantry and pomp of a constituted society in which the glory that people seem to have forgotten will have its place. The attitude of a poet in an epoch like this one, when he is on strike against society, is to put aside all the vitiated means that may present themselves.[33]

Later, in the same inquiry, he said of Paul Verlaine that his attitude as a man was "the only one, in an epoch when the poet is outside the law: to force acceptance of all pain with just such haughtiness and just such nerve."

These are such cool remarks that the implications might be missed if we did not know what was literally involved in the poet's being "on strike against society." With the history of alienation in *A Rebours* and in the lives of Verlaine, Rimbaud and Corbière, we recognize that Mallarmé accepted a culturally shattering upheaval in literature as necessary. A youthful essay on Baudelaire had previously indicated his own sense of alienation:

> Finally, the darkness like ink, where one hears only crime, remorse, and Death flying, invaded everything. Then I hid my face, and sobs, torn from my soul not so much by that nightmare as by a bitter sense of exile, cut through the black silence. What, then, is the fatherland?[34]

He felt exiled, not by Baudelaire's nightmare vision, but by what lay behind that vision. As Baudelaire had read Poe, so Mallarmé had read Baudelaire—as mirror-writing, intended to reveal the reverse of what was said. Similarly, the poets' proclamation of their role as outlaws is a nightmare vision, the reverse of what should be. Mallarmé's choice of words alters the situation only slightly: *exile* is merely less brutal than *pariah*.

The echo recurs under various forms in the Symbolists. Many

critics have noted the sense of the elite in these poets—"contempt for the masses," as G. Turquet-Milnes expressed it[35]—and have pointed out that Mallarmé incorporated it into his literary theory by opposing the language of the mercantile world with his own poetic language, inaccessible not only to the vulgar vocabulary but also to the vulgar thought pattern. It is true that the Symbolists found another means of striking back, a means independent of the moral refusal implicit in the Poe myth, and they used it. Nevertheless, the tradition of personal defiance did not wither. As Jacques Rivière explained Rimbaud's Bohemianism: "Bohemia is a protest against society and its ways, against the hierarchy of class, against the organization that men have imposed on themselves."[36] Rimbaud illustrates this thesis more dramatically than anyone except Huysmans:

> Industrialists, princes, senates:
> Perish! Power, justice, history: down with you!
> That's our due. Blood! blood! the flame of gold![37]

Rimbaud inherited Baudelaire's Demon of Combat; like Baudelaire, he imagined himself as the conqueror of his country. He refused to be pathetic and refused to be a victim. Unlike the truly outcast Corbière, he was a defiant pariah. Although he is thought to have used Poe's work as a source for "le Bateau ivre,"[38] Rimbaud's opinion of Poe is not known. Whether he admired Poe or not, he carried on the Poe tradition as Baudelaire understood it and propagated it.

The changes Baudelaire made in the established image of the martyr-poet made it dangerous. The threat was evident in Baudelaire's essays and led to real persecution in the last decade of his life, but his propositions became a matter of serious concern when the most important school of poets since the Pléiade began to treat him and his idol as spiritual ancestors. In the interweaving of the two identities that followed Baudelaire's declaration of their mysterious affinity and their identical poetics, the Symbolists did not always distinguish between Baudelaire and Poe. When myth has been separated from actuality, we find that the confusion has made little difference in the Symbolists' understanding of Poe, and it has not distorted his person appreciably.

In speaking of the "Poe myth," I have been discussing Baudelaire's interpretation of Poe's life and work. This is not to imply that Baudelaire's interpretation falsifies the biographical or artistic

facts. Any biographer tends to see significant designs and patterns
of cause and effect in the life of his subject, and when the biographer is a symbolic poet, and an angry one, we might reasonably expect some distortion. However, the only fundamental element of Baudelaire's interpretation that seems questionable is the
assumption that Poe recognized himself as an outlaw and, *accepting his alienation from society,* set out to fulfill his own nature.
This may indeed be the correct assumption, but it is not in accord
with the Poe myth that has evolved in America, where his actions
tend to be interpreted as desperate attempts to make himself acceptable to society. The distinction is a radical one, and the evolution of Poe's influence in France depends on Baudelaire's having
made it. The American version of the outlaw-myth is that of the
poet who recognizes himself as an outcast—and object of scorn,
pity or patronage—and accepts society's judgment while continuing to try to please society; this poet is Chatterton or Gérard de
Nerval. The French myth is that of the poet who recognizes himself as an outcast and responds by rejecting the criteria of society
and by using his own nature as the measure of truth. This poet is
Rimbaud. Much as he wanted to be the second kind of poet, Baudelaire vacillated between the two. Whether or not Poe fell into
the second category of poets, Baudelaire placed him there and
was bold enough to describe that category as the proper one for
great creative minds.

This is the basis for the Poe myth that was bequeathed to the
Symbolists. These poets were dissatisfied with their society; they
felt that the artist was the natural and inevitable aristocrat and
that a debased society was displacing and destroying him. They
resisted, esthetically and philosophically, and they needed a great
figure who could epitomize their situation.

The choice of Poe was not fortuitous, nor was it merely an
exploitation of his tragic destiny. Poe had qualities that made him
peculiarly compelling and set him apart from the Chatterton ster-
eotype with which the nineteenth century was a little bored. Instead of being a helpless dreamer or visionary, he was a man of
strong intellectual faculties and scope, so that he could be de-
lineated as a giant subdued by a horde of pygmies.[39] The fury of
some of the personal attacks on Poe originated in the critics'
awareness of Poe's intelligence. His intellectual scope and analytic
power did not have to be demonstrated to the public by Baudelaire; almost without exception, the writers who examined Poe's

tales were struck by his rational power. Whereas a distorted spirit and life could provide antagonistic writers with complacent moral homilies, Poe's logic and control were profoundly disturbing. The two essays by E. D. Forgues illustrate the ambivalence of the response of the French man of letters; the exercise of logic, which seemed new and exciting in 1846 as a fictional device and as an approach to all the unknown quantities of the universe, seemed a deception in 1852, and Forgues lashed out bitterly at the reader:

> And don't you, sensible man that you are, feel some secret remorse for having allowed yourself to be tricked by that mocking and perfidious madness which makes fun of you when it has captured you in the net in which it is captive?[40]

Poe was a dangerous man, for he had perverted the sacred tool of reason.

Poe was also peculiarly modern in his tragedy because his immolation was as much psychological as material. The perversion of society was vitally connected with the eccentricity of the individual, as in a two-way circuit; even further, the blocked impulses of the poet made him turn back deliberately upon himself, like Baudelaire's self-executioner, and upon the society which had ruined him. All these factors contributed to the final image that Baudelaire formed, and all of them inspired fear.

Thus Poe's identity as a man and a poet, as it served the nineteenth century symbolically as Poet, was a combination of existence, ideas and creations. Poe's philosophic tendencies and artistic techniques, which will be discussed in the following pages, are ultimately more important to literary historians because their dynamic effect and their mutations are more readily documented. But without the affective power of the Poe myth, Poe's theories would not have been championed with the fervor and coherence that the Symbolists gave them. On the other hand, because his ideas gave French writers a new approach, a new series of germinal ideas, he did not assume the inert venerability of a tombstone.

NOTES

[1] Charles Asselineau, *Charles Baudelaire* (Paris, 1869), p. 39.
[2] Charles Baudelaire, *Correspondence générale*, IV (Paris, 1948), 277. Letter to Thoré dated 20 June 1864.

3 Baudelaire, "La Révélation magnétique," *La Liberté de penser,* July 1848, pp. 176-178.

4 Baudelaire, "Bérénice," *L'Illustration,* 17 April 1852, p. 254.

5 Baudelaire, "Edgar Allan Poe, sa vie et ses ouvrages," *Revue de Paris,* VII (April 1852), 110.

6 Baudelaire, *Oeuvres complètes* (Paris: NRF, 1954), p. 1199. This edition will henceforth be referred to as the Pléiade.

7 Baudelaire took an active part in the revolution, both physically, in action on the barricades, and journalistically, in publishing a revolutionary paper, *Le Salut publique,* which was extinct after two issues. The issues of this paper are characterized by violence and incoherence, however, rather than by serious political aims.

8 Baudelaire, Pléiade edition, p. 605.

9 *Ibid.,* p. 674.

10 *Ibid.,* p. 908.

11 *Ibid.,* p. 680.

12 *Ibid.,* p. 1209.

13 *Revue contemporaine,* XX (30 June 1855), 266. The authors were Dickens, Charlotte Bronte, Thackeray, Anna Stephens, Miss Cummings and Poe.

14 Alfred de Vigny, "Dernière nuit de travail," *Chatterton.* In *Théâtre,* ed. Gauthier-Ferrieres (Paris, n.d.), p. 138.

15 Baudelaire, Pléiade edition, p. 1115.

16 See W. T. Bandy, "New Light on Baudelaire and Poe," *Yale French Studies,* X (1953), 65-69.

17 Baudelaire, *Lettres 1841-1866* (Paris, 1906), pp. 33-34.

18 Armand de Pontmartin, "Causeries littéraires," *L'Assemblée nationale,* 12 April 1856.

19 Barbey d'Aurevilly, "Bibliographie," *Le Pays,* 10 June 1856.

20 See E. and J. Crépet, *Charles Baudelaire* (Paris, 1928), pp. 282–283.

21 Baudelaire, *Oeuvres posthumes,* ed. E. Crépet (Paris, 1887), p. 239. Stated in a letter to Sainte-Beuve, 26 March 1856.

22 Baudelaire, Pléiade edition, p. 357.

23 *Ibid.,* p. 1210.

24 Barbey d'Aurevilly, "Le Roi des bohêmes ou Edgar Poe," *Le Réveil,* 15 May 1858, pp. 231-233.

25 Thalès-Bernard, "Revue critique," *Revue contemporaine,* XXIX (December 1856), 383-388.

26 A. Granier de Cassagnac, "Chatterton, ou la bohême au théâtre," *Le Réveil,* 2 January 1858.

27 Felix Platel, "Jeunes paroles," *Revue internationale,* I (1 August 1859), 5.

28 E. Blémont, "Littérature étrangère," *Renaissance littéraire et artistique,* I (8 June 1872), 53-55.

29 "Courrier social," *La Vogue,* 11 April 1886, pp. 27-28.

30 Thomas Carlyle, "Deux Hommes," *Entretiens politiques et littéraires,* I, no. 4 (1 July 1890).

31 Francis Vielé-Griffin, "Inutilisations," *Entretiens politiques et littéraires,* I, no. 4 (1 July 1890), 131.

32 Vielé-Griffin, "Les Forts," *Entretiens politiques et littéraires,* I, no. 5 (1 August 1890), 163.

33 Stephane Mallarmé, *Oeuvres complètes,* ed. Henri Mondor and G. Jean-Aubry (Paris: NRF, 1945), pp. 869-870. This edition will be referred to as the Pléiade.

34 *Ibid.,* p. 263.

35 G. Turquet-Milnes, *Belgian Writers* (London, 1921), p. 53.

36 Jacques Rivière, *Rimbaud* (Paris, [1938?]), p. 32.

[37] Arthur Rimbaud, *Oeuvres complètes,* vol. 1 (Lausanne, 1948), p. 132.

[38] Célestin Pierre Cambiaire, *The Influence of Edgar Allan Poe in France* (New York, 1929), pp. 123-124.

[39] The Image was used by Thalès-Bernard in "Revue critique," *Revue contemporaine,* XXIX (December 1856), 387.

[40] E. D. Forgues, "Poètes et romanciers Américains," *Revue des deux mondes,* 15 April 1852, pp. 339-340.

THE AMERICAN

In the first period of Poe's reputation in France, the philosophic inclinations of the American came under dispute, Poe appeared at a moment of philosophic unrest in the old world and re-evaluation of the new world and its possible contribution to European culture. In spite of his mocking satire of progress and democracy, many Frenchmen considered him a product and a prophet of the new world, the new age. In some ways their view of the new world seems grotesque to an American; in other ways, however, it seems highly perceptive. We might say that America was as much a myth as Poe, but with less variation in judgment: almost no one spoke well of America.

By 1850, the Romantic America had virtually disappeared from French literature; even 23 years before, at the end of his *Voyages en Amérique,* Chateaubriand had noted the change in the exotic land of Indians:

> If I were now to see the United States, I would not recognize it: where I once left forests, I would find tilled fields; where I slashed my path through the underbrush, I would travel on highways.

No longer a strange and beautiful primitive society to be studied, but a European offshoot to be judged, America now suggested pointed questions:

> Are the Americans perfect? Do they not have vices like other men? Are they morally superior to the English who are their ancestors? . . . Will they be dominated by the commercial

spirit? Has desire for profit not begun to be the major national fault?[1]

Chateaubriand does not answer the questions except by implication, and he concludes in a declaration of faith in American freedom, born of enlightenment rather than circumstance.

The following generation, however, did not hesitate to answer the questions more rudely. In spite of their knowledge of
Longfellow and Cooper, neither the forest primeval nor the conquest of the great west forms a part of the image of America
revealed in the French commentary on Poe in the 1850s. The
idyllic wilderness inhabited by a Rousseauesque innocent scarcely
appeared in their commentary, and the pioneer was unknown.
The United States was emerging as a political, economic and social entity, and it did not inspire affection. Soul-less, measuring
its being and its achievement by quantity (of wealth, power or
space) instead of moral standards or metaphysical concepts, the
French image of the United States was a caricature of the industrial east. The American was a man of raw enegry and unlimited
ambition and conceit; he was uncouth, ignorant and inaccessible
to traditional values.

It was bad enough to consider that American society was
thoroughly misguided by its materialistic philosophy and its denial of the traditions of the parent-continent, but it was worse to
foresee the corruption of the parent by the child. Baudelaire's
interpretation of the trend, indicated in a passage from the *Exposition universelle de 1855,* is characteristic of the attitude of the
time:

> Ask any good Frenchman who reads his newspaper
> every day in the café what he understands by progress, and
> he will reply that it is the steamship, electricity, and gaslight
> —miracles unknown to the Romans—and that these discov-
> eries fully prove our superiority over the Ancients. So much
> darkness has he in his unfortunate brain, and so strangely
> confused are the things of the material order and the spiritual
> order! The poor man is so americanized by the zoocratic
> philosophers and industrialists that he has lost the notion of
> the differences between the phenomena of the physical world
> and of the moral world; the natural and the supernatural.[2]

Thirty years later Huysmans took the same view and the same
tone in blaming America for the corruption of contemporary
values:

It was the great penal colony America transported to our continent; it was, in short, the immense, profound, boundless campfollowing of the financier and parvenu casting its light, like a vile sun, on the idolatrous city flat on its belly spewing impure canticles before the impious tabernacle of the bank.[3]

What was the source of these concepts? Certainly it could not have been the American literature known to the French— Cooper, Hawthorne, Irving, Holmes, Stowe, Longfellow. Most American literature was considered imitative and not very interesting. However, there were curious travelers to explore and document the new world of American society. Alexis de Tocqueville was the most incisive and the most highly credited. Like other European visitors, de Tocqueville portrays American society in action. Although he is inclined to theorize rather than to describe, there is enough detail in his work to reveal what obviously appeared to him as barbaric, if liberating, social structures and habits. Furthermore, in the second volume of his work, which was published in 1840, there are many general concepts which became significant in French criticism: the tyranny of opinion in the United States, the public demand for the sensational and the unexpected in literature, and the emphasis on utility in art as in action. He also suggested a problem that haunted nineteenth-century France—decadence. The old world seemed to have reached its limit, he said, while Russia and the United States were "proceeding with ease and celerity along a path to which the human eye can assign no term."[4]

If European society was waning and the immense new worlds were growing endlessly in their own pattern distinct from the traditions of the old world, the latter had two reasons to fear. The glory of French intellectual ascendancy would be diminished, for it would have no reflection or progeny in the new order; the old world itself would become subject to the new order, a prospect all the more disturbing because it was undefined. It was necessary to discover the nature of the new civilization, and it was necessary to confront the cause of French decline, if there was a decline.

Even before Baudelaire took up the banner of decadence and turned the concept to his own literary uses, magazine and newspaper writers had considered it directly or indirectly. For example, Emile Montégut, surveying the cultural scene in 1849, posed the question of decadence as well as that of America. Although ostensibly writing on Hawthorne, he was concerned with contemporary French literary sterility, and considered the possible causes: (1) the rule of the masses, (2) an exhausted civilization, (3) the revolutionary spirit and, finally, (4) industrialization, where the threat seemed ultimately to lie. Here was the threat of the new, unknown societies, Russia and the United States, which might depart from the European tradition. But, Montégut said, they are only "prolongations of Europe. That is the only thing, perhaps, that might reassure the old European civilization. We cannot deny that in many ways these two countries are a danger for the old societies; until now, however, the signs and symptoms which would point to the seeds of a new and original civilization do not show themselves."[5] Others did not find the same reassurance of American dependence on European culture, nor did they see the same imitativeness. Whereas Montégut dismissed Poe's work as a pastiche of European thought, others found it new and disquieting; and whereas Montégut was pleased to reduce the United States to a mixture of all Europe, others, such as Baudelaire, Barbey d'Aurevilly and Renan, found it to be the breeding ground of a perverse philosophy.

Certainly the founding of American society and its development through the eighteenth century were not shocking; these were the products of European dreams. America had no laureate philosopher who directed its destiny. Instead, in the process of self-determination, it used and transformed European thought, so that Europe seemed to see its ideas embodied—and, after a time, terrifyingly embodied. America came to mean variously, materialism, positivism, individualism, collectivism and protestantism. Fundamental to all the *isms* was the venerable idea of progress.

For Americans even now, the idea of progress—the optimistic idea that humanity follows a constant or consistent upward movement—is nearly sacrosanct. For the French there was an early disillusionment. The question of progress came to a crisis in the 1848 revolution. In the 1830s and 1840s the idea had been associated with the emergence of the middle class as a cultural force. Disillusionment came when it became apparent that the middle-class exercise of force was economic and that cultural values were succumbing to a marketplace materialism. For this unpleasant turn of events, America very naturally became a symbol, for America had been the proving ground for the philosophy of progress, and the materialism found in mid-century France was even more pervasive in America.

Although the idea of progress is simple, the manifestations of its errors were complex, involving all areas of human action. America had been like a gigantic scientific experiment, with controls established to eliminate the inhibiting effect of old, perhaps outmoded, institutions and traditions. In America, man was freed of the authority of Catholicism; the Protestant was a questioner, a seeker, subject to the opinion of his contemporaries rather than to the doctrine of a church that represented the accumulated virtue of great and illuminated minds of the past. Moreover, there were no political institutions to form the individual citizen; instead, the rebels who formed the citizenry constructed the new country's institutions. Finally, the new land offered material conquest the boundaries of which were not yet visible. However, with another perspective after the French adventure of 1848, progress seemed illusory and the American adventure appeared less beneficent. Some French writers recoiled from the entire concept of progress and took refuge in absolutes. Baudelaire was one of these. Rejecting progress, which would inevitably lead to a questioning of the unalterable value of any traditional culture, he affirmed that man "is always like and equal to man, that is to say, always in the savage state."[6] Even though Baudelaire tried to imagine an authentic progress in the "diminution of the traces of original sin,"[7] it was never more than a remote and visionary possibility. It was not progress as the nineteenth century understood it. For most people, then as now, progress meant material advance, measurable in communal life. With its sense of deception about material progress, the intelligentsia became hostile to America, its symbol.

To a great extent, the dangers and the symptoms of cultural change in America remained objects of speculation, but there were irrefutable facts that could be interpreted. One was the composition of the new society. It was made up of rebels: charitably seen, the rebels were men of unshakeable principle who sought a new world to house their ideals; seen skeptically or cynically, they were opportunists, outlaws and troublemakers who could not or would not accept the accident of social status. This was true in religion as well as in economic and political life. At the extreme of religious deviation, for example, illustrating the boundless hubris of a people who intended to create everything anew for themselves, was the Mormon sect, which found its own revelation in the New World, thus entirely freeing itself of the old. Barbey d'Aurevilly had only to mention the name in order to indict a whole society: "One asks oneself pityingly what his [moral education] was . . . in a society that one morning awoke to find the Mormons in the depths of its morality."[8]

But Mormonism was merely an exceptionally dramatic example; in other ways the individual, or the new group thrust himself into the world uninhibited. The eccentric, sectarian or partisan character of American literature is mentioned casually by Charles de Moüy almost as though it had been a kind of regionalism in literature—the Methodist novel, the Abolitionist novel, the Transcendentalist novel.[9] Elsewhere the tendency of each group to make itself a special genre is seen as the tendency of an entire people to aspire beyond its capabilities and, further, to make literature a tool of special interest—monetary or social— rather than the result of a superior and disinterested vision. Baudelaire, referring to Rufus Griswold's comment that Poe was too far above his compatriots in style to be a money-making author, uses it as a defense of Poe and an indication of the values of his society. In contrast, Barbey d'Aurevilly sees Poe as a server of those very American interests. It must be remembered that the French were well acquainted with the Benjamin Franklin of "Honesty is the best policy," the practical businessman, who, in the popular view, subordinated morality to monetary gain. This American is typified in Baudelaire's sarcastic quotation in English in his 1852 essay, *"Make money, my son, honestly, if you can,* BUT MAKE MONEY." This view of the typically American attitude has persisted until the present time. If fact, Remy de Gourmont went so far as to find Poe literally a representative of the American type, and to say that he would have been a fine businessman if he had been cut off from literature.[10] If one weighs this attitude in balance with de Tocqueville's interpretation of the restless spirit of the Americans, devouring, conquering, discarding aspects of the material world in a ceaseless and fruitless effort to achieve an ideal political and spiritual destiny, one has a partial sketch of the strange New Man that must have seemed monstrous to a traditional French man of letters.

The American experiment seemed to have ended in an untidy and contradictory welter of individual whims. It is not easy to find any philosophic coherence in the religious sectarianism, the individual opportunism or the social instability that the French gleaned from American and European literary sources, but the French made the hypothetical leap necessary to form a theory. Thus they wrote of a nation composed of religious and social deviants who had lost all footing in the moral ground of western history—a nation that had forgotten the soul and put faith only in power over its world, a power that depended on fact, perception and exploitation rather than on sentiments or ideals. In general, French writers were content to call America materialistic for these reasons. And, as a further refinement of America's ignorance and practicality, it could not or would not distinguish between spirit and matter. An article on magic in 1857 illustrates this attitude more specifically; it excoriates the Puritan pride as the source of the vicious spirituality of the American:

> Its final word is thus deification of man and nature, that is to say pantheism. We should not be surprised if the spiritualist madness is joined by aspiration to endless progress, attempts at social reorganization, hopes for human regeneration. All these dreams have the same source, the immense pride of man who, misunderstanding his own nature and the condition of his earthly existence, tries by every means to raise himself to a perfection not given him to achieve; and since, according to Pascal, he who desires to become an angel becomes a beast, he falls into the grossest absurdities, having intended to win a chimeric knowledge. Thus the words of a great writer are confirmed: "Man has such great need to believe that when he deserts the holy sanctuary of the temple, it is to visit the witch's den."[11]

The author of this article very readily links a bewildering variety of ideas, from spiritualism to social reform, but he indicates fairly clearly the train of association that made it possible for *materialism* to be the cover-all label for America and also made it possible for Poe to be considered thoroughly American. In brief, the associations follow this pattern: the Puritan, in breaking away from the established church, declares his faith in his own power to know and fulfill God's will; once placed in this perilous position by his pride, he can no longer distinguish

the area of his mastery. Because in reality his area of mastery
is the material world—and not all of that—he attempts to extend
his power by approaching spirit and society as though they were
subject to the rules applicable to matter, or even as though they
were matter.

Because this intepretation of the paradox within the American character (which approaches spirituality through materialism)
proves to be important in understanding the French reaction to
Poe, I have retraced the underlying process of thought. Even
where there is no overt religious censure, the basically Catholic
religious attitude seems to determine the first premise. While the
article just quoted is primarily concerned with table-rapping and
spirit-materialization instead of literature, it makes no distinction
between that kind of hocus-pocus and the spiritual preoccupations
of the Transcendentalists. Similarly, Poe had already been placed
among the table-rappers by Philarète Chasles in 1856. In 1858,
Barbey d'Aurevilly, in an attack on *le Siècle,* again associated
America with spiritual and intellectual charlatanry:

> In fact it seems impossible that the art for art men who
> have produced all the literature of the last thirty years, the
> rope-dancers of transcendental fantasy, the opium-eating
> poets, all the various types of contemporary degradation,
> will let your claim go by without disputing its passage. The
> decadence of these times is the only thing that gives us
> courage in our claim, which is that we must finally sweep
> out all that dust—art for art, sensation, imagination, magnet-
> ism, and all the American imitations; for America gnaws at
> us by its ideas as well as by its customs.[12]

On the face of it, opium-eating poets would seem properly
to belong to a different class from Transcendentalists; but beyond
the level on which this tirade was spoken it has a kind of validity.
Both were attempting—like Ahab—to arrive at ultimate reality
in the material world.

Certainly, the French found among other American traits
the confusion of spirit and matter presented to them with unquestionable force and coherence in the stories of Poe. In spite of
all that Baudelaire could say to fend off the danger, Poe was identified with America by most of the French writers before the
Symbolists. Although his American origin was thought to have
determined Poe's morality and temperament, the point that im-

mediately concerns us is the extent to which he reflected the
philosophic temper and tendency of his country. Instead of attempting to trace Poe's knowledge and acceptance of formal
philosophy, which were largely idealist, we will look for his
philosophy in the way that the French found it—revealed in his
mode of handling the elements of experience and art—with the
assumption that man often assimilates the intellectual habits of
his contemporaries without deliberately deciding to do so. And
sometimes his consciously cherished ideas do not coincide with
the ideas underlying his action.

Just as there were two camps in the literary quarrel over
Poe's character as outlaw, there were contradictory attitudes toward his Americanism in the articles of the 1850s. Some critics
found no evidence of his American identity, and condemned him
for imitating the Germans instead of being American; the major-
ity found him thoroughly American either because of his sensa-
tionalism or his materialism. Baudelaire, of course, claimed that
Poe was in revolt against American vulgarity, mechanization,
democracy and materialism. At this point some careful distinctions
must be made. When the charge against America was very simply and explicitly that of *materialism,* we find the reviewers uni-
formly contemptuous of America; they agreed that Poe was a product of that materialism, but he was discussed as though he were
a by-product, for the spirit of calculation, the love of facts and
the exploration of sensation were branches of materialism. As
materialism began to reveal these ramifications, Realism and
Naturalism became implicated and were associated with Poe or
America. Baudelaire, who opposed materialism so violently, could
be charged with it himself when it included science and sensation.

The irony of the situation did not become apparent until
many years later, when generic traits in the new literature could
be distinguished and some of the bewildering clashes of detail
and emotion fell into their proper places. There was, in reality,
a fundamental ambiguity in the attitude of many writers. What
they despised in American democracy, American mechanization
and American materialism, they welcomed in literature by rejecting highflown language and heralding rigorous rational control
and the concreteness of perception, sensation and experience in
art. Therefore we find that even as an American, Poe was a new
force in literature.

In spite of their preoccupation with the threat of materialism as it implied the commercialization of values dominating mid-century France, the French did not see marketplace materialism in Poe's work. If they had wanted to insist, they could have found it in "The Gold Bug," for in that story a mathematical genius agonizes and grows impassioned over a cryptograph and a box of buried treasure. "Philosophy of Furniture," one of the first works to be translated by Baudelaire, could also be charged with materialism in the popular sense of the word, but it is to the credit of the French writers that they did not attempt to fix Poe in that sort of materialism.

The charge of materialism first arose over the stories of mesmerism, "The Facts in the Case of M. Valdemar" and "Mesmeric Revelation." Since they are among the most shocking of Poe's stories in horror of physical detail as well as in weirdness of idea, these stories of hypnotism were among the first to be translated for the French periodicals. The stories that were to appeal to the Symbolists ("Silence," "Shadow," "The Fall of the House of Usher") did not appear until Poe's reputation was already established. The stories of hypnotism are also the ones that lend themselves most readily to the interpretation that the author refused to recognize the limits of mind and matter, but tried to subdue death and spy on eternity through acts of will. The traditionalist and the solid middle-class critic (most of the literary critics for French periodicals in the middle of the century fell into these categories) found the attempt impious rather than psychologically interesting.

"Mesmeric Revelation" is unquestionably an attempt to reduce spirit to matter in a search for unity; in a less obvious materialism, "Ligeia" attempts to control the ultimate life, the life of the spirit, through a willed control of the physical life that corrupts in death. In a fantastic guise, "The Power of Words," "The Colloquy of Monos and Una" and "The Conversation of Eiros and Charmion" also confound the realms of spirit and matter. There can be no doubt that Poe was not satisfied with any kind of dualism and that he used many devices in his efforts to dramatize the inseparability of spirit and matter. This tendency in Poe's thought is too pervasive to be denied, and it is precisely the tendency Baudelaire had associated with America in speaking of the average Frenchman's materialistic bent in desiring progress. However, it is now evident that Baudelaire's statement cannot be taken at precisely face value. The very story that brought sharpest censure from other French reviewers ("Mesmeric Revelation") had been the one first chosen for translation by Baudelaire. Furthermore, Baudelaire's theory of correspondences—to say nothing of his interest in word-magic—would be subject to the accusation of materialism if his statement were strictly interpreted. Therefore, we must read his criticism of materialism in contemporary society as a moral one: that is, he condemned society for valuing utilitarian objects as though they were proof of cultural advance and man's moral superiority. On this basis he was right in considering Poe the opponent of his country's materialism.

In the larger and vaguer sense, however, the other critics were right to call Poe a materialist, and to proceed to find the same tendencies in French literature. Fortunately, less misleading terminology was applied as soon as they left general statement and turned to literary works. As has been suggested, two of the key words in articles on Poe were *sensation* and *science*.

In Poe they found the life of man in the universe seen not spiritually nor sentimentally, but with the nerves subjected to the faculty of rational analysis. Pontmartin satirically noted this tendency: no more love, he said, or lost children or soul-seeking: "Instead, a chain of reasoning, a calculation of probabilities, a series of physiological, metaphysical, and mathematical demonstrations become chapters in a novel and do not permit us to regret the absence of other sources of feeling or interest."[13] Cartier, who also felt the emotional aridity of Poe, concludes that Poe is a reasoner, even about his sensations, and that facts displace feelings in his stories.[14]

In the evolution of literature, the emphasis on fact and sensation, as opposed to emotion, marks the transition from Romanticism to Realism. Sensation also provides a thought-link between science and materialism. Since these words were used rather freely in the articles on Poe, it is necessary to indicate that the trait one writer called *materialistic* might be called *factual* or *scientific* by another. In fact, the distinctions are difficult to draw in literature, since all of these terms relate to the phenomena of the world, which are primarily subject to the senses, and on experience rather than thought. In the French criticism of Poe, *science* could be called a euphemism for materialism because while America was seldom called scientific, its materialistic attitudes were often termed scientific when found in literature. For example, in speaking of the literature of voyages—which he considers a peculiarly American literary genre—Louis Etienne says:

> We have the gay lie, they have the scientific lie. La Fontaine's voyager had to be French:
>> I saw, he said, a cabbage as big as a house.
>
> If he had been American, he would have given the measurements within half a yard; he would have shown a piece of its leaf carefully pressed in his notebook; he would have measured it before your eyes, and he would have succeeded, by calculations like those of Cuvier with a fossil fragment, in reconstructing his colossal cabbage, with its shape, its size, and its three dimensions.[15]

His article ends by protesting against the scientific and sensational tendencies in French literature which he has just traced in the works of Poe. Essentially, he is recoiling from the cold mind and nerve of Poe and crying out against a change in the moral climate of his time; he senses the abandonment of the soul and the transfer of allegiance from religion to science. In addition to the question of world views and moral values, however, the encroachment of materialism and science seemed to have very specific effects on the structure and detail of literature.

Literature began to translate the world of nerves; it emphasized sensation rather than emotion. Sometimes the critics did not find the dangerous shift purely by an effort of interpretation, but were told specifically that it was there. In 1855, a review of Maxime du Camp's *Chants modernes* worried over the poet's manifesto—his attack on Academicians, his desire to break from the past and the old rhetoric in order to belong to the new scientific world. The critic's judgment was that "instead of finding [in du Camp's poetry] the triumph of science over nature, one really sees the soul conquered by matter and disappearing before it."[16]

Thus many of the French writers gladly identified their art with science. In 1856, Baudelaire said in a letter, "A long time ago I said that the poet is *sovereignly* intelligent, that he is *intelligence* par excellence, and that the *imagination* is the most *scientific* of the faculties, because it alone understands the *universal* analogy, or what a mystical religion calls *correspondences*."[17] There is other evidence that Baudelaire welcomed Poe's "Philosophy of Composition" and "Poetic Principle" as the expression of his view of what art could and should do, and that he accepted literally Poe's statements about the scientific construction of poetry.

An anonymous reviewer in the *Bibliothèque universelle* discussed these tendencies in the Goncourts, Stendhal and Nerval, using exactly the same terminology that other critics had applied to Poe. Of Stendhal, for example, he said, "Sentiment is lacking, the heart is arid, a cold irony dominates all inspiration. He is a materialist who believes only in sensation. . . ."[18]

The Goncourt brothers, Stendhal and Poe have one thing in common: precision and minuteness in examining the exceptional or the excessive sensibility. All use a technique that has been called scientific in the first, analytic in the second, and scientific, analytic and mathematical in the last. It is not always easy to see literary tendencies or causes and effects until time has shown the patterns, and Poe was tossed into one heap with Realists, Romantics and Naturalists. One critic claimed that the combination of algebra and horror in Poe had already been created by Hugo, and the supplanting of the soul by facts and sensation was the work of the Realists.[19] There can be no question of absolute newness in Poe's conceptions and techniques, but even the combination of Romantic and Realist tendencies was original and the writers were more aware of it than were the professional critics. An entry in the journal of the Goncourt brothers in 1856 reveals the excitement Poe's scientific technique aroused:

> After having read Poe, the revelation of something that criticism does not seem to have suspected. Poe, a new literature, the literature of the twentieth century: the scientific miracle, the creation of fable by A + B, a literature which is at the same time monomaniac and mathematical. Imagination by dint of analysis, Zadig as prosecuting attorney, Cyrano de Bergerac as student of Arago, and things playing a greater role than human beings—and love, already somewhat diminished by money in Balzac's work, love giving way to other sources of interest; finally, the novel of the future called upon to tell the history of events that occur in the brain of mankind instead of in the heart.[20]

Even the critics who had not read Poe's theoretical essays had little difficulty in finding some reflection of this principle at work in Poe's stories. The refrain "mathematician-poet" in all its variations becomes so monotonous to one who studies French criticism of Poe that it begins to seem no more than a commonplace. While it is true that Americans have occasionally noted this characteristic—James Russell Lowell's introduction to the 1853 edition of Poe's works mentions it as a duality of analysis and imagination—more frequently they have reacted as Louis Etienne did, with derision at the improbability of the events or at the excessiveness of the element of horror. The nearly universal French awareness of the peculiar bent of Poe's genius is important, for it indicates that they were ready to see that Poe was not simply Gothic Romantic, but original and contemporary. The ordinary critic can see only what his training has prepared him to see, and the ordinary critics saw in Poe the application of a rigorous scientific method to themes, plots and emotions, which should have been the stock in trade of a Gothic imagination; and they were much shaken by the discovery. Barbey d'Aurevilly, who had little favorable comment on Poe (or on anyone, if we are to believe Emile Zola), gave grudging and qualified admiration to Poe's "method," which he compared to that of a watchmaker and a surgeon. Poe, anatomizing the human brain, is a realist and scientist only as a surgeon is a scientist: the reality of surgery is not the reality of human life. The critics who recoiled from that agonizing reality may have been quite justified; one sympathizes with Etienne when he cries: "Life does not exist merely in the blood and the nerves." Nevertheless, art's direction was scientific, in one way or another, and its tendencies were anything but reactionary. The world's new infatuation was the idea of science, and poets shared it and used it in their fashion.

It is commonly thought that these principles are the property of Zola and the Naturalist movement; it is true that the scientific spirit informed the entire work of art for Zola—its intent, its structure and its technique—whereas it was more exclusively a technique with Poe. Here is Zola's famous definition of the technique of the naturalistic novelist:

> The observer in him gives the facts as he has observed them, suggests the point of departure, displays the solid earth on which his characters are to tread and the phenomena to develop. Then the experimentalist appears and introduces an experiment, that is to say, sets his characters going in a certain story so as to show that the succession of facts will be such as the requirements of the determinism of the phenomena under examination call for.[21]

Later in his essay he is to conclude, "The metaphysical man is dead; our whole territory is transformed by the advent of the physiological man."

Fortunately, these theories would scarcely serve for poetry. Even the Parnassians, who were responding to the same cultural stimuli, could not have been so physiological in their poetry of perception and yet have been poets. The kind of scientific approach that Poe used and gave others the pattern for did not depend on physiology. It was (in the terms set by the French) more American. His scientific impulse was not content with the data of sensible experience or even rational experience, but intended to operate within the realm of the spirit, and this is precisely the aspect of American materialism that most outraged the French. It was a breach of intellectual decorum. Therefore, a dedicated scientist like Zola was not likely to appreciate Poe; and Zola did not. Although science-fiction originated with Poe, and many Frenchmen found a childlike delight in his ingenious inventions, that aspect of Poe's mind, revealed in "The Balloon Hoax" and "Hans Pfaall," could have only a momentary and minor interest. This aspect, as well as the Gothic, was subordinated in Poe's work to the primary interest in the interaction of matter with spirit or thought.

Poe's exploitation of the scientific spirit is complex, and the aspects must be considered in isolation even though their influence is in combination. Aside from the emphasis on sensation, which has already been discussed, and the theory and practice of poetry, with which the following chapter is concerned, the most important elements in Poe's scientific approach to fiction are his choice of descriptive facts or details, and his style.

As the French were quick to notice, Poe brought an American literal-minded rationality to bear on fantastic situations. Entertaining an image of the wildest imagination, such as the annihilation of a phantom ship and its crew in the mythic river-vortex ("Ms Found in a Bottle"), he declines to give it the tone of delirium or even to treat it as myth or dream. The narrator, in the first paragraph, indicates his bias and his nature:

> I have often been reproached with the aridity of my genius; a deficiency of imagination has been imputed to me as a crime; and the Pyrrhonism of my opinions has at all times rendered me notorious. Indeed, a strong relish for physical philosophy has, I fear, tinctured my mind with a very common error of this age—I mean the habit of referring occurrences, even the least susceptible of such references, to the principles of that science.

The narrative proceeds with detailed physical description that is convincing, at least to one not versed in sea matters; there is straightforward description of the vessel, the cargo and the warning of storm that convinces a reader of the precision of the narrator's observation. The quasi-scientific observation continues with no false note until the day when the sun is extinguished. Thus the first half, or nearly half, of the story is handled with the realism of a precise and rational observer. The transition can be immediately detected in the language:

> About noon, as nearly as we could guess, our attention was again arrested by the appearance of the sun. It gave out no light, properly so called, but a dull and sullen glow without reflection, as if all its rays were polarized. Just before sinking within the turgid sea, its central fires suddenly went out, as if hurriedly extinguished by some unaccountable power. It was a dim, silver-like rim, alone, as it rushed down the unfathomable sea.

After this point, the description, while remaining detailed and powerfully imagined, no longer has the quotidian realism of the first part, nor its coldly factual language. Precisely that shift in technique seemed a deception to many Frenchmen. Poe was a literary juggler because he misled the reader with a pretended realism, a mere stage-setting. Yet in fact Poe is forcing the scientific techniques associated with realism to support the evidence of dream, to prove myth. He was sufficiently bold, and American, to test the possibilities of science beyond the approved limits.

Many of his stories of human perversity—"The Black Cat," "William Wilson," "The Tell-Tale Heart," even "Berenice"— repeat the pattern of the tales of fantastic adventure by employing keen objective observation and profound psychological insight as the mold for experiences beyond the boundaries of nature. His technique in establishing psychological credibility is both like and unlike his technique in creating a sense of realism in fantastic action. He begins "The Black Cat" with a similar effort to establish the observable truth of the narrative, and the narrator is at pains to explain the events in their natural causes, as, in seeing the bas relief of the cat on his wall, he says, "When I first beheld this apparition—for I could scarcely regard it as less—my wonder and my terror were extreme. But at length reflection came to my aid." Every effort is made to narrate the events on the level of scientific observation. If there is a supernatural element in the story, it is because the deep current of human nature impinges on the supernatural, and a full and objective description of events leads to the dark world where mind and matter have a mysterious unity.

When the sensations and motives of men are subjected to detailed observation and rational analysis, the effect is more compelling than in the apocalyptic fantasies. Although human motive in Poe may have seemed as fantastic as the mythic sea to the traditionalist whose concept of human virtues, vices and motives scarcely differed from those in the classical scheme, its observation could be more closely verified than could the fantastic in nature, which, in "The Conversation of Eiros and Charmion" for example, had to rely on its scientific and logical possibility. The psychologically fantastic could be verified by the reader, Baudelaire's "Hypocrite reader, my likeness, my brother."

In part, Poe's scientific effect depends on choice of detail, but it also depends on style and manifests itself in language. While Poe's style is a constant irritant to English-speaking critics, the French have generally admired it:

> His sentences are, in general, firm, bare, and sober, without ornament or over-writing; they move directly to the conclusion, and if an image appears, the thought absorbs it without effort. This scorn of artifice is itself an artifice, for the commonplace is relieved by sincerity of detail, whereas a brilliant style could curb the rapid pace of the story and mar the intensity of observation. Impossible to have a manner *too* quick and decided, when one is reporting facts. One must avoid the charm characteristic of tales of passion.[22]

It has so often been claimed that Baudelaire improved Poe's style and made it palatable that the idea is now rather completely accepted. However, an examination of the style of "The Black Cat" reveals a restraint, precision of narration and fineness of psychological distinctions which directly serve the narrative; even the traces of pedantry contribute to the authenticity of the facts. The same paradox of cool scientific observation and analysis contributing to inexplicable terror occurs in a story as poetic as "The Fall of the House of Usher." Through the narrator's rationalistic deprecation of his own mysterious dread, and through the specific observations of a character of such a skeptical turn of mind, Poe practices, as a method of persuasion, the psychological paradox that his character analyzes: the analysis itself accelerates the sense of foreboding.

The purpose of these remarks on Poe's narrative technique has been to show that the scientific approach he took in the "Philosophy of Composition" was not merely a momentary hoax, but that, although he may sometimes have been mistaken in the formulas he decided upon, he was deliberately using a type of introspective psychological analysis that is almost clinical, in determining the element of style, as well as the elements of subject and structure in his stories. The intention must be understood in order to see how the Symbolists interpreted his work and what effect he had on their technique.

An examination of the essay on Poe by Gustave Kahn will illustrate some of the effects of artistic preoccupation with science, and their relation to Poe. Kahn's acceptance of a much-disputed theory, that of evolution, is immediately evident, and the argument for which Mallarmé's translation of Poe's poetry is a pretext is that poetry is a living thing which must either become fossilized or evolve. His contention is that Poe, free in the new intellectual world, had begun to revolutionize poetry, to remove it from the control of unjustified rule-makers, and Kahn implies that the natural evolution of the form of poetry would be in the direction of prose poetry.

The style of Kahn's article reflects the desire of many nineteenth-century poets to apply experimental control to the shifting, impalpable area of human emotion. One of Poe's translators, William Hughes, had a fleeting glimpse of the tendency in Poe. In contrasting Hoffman and Poe in the introduction of Contes inédits, Hughes said that Hoffman stops at the outer image of his hallucination, while Poe fixes the image in his mind and tries to determine its essence. "That is why the fantastic rises so easily beyond the object in order to take possession of the human spirit; for all its power is born of this reciprocal and simultaneous penetration. Moreover, what we can really call its value and its scientific explanation are born of that interaction."[23]

This was also very nearly Mallarmé's intent—with an obscurity different from Kahn's—when he wrote the preface for René Ghil's Traité du verbe and asked, "To what end the miracle of transposing a natural event into its vibrating near-disappearance by the play of words, however, if not to elicit, without the hindrance of a close or distant recall, the pure idea?"[24] Mallarmé's statement is a late definition (1886) and mysterious because it is an algebraic solution whose preliminary steps have not been given. In some early notes on linguistics, he has already revealed that he was exploring the possibilities of a scientific refinement of language.

So far, our investigation has been largely devoted to techniques in Poe's narratives that could be called American—the factual, logical or pseudo-scientific, and the materialistic—and their relation to similar tendencies in French literature. The discovery of an interest in science among French poets from Baudelaire to Valéry is not new; in his study of Symbolism, Edmund Wilson has pointed out that "there is something akin to the scientific instinct in the efforts of modern literature to render the transitory phases of 'a world of fine gradations and subtly linked conditions, shifting. intricately as we ourselves change.' "[25] Paul Valéry says of Mallarmé: "The obscurity found in his work results from some rigorously maintained requirement of his, just as it happens in science that logic, analogy and careful following of consequences lead to results very different from those with which firsthand observation has familiarized us."[26] With Poe's strong influence on this tendency established, only one significant aspect remains to be discussed. It is a shift in emphasis which, although it marks a change in literary craft, make a distinction between two world-views. The shift can be seen in the imagery used in speaking of the artist as scientist: there are dissectors and mathematicians. Both categories contain Poe.

In Jacques Rivière's study of Rimbaud we find a relevant interpretation of that poet's interest in science. Rimbaud's poem "Angoisse" in Les Illuminations presents a question: "Is is possible that the accidents of scientific fairyland and a movement toward human fraternity will be cherished as the progressive restitution of primal freedom?" And Rivière explains the attraction of science:

> Human life by its very imperfection is pliant and thoroughly bound . . . but in science everything is as pure, new, sharp, keen, and atrocious as (on the operating table, under artificial light coming from the ceiling) the naked child that the scalpel cuts. Science, then, is designed for expressing the inhuman cleanness, the brightness, the horror of that antithesis of life—virginity.[27]

We may disregard the end of the last sentence, which has particular reference to Rimbaud and cannot apply to others—to

Baudelaire, for example, who is forcibly brought to mind by the surgical image. His first essay on Poe used the same image in speaking of the spirit of inquiry in philosophic writers, some of whom "examine the tumorous soul, as doctors examine the body, and put out their eyes looking for the source."

Surgery is an act of controlled cruelty, useful but, in a sense, inhuman. It is a remarkably good metaphor for some aspects of the relationship between nineteenth-century literature and society because it conveys the idea of disorder, of agony, while at the same time conveying the idea of the cold, analytic, unmoved operator. The surgeon is a *dandy*. Yet even in Zola the metaphor occurs when he compares the two Romantic masters of the novel, George Sand and Balzac. Whereas George Sand is an idealist who wants to change society—a healer—Balzac is an anatomist: "He operates on the human body, without pity for that palpitating flesh. . . . He verifies and explains, like a professor of surgery who describes a rare disease."[28] The cure, he indicated, would come later; but the anatomist could not be concerned with it. He has expressed the unadulterated scientific view of literature; when his earnest and literal moral view is replaced by a demonic imagination, as in Baudelaire and Rimbaud, the surgeon takes on some of the traits of a punisher or torturer. In this connection it is interesting to note that Baudelaire was so fascinated by "The Black Cat" that he memorized it and recited it for his friends. The story is related to the surgical symbol because Poe described insane crime and concealment with the same amoral rationality and cold calculation that a surgeon would use, and because the gouger of Pluto's eye represents the essential nature of the Surgeon without the restriction or direction of morality. The pattern was not always so brutal and sadistic. In "Mesmeric Revelation," for example, there is a combination of medicine and metaphysics which, as Baudelaire indicated, is highly original. There was something new in a writer's asking casually, "But where, meantime, was the soul?" as Poe did in the "Premature Burial," and then setting out to answer the question by means of fictional induction. In the "Mesmeric Revelation," Poe set his stage with all possible scientific apparatus—the fact of hypnotism (that is, the fact that such power of one individual over another exists), the stiff, cold language used in an objective description of an experiment, the formal medical analysis of the patient—as a basis for the experiment. After the sober medical scene has been set, the doctor proceeds to wrest the truth from his patient: "What, then, is God?"

No one would seriously contend that this is proper medical science. Yet the technique is that of presenting evidence to support a hypothesis, and it arrives at metaphysical statement through the phenomenal world. It is in harmony, as technique and symbol, with the surgical pattern. The impulse behind this pattern is one of emotional refusal of human life combined with a desire to know, a curiosity that approaches its desire by force, by anatomizing the flesh, blood and nerves of humanity.

In contrast, *Eureka,* which extends the inquiry of the "Mesmeric Revelation," arrives at metaphysical statement by means of the mathematical pattern. In spite of the fact that Poe's mathematical calculation was noted from the first—Forgues made much of it in his essay in 1846—it did not take hold imaginatively as Poe's dissecting method did until later in the century. Although Baudelaire wrote about mathematical form in poetry and accepted Poe's poetic theories, they remained for the Symbolists to assimilate actively, just as the appreciation of *Eureka* was left to them.

Both Mallarmé and Valéry write of their methods as mathematical; Valéry clearly states that Poe provided his introduction to the creative possibility of mathematics. The intellectual development of these two poets exploits fully a tendency which, in Poe, is sometimes obscured by other traits. It reflects an impulse toward dehumanization or withdrawal from the inevitable fluctuations of feelings, values and truths in human action. In short, it rejects mortality. The distinction between the surgeon and the mathematician parallels the distinction between Baudelaire's outlaw and Mallarmé's exile. Spiritually and artistically, the latter dissociated himself by withdrawing into forms having no human equivalent or reflection—music, mathematics and pure poetry.

Thus the scientific method applied to literature and human action had a very widespread interest for French writers in the second half of the century; such dissimilar poets as Gustave Kahn and Paul Valéry found equally dissimilar patterns of scientific approach in Poe. The image of America and the work of Poe contained two contrary potentialities: literature of hard clinical analysis, and literature that combined science and imagination. Poe had much to offer in both methods, but he was not an isolated pioneer in any of the uses of science we might associate

with Naturalism or with the poetry of sensation. In those areas
his influence was supplementary; there were also French experi-
menters. He was, however, a major influence in the development
of psychological analysis. And in one of its aspects he was more
than a revolutionary influence. He was the source of a method
for unifying the scientific and the spiritual. For this reason he was
ultimately rejected by the dedicated materialists at the end of the
century—those who believed that idealism was outmoded and
false to the physiological reality, and said, "There is the same
distinction between them and the naturalists as there is between
orthodox philosophy and the true modern philosophy, scientific
positivism."[29] It so happened that positivism was not the true
modern philosophy, and the poets who followed the dogma of
sensation and realism—Jean Richepin, for example, another ad-
mirer of Poe—were not destined to dominate the poets who
followed Poe in fusing the two modes, or found a means of
expressing the contradiction. Jules Laforgue combined idealism
and naturalism in a synthesis that is found in these lines:

> Ah! what rich treasure the artist Love displays!
> Red or sulphurous oranges, or bruised rose,
> The white of cold-cream; and the oriental splendor
> Of greens, black lilacs, and rotten yellows![30]

Rich treasure, the artist Love derive from Renaissance amor-
ous esthetics; the rose in idealist symbolism is nearly universal
in western poetry. These in conjunction with the commonplace
realism of *cold-cream* and the Naturalist physiological analytics
of *bruised* and *rotten yellows* provide an effect which Laforgue
himself found in Baudelaire and called *American*:

> "Your skin glistens, your gait—a serpent at the end of
> a stick, your hair an ocean, your head poised with the soft-
> ness of a young elephant, your body bends like a fine ship
> that dips its yards to the water, your saliva rises to your
> lips like a river swollen by the thaw of growling glaciers"—
> It's americanism applied to the comparisons of the Song of
> Songs.

Baudelaire
cat, Hindoo, yankee, episcopal alchemist

yankee his "very—" before an adjective
his brittle landscapes—and this line

   "My heart, you move with agility"
which the initiate parcel out in metallic voices.
   "Clear emblems"
hate of eloquence and poetic secrets.
   "The vaporous pleasure will fly towards the horizon
    Like . . ."
Like what? Before him Hugo, Gautier, etc., would have a
French comparison—oratorical—he makes it yankee, with-
out preconceptions, even while remaining aerial
   "Like a sylphid behind the scenes."
One sees the wires and the machinery.[31]

Thus the American who "poeticized science"[32] prepared the
literary world, by both theory and practice, for literature that
would be almost mystical in its intent, as well as scientific in its
technique and materialistic in arriving at the ideal through sensation rather than through didactic or abstract statement. It is important to note that thus far this particular tendency was not seen
in Poe's poetry, but rather in his tales. Mallarmé is justly famous
for his "discovery" and dissemination of Poe's poems because he
succeeded in transposing their distinctive virtue. For many years,
however, even the poets were more influenced by his prose technique, with their detailed physical and psychological analyses,
often dryly presented, leading deliberately to a terrible vision of
the extra-sensory world.

  America, then, represented a new cultural trend that many
Frenchmen feared. Almost all distrusted the fundamental tenets
of individual disengagement from any tradition and material
progress as they saw those principles in action in an entire society.
The factual, practical and rational aspect of American character
was not so distressing as its ignorant mingling of material idolatry
and spiritual covetousness. The early French identification of Poe
with America was not detrimental to Poe, however, because it
emphasized his dominant intellectual qualities while leaving his
character as outlaw intact.

  It is a fine irony that in reacting against America and naturalism (both being fundamentally materialistic) the most unmater-
ialistic and nonrational school of French poetry should choose
an American as standard-bearer and chief witness against America, and yet that it should use America's own tools of sensation,
science and the untrammeled spirit of conquest. That was the
paradoxical and fruitful situation of Symbolism.

NOTES

[1] Francois-René de Chateaubriand, *Oeuvres complètes,* XII (Paris, 1836), 279, 290.

[2] Baudelaire, Pléiade edition, p. 693.

[3] J-K Huysmans, *A Rebours* (Paris, 1953), p. 268.

[4] Alexis de Tocqueville, *Democracy in America,* trans. Henry Reeve, ed. Henry Steele Commager (New York, 1947), p. 242.

[5] Emile Montégut, "De la littérature en Europe et en Amérique," *Revue des deux mondes,* 15 October 1849, p. 322.

[6] Baudelaire, Pléiade edition, p. 1201.

[7] *Ibid.,* p. 1224.

[8] Barbey d'Aurevilly, "Le Roi des Bohêmes."

[9] Charles de Moüy, "Etudes contemporaines; XX: Edgar Poe," *Revue française,* VI (1 October 1853), 147.

[10] Remy de Gourmont, *Promenades littéraires* (Paris, 1904), pp. 348-382.

[11] Adrien Delondre, "La Magie et les magiciens," *Revue contemporaine,* XXXII (15 June 1857), 284.

[12] Barbey d'Aurevilly, "Les Romantiques du *Siècle,*" *Le Réveil,* 16 January 1858.

[13] Armand de Pontmartin, "Causeries littéraires."

[14] L. Cartier, "Edgar Poe, Romancier américain," *Le Figaro,* 21 March 1856, p. 1.

[15] Louis Etienne, "Les Conteurs américains—Edgar Allan Poe," *Revue contemporaine,* XXXII (15 July 1857), 492-524.

[16] Auguste Laucassade, *Revue contemporaine,* 15 October 1855, p. 96.

[17] Baudelaire, *Lettres 1841-1866* (Paris, 1906), p. 83. Letter dated 21 January 1856.

[18] *Bibliothèque universelle,* 4 series, XX (May 1852), 105-116.

[19] L. Etienne, *op. cit.,* p. 524.

[20] Edmond and Jules de Goncourt, *Journal,* I (Paris, 1891),.137-138.

[21] James H. Smith and Edd W. Parks, eds., *The Great Critics,* 3rd ed. (New York, 1951), p. 906. The passage is to be found in "Le Roman experimental" in Emile Zola, *Oeuvres complètes,* ed. Maurice Le Blond, XLV (Paris, 1928), 16.

[22] L. Cartier, *loc. cit.*

[23] *Contes inédits d'Edgar Poe,* trans. William L. Hughes (Paris, 1862).

[24] Mallarmé, Pléiade edition, p. 857.

[25] Edmund Wilson, *Axel's Castle* (New York, 1948), p. 295.

[26] Paul Valéry, *Variété II* (Paris, 1930), p. 199.

[27] Jacques Rivière, *Rimbaud* (Paris, [1934?]), pp. 69-70.

[28] Emile Zola, *Oeuvres complètes,* pp. 155-156.

[29] Fantasio, "Quelques mots sur le roman moderne," *La Revue blanche,* II (15 February 1886), 59.

[30] Jules Laforgue, "Rosace en vitrail," *Oeuvres complètes,* I (Paris, 1951), 33.

[31] Jules Laforgue, "Notes sur Baudelaire," *Entretiens politiques et littéraires,* II (1891), 97-120.

[32] F. Bachelier, "Le Scarabée d'or," *Le Moniteur universel,* 7 September 1853, p. 994.

THE POET

By 1885, Poe had assumed the legendary role he was to play in France, the cultural challenge of America had settled into the background and various post-Romantic literary experiments had been made which had no relation to Poe's theories or poetic experiments. Then, in that year, a new school declared itself and based its program on Poe's poetics. However, the emergence of Poe in his new position was not so sudden as it seemed. In the interval between Baudelaire's death and the ascendancy of the Symbolists, Mallarmé had been persistently translating Poe and talking of Poe in his intimate circle, and Verlaine had also admired and studied Poe and kept alive the tradition of the "accursed poet." Although the poets and theorists who were to be grouped together as Symbolists were also drawing idealist and mystic ideas from other sources, notably Carlyle and Schopenhauer, Poe was a more impressive influence for he satisfied the Symbolist inclination both as theorist and as artist. When the philosophic heritage had been assimilated and the poetic movement had maturity and some coherence, the Symbolists launched the manifestos that aroused new controversy over Poe and the concepts he represented.

In the notes to his translation of Poe's poems, Mallarmé speaks of the "new poetic theory that suddenly arrived from a distant America" and caused a crisis in French esthetics. The crisis he is apparently referring to revealed itself in the exchange of articles among the traditionalists and the new poets in 1885 and 1886.[1] Sutter Laumann and Anatole France had attacked the new "decadent" school of poetry; Paul Adam, Jean Moréas

51

and Gustave Kahn had asserted their identity as "symbolists" and had drawn much of their theory and support from Baudelaire and Poe.

However, Poe's two essays on poetics, "The Poetic Principle" and "Philosophy of Composition," were not equally well known or completely adopted. When Mallarmé speaks of the new poetic theory, he is referring to the key concepts of "The Poetic Principle" and the idea *behind* "Philosophy of Composition." In the first essay, the Symbolists ignored certain elaborations and examples of the major ideas—the poetic inducement, for example, of "the bright orbs that shine in Heaven" and "the sighing of the night wind"—and they gave little attention to the question of length. They pointedly ignored one idea in "The Poetic Principle": Poe has commented on naturalness of style, saying *"the tone,* in composition, should always be that which the mass of mankind would adopt." Poe's own style does not obey his edict, and the Symbolists were far from entertaining this attitude.

In limiting their acceptance of Poe's theory to its essence, the Symbolists followed Baudelaire in appropriating the two master ideas that beauty, not truth, is the province of poetry, and that true poetic effect is an exaltation of spirit through the creation of beauty. At the outset it must be acknowledged that Poe's theories had already been interpreted by Baudelaire; in the process of interpretation, he had emphasized these major ideas in such a way that their application was made easier. For example, Poe's statement that beauty brings tears of sorrow "at our inability to grasp *now,* wholly, here on earth, at once and for ever, those divine and rapturous joys" is interpolated between two of Baudelaire's own favorite ideas. First, "This admirable, immortal instinct for the beautiful makes us look upon the earth and its spectacles as if they were glimpses or correspondences of Heaven. The insatiable thirst for the beyond—which life reveals—is our most active proof of immortality." Second, "these tears . . . testify to an aggravated melancholy, a cry of the nerves, of a being exiled in the imperfect and wanting to grasp at once . . . a revealed paradise."

"Philosophy of Composition" underwent an even greater change. Whereas Baudelaire had merely translated large passages from "The Poetic Principle," he interpreted "Philosophy of Composition" thoroughly, explaining Poe's motives and the implications of the essay. Having drawn from it the principle that the poet works in full and deliberate consciousness, he ignored such details as the dictum that the death of a beautiful woman is the most poetic subject.

The Symbolists, therefore, had the advantage of Baudelaire's interpretation of Poe's essays, as well as the original statements. They were nurtured on those theories, whereas Baudelaire had come upon them in his maturity, so that they served largely as confirmation of his own ideas. Since the Symbolists treated Poe as the Source, it is necessary to see how closely their theories coincided with his.

There were various manifestoes, but the earliest and probably the most important in presenting the central Symbolist doctrine was that of Jean Moréas, one of the lesser poets, in 1885. According to Moréas, the Symbolists accepted Baudelaire, with his poetry for poetry's sake, as their master, sought "the pure concept and the eternal Symbol" with Poe's limitation of poetry to Beauty, attempted to use suggestion as a technique replacing direct statement and worked for metrical liberation beyond that of Romanticism. The first three ideas bear unmistakably the mark of Poe.

In reality, the declaration of the independence of art was a necessary preamble to the other principles. If the artist was to claim a position above society, to claim to be the spiritual and intellectual aristocrat at least, and a transcendental seer at most, he had to cease being a public servant, celebrating the values of society and humbly effacing himself. As the previously quoted statements of the School of Good Sense indicate, the artists were not fighting straw men; there was a strong public opinion attempting to hold the writer to his function as the supporter and disseminator of right attitudes toward life. In rejecting Morality and Truth as the concern of the poet, Poe was protesting this rein, rather than refusing all morality and all truth. To judge by their analyses of his statements, there was never any question about this in the minds of the French adapters of his theories. As the artist became progressively more dissatisfied with his society, and as the distance between commonly accepted ideas and avant-garde ideas noticeably widened, the poets detached themselves more determinedly from the limitations of public concepts. For this reason the Symbolists found Poe's "Poetic Principle" new and prophetic, as if created for their moment, even though Baudelaire had advanced it twenty-five years earlier

as a solitary protest; Poe's theory had gained little credence
through being supported by such Bohemians as Charles Baudelaire and Théophile Gautier.

Having thrown out the most venerable of literary standards
—the social and moral ènd of literature—Poe had replaced it
with the statement that the esthetic experience has no other end
than itself. Although Moréas spoke of "poetry for its own sake"
in his manifesto, such terms suggest a false interpretation of the
theory. Poe no more worshipped art than a religious man worships
images. He made it clear that the experience of true poetry is the
closest possible approximation to a total religious and philosophic
experience that man can have. Poetry is the creation of beauty,
which in turn is the gate to the supernal. The last two propositions that Moréas makes ("the pure concept and the eternal
Symbol,") are techniques for fulfilling this poetic ideal. They are
an outgrowth of the first proposition and of Baudelaire's theory
of correspondences, which had been added to the transcription of
Poe's theory. If the beautiful object becomes a means of a transcendent experience, it follows that one task of the poet is to find
and represent the essence of that object. Since it is a transcendental experience that he must convey, and not a lesson that he must
teach, no direct statement will serve.

This is the basic principle of the Symbolists, and it is Poe's.
Once we leave broad general statements, however, and consider
specific applications, we find a great deal of variety in the temperament and inclination of the Symbolists, and consequent
modifications by them of Poe's theory. Gustave Kahn, who placed
more emphasis on revolutionary metrics than Moréas, suggests
another area of Poe's influence. Kahn thought the poets united
by "denial of the old, monotonous techniques of verse and by
the desire to vary rhythm and to give the diagram of a sensation
in the design of a stanza."[2] He also declared the intention of the
group—similar to that of the Pléiade—to renovate and restore
the French language. The latter aim is characteristic of many
Symbolists (Mallarmé, Adam, Laforgue, Ghil) and provided
ample grounds for satire. Brunetière, in 1891, defined the group
by aping its language:

> Above all intent on pledging the art dying of secularity,
> in urgent reaction, or better called revolt, against the torpid
> bondage of Alexic and Zolist naturalism to tasks of duplica-
> tion of an unfixable reality, Symbolism is the reintegration

of the indefiniteness or the fluidity of things, to be registered
in the comparative or the suggestive by means of a poly-
morphic rhythm allied to a language undulating to the
incessantly promised limits of metaphorism emancipated
from trivial usage.[3]

Brunetière's parody is, of course, highly exaggerated, but he has
reflected the attitude and some of the faults of Symbolism. There
is some possibility of Poe's having influenced Symbolist language
in his use of the jargon of science and of rare and archaic words;
indirectly, he may have influenced it through his translators, for
Baudelaire was accused of neologism by Pontmartin, and Mallarmé has been accused of introducing foreign syntax into
French. But the convoluted syntax and forced vocabulary cannot
be ascribed to Poe's poetic theory, nor can the self-determinism
of line and stanza. It is very probable that Kahn is referring to
free verse. If so, the statement is relevant to Poe's poetry, for
Kahn speaks of Poe's verse as if it were freed from traditional
laws, as if brief evocative stories such as "Shadow" and "Silence"
were experiments in a new poetic form, and as if Poe had begun
to evolve a form combining metric poetry and prose narrative,
as in "Ligeia."[4] It is uncertain to what extent Kahn believed that
Poe was an innovator in poetic form and to what extent he was
constructing a convincing precedent for his own innovations. In
fact, we cannot even say with assurance that Kahn was mistaken.
It is quite possible that Poe *was* attempting a new form, the prose
poem. It has also been suggested that Mallarmé's translation of
the poems, which is in prose, caused some confusion and led to
the belief that Poe was a vers-librist.

Although Poe's relation to the revolution in metrics is
questionable, it is evident that Moréas and Kahn are in agreement in their fundamental concepts, and that they believed they
were pursuing the course that Poe had outlined. Both poets are,
in their own way, seekers after essence; they share a desire to
cast off not only society's requirement of didacticism, but also
the old prosody and rhetoric that served the poetry of the past.
Since psychic experience is intangible and is to be captured not
by photography or description but by evocation, the poets struggled against rhetorical patterns associated with dogma and description. Verlaine's exuberant "Art poétique" states the position:

Prends l'éloquence et tords-lui le cou!

Mallarmé, in his preface to Rene Ghil's *Traité du verbe,* excludes the "brute" word from poetry, and the brute word is the word rhetorically used. Rhetoric implies personal communication, which Mallarmé rejected. "Pure work implies the elocutionary disappearance of the poet, who gives the initiative to words, mobilized by the shock of their inequality."[5] There is nothing in Poe's essays to suggest a rejection of rhetoric; the poems cited in "The Poetic Principle" are, in fact, largely rhetorical. But the procedure described in "Philosophy of Composition" clearly indicates composition by the sound and effect of words, with emphasis upon the sublimity of the evocation of an essential emotion rather than on the truth of the concrete situation which gives rise to it.

Although they were unanimous in rejecting the old rhetoric (the oratorical and direct statement), they were divergent in the means of replacing rhetoric and in the extent to which they disintegrated the old forms. Mallarmé is at one extreme, with his cult of the word and his definition of poetry which echoes Poe and Baudelaire:

> Poetry is the expression, in human language recapturing its essential rhythm, of the mysterious meaning of the aspects of existence: thus it offers authenticity to our stay and is our only spiritual task.[6]

Mallarmé is interested in a spiritual absolute, and he goes farther than Poe in abstraction of esthetic feeling. He adheres to Idea rather than sensation:

> I revere Poe's opinion, no trace of a philosophy, of esthetics or metaphysics appears; I must add that it is necessary, inherent and latent. . . . The intellectual armature of the poem is hidden and holds—occurs—in the space that isolates the stanzas and in the white spaces of the paper. [7]

At the other extreme, far from the occult, is Gustave Kahn. In analyzing Poe's stories according to the principle of "Philosophy of Composition," Kahn evolved the theory that Poe's work, and all true modern poetry, is "an attempt to translate pure sensation: love without the contingencies that might limit it to such and such a person. . . ." He then defined poetry as "the elaboration of feeling in its essence, purified of the environment and the accidentals that are the cause of error." The key words in Kahn's analysis are *sensation, feeling, true nature* and *essence.*

For him as for Mallarmé, but on a different plane, all precisions of prosody were attempts to capture the essence of experience rather than existence.

Others elaborated Poe's theory of the calculation of verbal and musical effects. In his defense against attacks made on *Le Thé chez Miranda,* Paul Adam stated the requirements of a Symbolist poet, beginning with the major one, that the poet be a complete master of language. With that mastery he created sensation and an inscape:

> Sensations should be at once complex and single; the individual should live within the external world and construct it according to his particular configuration. And, since dream is indistinguishable from life, the poet should portray the state of dream and also the state of hallucination and the constant dreams of memory. Then he must give the phrase the cadence of the idea; use a certain tone for one sensation, a melody for another; ban sounds that are repeated without deliberate harmony; recall a previously expressed idea by a word of a different meaning, but similar to the first through assonance.[8]

Both Kahn and Adam, though minor poets, speak for the Symbolists as a group more than Mallarmé does, for they indicate the fundamental interest in the specifics of sensibility—sensation, knowledge, feeling—whereas Mallarmé tends to speak only of the ultimate intentions. Paul Valéry follows the tendencies of Kahn and Adam in this respect when he states: "The duty, the labor, and the function of the poet are to reveal and enact the powers of movement and enchantment, the arousers of the affective life and intellectual sensibility."[9]

When the poet was no longer held back by the dogma of his society and by its practical demands, and had freed himself from traditional art forms he would be able to use Poe's last great principle and achieve his destiny as creator rather than entertainer or teacher. For the Creator, there could be no question of inspiration; there had to be mind in full power. Poe's "Philosophy of Composition" had various repercussions because, like "The Poetic Principle," it was fortunately susceptible to many interpretations. The influence of technical aspects of the poems will be considered briefly, but the adoption of specific techniques is less significant than the poetic intention because of the overriding metaphysical or philosophic impulse of the Symbolists in applying Poe's doctrine of conscious control.

As the preceding chapter suggests, the French poets were stirred by the idea of a scientific approach to literary creation. Paul Valéry's statement on Romanticism and the reactions against it in his essay on Baudelaire summarizes the self-determination of a literary movement and indicates Poe's vital role. First, as Valéry describes the process, the Romantics having appropriated certain large areas of poetry and exhausted them, their successors had to explore other areas; second, the excesses and enthusiasms of Romanticism brought a revulsion; third, a "reflective action" inevitably took the place of a "spontaneous action." That is, the spontaneous, in the sense of a surge of expression that has not undergone an analytic test and in which "inspiration" plays a major role, must give way to a highly intellectual action in which the original inspiration becomes the subject of an analytic construct. Poe's contribution in this literary evolution was to give the new school a method: "Before Poe, the premises of literature had never been examined, reduced to a problem in psychology, and attacked by means of an analysis in which logic and the mechanics of effect were deliberately employed."

The immediate, ponderable effect was evident in the enthusiasm with which the poets avowed their credo of poetic *calculation*. A certain possibility of cynicism is implicit in the concept of the artist's dispassionate control of his craft, especially if he is intent on affecting the reader. In a comment on a line by Baudelaire, Verlaine makes light of this attitude and avoids the problem it poses by mocking the sentimentality of the opposition. Baudelaire's line, from "Les petites vieilles," is "Have you noticed that many shrouds for old women/Are nearly as small as those of children?"

> "Have you *noticed,* etc."—a superb phlegmatic impertinence, which would have ravished Poe . . . . I can hear the passionists from here, those everlastingly disappointed ones: "Damn the insolent artist, spoiling our pleasure like that, making fun of the tears he wrings from us, and trampling on our emotions, which he has aroused!" And there they are, all frothing. . . . And the inspired ones! I don't dare imagine what they think.[10]

Curiously enough, accusations of intellectual cynicism and complaints of inconstancy have been directed against Poe and Baudelaire, more than against Verlaine, Rimbaud or Valéry. Verlaine, who is scarcely notable for his integrity or rigor of thought, comments on Poe as if he were a fellow minstrel with some rather good tricks up his sleeve.

In contrast to Verlaine's essentially adolescent attitude toward highly conscious technique, other poets employed it more intellectually or more subtly. They were turning to the exploration of the reach of man's mind. Some were engrossed in the inner drama of thought and feeling:

> We want to substitute the struggle of sensations and of ideas for the struggle of individuals, and for the scene of action, instead of the overused stage of crossroads and streets, part of a brain or all of it. The essential aim of our art is to objectify the subjective (the exteriorization of the Idea) instead of subjectifying the objective (nature seen through a temperament). . . . It is literature's adhesion to the scientific theories constructed by induction and controlled by experiment.[11]

On the other hand, some were intent on descending into consciousness to infinity; they found a pioneer in Poe, but, as with most pioneers, he was revered on their own terms by the men who followed him. Kahn had an almost scientific detachment; although he was fascinated by the bizarre and morbid elements in Poe, he tended to deny the powerful moral basis of such stories as "Berenice," thus denying the coherence given Poe's exploration of consciousness by his concept of evil. In contrast, Maeterlinck and Mallarmé ignored the grotesque, the baroque and the evil, equally. In Maeterlinck consciousness became a mystic unconscious; in Mallarmé it became a means of transcending consciousness.

Poe's anatomizing of the perverse and of the inverted consciousness and his exploration of the levels of the human mind, from intuition probing the subconscious to reason suing the cosmos came at a time when the relationship of mind to matter, of idea to reality and of earth to universe seemed very uncertain. Psychological conflict provided a new and unknown area of art, as Valéry implied, for writers who felt overwhelmed by their Romantic predecessors. But it was much more than that. For some idealistic poets it was a method of approaching the absolute at a time when a traditional religious approach was impossible, and for some it led to a terrible intoxication and to an inescapable

and deceptively enchanting labyrinth. Albert Samain recorded
the latter attitude in his two responses to *Eureka* and its effect of
transcendent consciousness. In the first encounter, he felt that
the realm of rarified reason was a death, and he had difficulty
in re-establishing contact with his earthly routine; in the second,
he had been captivated by the "compelling and vertiginous
beyond" and he was exhilarated by the feeling that "space opens
out. . . . One advances forever, forever." Samain's response was
the reaction of the School of Good Sense exactly reversed; both
felt the unearthly compulsion, but Good Sense rejected it, perceiving that the disengaged mind would refuse the world. Among
the Symbolists, Charles Morice gave strongest and clearest expression to the mystical instinct of the seeking mind:

> [People] understand that the work and the spirit of the Poet
> are, for society as it has decided to be, a social threat: if
> genius should achieve its own perfect realization—that is,
> its own advent in the Absolute—the embrace of Man and
> God would intoxicate all other men with distaste for living
> outside of God, and this would be the fall of appearance
> into Reality.[12]

Morice interpreted the Symbolist poetics according to his own
bent, which was philosophic and discursively mystical, and he
was more inclined toward German masters than toward Poe.
Although he relegated Poe and Baudelaire to a subordinate position as predecessors of the New Art (the philosophic ancestry of
Goethe and Chateaubriand, precursors in science and mysticism,
was thought to be more important), it becomes clear, as soon as
Morice states the intentions of art, that Poe was also philosophically in harmony with Morice's version of Symbolism, which is an
attempt to reach the "forbidden beyond." Morice's contemporaries desired "l'art pour l'art," he stated, but only as it was "pour
l'au-delà."

Many of the Symbolists are evidently motivated by the
desire he indicates. The poetic platform of Rimbaud, serious
even in its irony, is art's calculation of the means of leaping to
the absolute through words:

> I regulated the form and the movement of every con-
> sonant, and with instinctive rhythms I prided myself on in-
> venting a poetic language accessible some day to all the
> senses . . . at first it was an experiment. I wrote silences, I
> wrote the night. I recorded the inexpressible. I fixed fren-
> zies in their flight.[13]

These lines are in the natural line of extension of Poe's theories. From the start, most of the French critics had seen in Poe's tales a combination of calculation and mysticism, but in the 1880s the purpose of that combination became significant. The impalpable psyche was submitted to every test-tube analysis not solely through scientific curiosity, but through a craving for ultimate knowledge. All of Poe's work bears this double character: deliberate control of means, and empyrean aim.

Poe's calculation, his discriminate choice of words for precision of effect—whether specific or indefinite—is a crucial characteristic. As Poe developed this technique, it is perhaps the root of all his originality. It is the characteristic above all others that enchanted French poets, but it is also, in some deep cultural substratum, antipathetic to Anglo-Saxon people, for whom Poe stimulates hostility, while the French poets arouse no such animosity. Deliberate manipulation of words for a predetermined effect makes Poe a charlatan but Valéry a poet of consciousness. There is some difference, however. Consciousness in Valéry is a mode of exploring life and the self, while consciousness in Poe is felt to be a mode of *acting upon others,* that is, of playing the unmoved mover. Any experienced perversity is more readily accepted than the pretense of feeling in order to lead others into feeling. All questions of sincerity aside—for the questions come at last to a question of technical competence—Poe's statements concerning the calculated effects of his poems condemn him for a Romantic reader. This is the reason for much of the adverse criticism of Poe, and although the antagonism is often caused by the tales—where he was often avowedly a hoaxer—"Philosophy of Composition" harmed Poe's reputation with its mockery as much as it benefited poetry with its analytic approach. The irritating tone of the essay and Poe's denial of its seriousness must be taken into account. Faced with the problem, Mallarmé considered it judiciously and emerged unshaken in his admiration for Poe.

When he referred to the novelty of Poe's ideas, Mallarmé indicated that the procedures of his composition are as old as art, and he insinuated that they had been partially determined by the poverty of art in America, particularly the lack of a theater. His suggestion that Poe transferred his architectural and musical talents (which Mallarmé equates with the dramatic) to poetry because lack of outlet cast him back to the poetic source

deserves some thought and returns to us what Baudelaire called
the *jongleur* in Poe. The emphasis on effect, the control of the
structure and tone of a poem with an eye to its effect on the
reader, does in fact reveal the dramatist's view. It is not the
traditional view of a lyric poet; at least the lyric poet has not
commonly declared his intentions. The writer of short poems—
and Poe claimed that there were no others—was a lyricist, a
singer. Although there have been dramatic lyricists—Baudelaire
is the most striking example—Poe gave the poetry of effect a
rationale and a metaphysical basis. Consequently, even Mallarmé,
the least public of poets, and the least theatrical, fully accepted
Poe's dramatic intent, judging drama to be the perfect art form
because it fused the multiple manifestations of consciousness and
sensibility into an essential unity. Although Mallarmé has been
compared to a choreographer rather than a dramatist, his own
suggestions on drama would lead us to assume that ballet could
not achieve the essential unity. His notes for *Igitur* define his
high conception of drama:

> Drama is in the mystery
> of the following equation—
> that theater
> is
> the development of the hero or heroes,
> the summing-up of theater
> as Idea and hymn
> so that Theater = idea
> hero = hymn
> and that makes a whole
> Drama or Mystery
> coming together again
> also[14]

Most of the major Symbolist poets attempted dramatic
structures, sometimes for the theater (Villiers de l'Isle-Adam),
sometimes in "closet-drama" (Mallarmé and Valéry), sometimes
in externally dramatic poetry. The dramatic experiments were
more successful in lyric poetry than in the theater because the
drama of consciousness is difficult to stage, requiring a dramatic
genius of the order of Beckett to find a form. Drama and transcendence have a venerable kinship in mystery and ritual, but
Mallarmé's mystery drama, *Igitur,* has no ritual because it has
no outward action, and his drama never achieved transcendence,

not only because it was never completed, but also because it had
no body to transcend. However, if we consider his poetry (the
"Herodiade," "L'Après-midi d'un faune" or "Le vierge le vivace
et le bel aujourd'hui" we find the drama of attitudes embodied,
even if tenuously so, and in the famous "Tombeau d'Edgar Poe"
there is a rather traditional heroic drama. If we compare the last
two sonnets, we come to the conclusion that Mallarmé understood Poe's darkly suggestive language and strongly highlighted
tensions and did them homage by imitation in the "Tombeau,"
but that his own inclination was toward a more allusive drama.
But in either case he accepted drama as an attempt to weld the
visible and the imagined, the creative consciousness and the
perceiving consciousness, in an essential event.

These elaborations illustrate the analysis and extension that
Poe's theory underwent. They reveal the Symbolists' fidelity to
the basic concepts of Poe's poetics: art's automony, the poet's
control, and his essential aim. They suggest how fully mistaken
an eminent American critic can be in judging Poe's theories to
be purely personal, without application to literature in general.[15]

Although all facets of the cult of consciousness are implicit
in Poe's work, his literary theory and the psychological exploration of the tales appear to have had a more widespread effect than
his poetry, whether consciousness was considered a means of
poetic creation or an end in itself. The reason is simple. Poe
followed his own theory only too well in eliminating Reason from
poetry, and his followers found it easier to use his dogma than
his poems as the pattern for their work. In the complete Symbolism of his better poems Poe was thoroughly understood by
only the most subtle of the Symbolists—Mallarmé. The other
Symbolists approached Poe's poetic originality primarily through
his theory and secondarily through the partial Symbolism of tales
such as "Shadow" and "Eleonora." However, since they saw
many of Poe's tales as poems of a new kind, the distinction between the two influences is blurred.

Célestin Pierre Cambiaire has studied extensively the imita-
tions of Poe and the allusions to his poetry that had a vogue in
the second half of the nineteenth century. They take the form
of subject borrowings, titles, refrains, English words and epi-
graphs, and allusions to Poe himself. On the whole, these imita-
tions either prove uninteresting or reveal a very superficial relation
to Poe. One example from Verlaine will suffice to illustrate. "Mon

rêve familier" is thought to reveal Poe's influence; some of the
deliberate vagueness ("Her name? I remember it was soft and
sonorous") reminds us of Poe's mysterious women, and the use
of words for their suggestive power is in the tradition of Poe, but
the effect, the tone and the intent are all very unlike Poe's. They
are too finite and too sentimental. The French response to Poe's
poetry in its primary function and practice—that is, as the
poetry performs what the theory promises—is more interesting.

Although the early critics had read little of Poe's poetry,
or had paid little attention, it was not completely unknown before
Mallarmé's translation. "The Conqueror Worm" and "The
Haunted Palace" were translated in "Ligeia" and "The Fall of
the House of Usher," while "The Raven," "Annabel Lee" and
"The Bells" had appeared in various periodicals between 1853
and 1862. Baudelaire's comments on the poetry were rather brief
and inconclusive. In his 1852 essay he commented sarcastically
that the traditional "To Helen" and the virtuoso "The Raven"
were highly valued in America because they were departures from
Poe's true poetic destiny, which was "eccentric and electric." In
the *Nouvelles histoires extraordinaires* in 1857 he remarked on
Poe's use of repetition and on the element of strangeness; and he
indicated that such consciously sought effects were not trans-
latable, at least not by him. He further characterized the poetry
as "deep and shimmering as dream, mysterious and perfect as
crystal."

The first essay devoted exclusively to Poe's poetry, Armand
Renaud's appreciation and summary, was published in 1864. His
approach—emphasizing as it did the poems that showed Poe as
a man of heart—was sentimental and partisan, but also perceptive. In analyzing the ultimate effect of Poe's art, Renaud indicated its purpose:

> Edgar Poe has found the poetic secret that Goethe
> possessed to such a high degree, that of composing the
> poem so that no positive meaning results, but giving it a
> mystic form which lends itself to interpretation. . . . We aré
> charmed as by the unreadable eyes of the sphinx, and we
> try to solve the enigma. . . . An effect analogous to music
> is produced. No apparent idea had been stated, but the artist
> has awakened sensations which lead to ideas.

Thus the profundities and mysteries of Poe's art were not invented by the Symbolists. Long before the ascendancy of Mal-

larmé, a French poet and critic had glimpsed the tendency of
Poe's poetry and had judged it without exploring its purpose or
significance deeply. In contrast, Charles de Moüy, in his keen
and sympathetic essay on Poe in 1865, considered him a failure
as a poet:

> Poetry, which seems essentially destined to express the
> nebulous, cannot endure too much of it. There are some
> things that would be said too obscurely; if poetry adds its
> rhythm to their nebulous grace, the entire meaning is not
> conveyed. . . . One feels, on reading Poe's poems, that the
> tenuous, misty idea evaporates in the very harmony of the
> form.[16]

These two contrasting responses have never been reconciled,
either in nineteenth- or twentieth-century criticism, for the writers'
expectations in art are basically divergent. Charles de Moüy
states his assumptions with more moderation than Somerset
Maugham or Yvor Winters, for example, but essentially all are
rationalists. They demand that a poem be rationally approachable,
that it speak strongly and clearly to the intelligence, as well as
to the sensibility. Such a critic is temperamentally incapable of
appreciating most Symbolist poetry. In order to see the real
worth and the potentiality of Poe's poetry, such preconceptions
must be set aside, for Poe did not write that kind of poetry and,
as far as can be judged, he did not intend to.

Unlike his prose method, Poe's poetic method is suggestive
rather than analytic or concretely imagined; ordinarily, it proceeds by indirection. While it achieves effects that would be
termed intentionally psychological, its field, in contrast to the
tales, is not "part of a brain or all of it," nor is his calculation of
effect a phonetic and semantic equation. His method is precisely
the opposite of that of the tales, aside from the ones that Kahn,
Mallarmé and Baudelaire recognized as prose poems. ("Ligeia,"
"Shadow," "Eleonora" and "The Island of the Fay" employ both
poetic and prose techniques.) In order to study his method, we
will examine a poem that Mallarmé placed "among the most
significant, unquestionably stamped with the seal of spiritual
maturity." It is "The Valley of Unrest."

> *Once* it smiled a silent dell
> Where the people did not dwell:
> They had gone unto the wars,
> Trusting to the mild-eyed stars,

5- Nightly from their azure towers,
To keep watch above the flowers,
In the midst of which all day
The red sunlight lazily lay.
Now each visitor shall confess
10- The sad valley's restlessness.
Nothing there is motionless—
Nothing save the airs that brood
Over the magic solitude.
Ah, by no wind are stirred these trees
15- That palpitate like the chill seas
Around the misty Hebrides!
Ah, by no wind those clouds are driven
That rustle through the unquiet heaven
Uneasily, from morn till even,
20- Over the violets there that lie
In myriad types of the human eye—
Over the lilies there that wave
And weep above a nameless grave!
They wave:—from out their fragrant tops
25- Eternal dews come down in drops.
They weep:—from off their delicate stems
Perennial tears descend in gems.

This is a particularly good poem for analysis because there can
be no question of logical paraphrase, or of a definite symbolic
key. Poe's technique and intention are obvious, however, and the
effect can be stated impressionistically, as Mallarmé indicated in
pairing this poem with "The City in the Sea" as troubled dreams:
"Here, painful instability, where the gaze is dissipated and lost
in futile agitation; there, the ponderous weight of an antique atmosphere, immobile and breathless, like the oblivion of somnolent
centuries."

The poem is composed of two scenes in fragments, only
partially described, and an implied narrative. Both scene and
narrative convey the sense of dread beauty, but this effect is
logically inexplicable. The human action cannot serve as guide
through the poem, for it stops at line 6, to be resumed only by a
suggestion in lines 21 and 23. There are certain basic contrasts
between the two scenes that provide a pattern for the mind—
sumptuous ease of the first scene opposed to the eerie movement
of the second—but the imagery is not simply consistent in either
scene. There is no easy contrast of idyllic and demonic scenes.

In short, the poem is an act of evocation in which the rational level is refused to the reader.

A prose approximation of this poem, "Eleonora," can furnish some clues to the purpose of the enigmatic structure and vocabulary, although it cannot explain the poem. "Eleonora" gives the reader two lines of progression to follow: narrative and scene. These two elements explain and intensify one another; the scene is, in a sense, the outward manifestation of the narrator's sensibility as he goes from the paradise of childhood to the erotic mysticism of adolescence, then to exile from paradise and finally a restitution of life. The story and the poem are not completely parallel; for example, there is no restitution of life in the poem. Nevertheless, there are striking similarities in the scenes ("eye-like violets," the crimson cloud, the flowers that "writhed uneasily and were ever encumbered with dew" in the story have echoes in the poem) and in the fundamental psychological movement. In the poem, however, the narrative has been suppressed, so that the symbolic scene alone—with an occasional narrative *hint*— must communicate the spiritual mystery.

Poe is seeking a *controlled imprecision* in the sense that his poem is intended to arouse contrasting and ambiguous feelings— Elysian and demonic—without a precise object and without a direct resolution. The scene, with its enigmatic relationships (the silent dell smiling *because* the people are gone?) serves as a gate through which one is led beyond the sensible world. There can be little question that the effect was deliberate. In "The Valley of Unrest" the mystery is the result of ambiguity in imagery; the objects are not permitted to be symbols, which, even when complex, can always be explained with logically perceivable equations. Poe's intention to avoid a satisfying symbolism is evident in his choice of words in the second part. The effect of "restlessness" and "brood" conflicts with "magic solitude," "fragrant tops" and "tears descend in gems." If one attempts to make an allegorical structure, he stumbles over the deliberate multiplicity of attitudes revealed in Poe's treatment of imagery, for the valley of unrest and death distills jewels from sorrow or pain. The poem can be interpreted symbolically, but on a rather abstruse level and without any assurance that a particular symbolic structure is the final one. Poe has attempted a form, then, that opens out indefinitely rather than closing in or limiting precisely.

There is other evidence that the technique was the result of

care and effort rather than of haste and indifference. The metamorphosis of the poem "To - - -" (beginning "Should my early
life seem") illustrates Poe's method very clearly. The version of
1829 is highly personal and obvious, an almost direct expression
of a defiant mood of self-recognition, diffuse even in its par-
ticularity. The parting, the nature of the questioner, the grandiose
stance are somewhat unified by the Byronic attitude and the
reference to Napoleon, but the whole effect is that of a schoolboy
pose. In the 1850 version of the poem, entitled "A Dream within
a Dream," Poe has discarded the first and last stanzas, with their
specific references to personal attitudes; he has retained only the
two specific acts which can readily be unified (the parting, the
grains of sand); he has severely restrained the expression of
emotion; and he has added the refrain and the references to
dream that are now indeterminately suggestive because they have
no Napoleonic context. Remy de Gourmont noted these particular
lines and commented on their oddness:

> I stand amid the roar
> Of a surf-tormented shore,
> And I hold within my hand
> Grains of the golden sand—
> . . . .
> O God! can I not save
> One from the pitiless wave?

But de Gourmount accepted the "futile and ridiculous incident"
because it led to an "obscure and profound revery." The poem
differs from "The Valley of Unrest," however, in that it employs
a simple symbol. The lack of explanatory apparatus or equations
gives only a hint of unresolved implication because the object in
itself is solid, unified and traditional.

These techniques of suggestion, although varying in their
degree of abstraction, are consistent efforts to arrive at the
"supernal' described in "The Poetic Principle." A poem launches
into sensory beauty and finite dream and emotion very briefly,
in order to depart for the infinite, and, as Poe states, poetry gives
the dubious joy of an attempt "to grasp *now* wholly . . . those
divine and rapturous joys, of which *through* the poem, or *through*
the music, we attain to but brief and indeterminate glimpses."

The attitude is thoroughly familiar to a modern reader, for a
lineage of anagogical poets stretches from the nineteenth century
to the present, with T. S. Eliot the most notable contemporary

poet attempting translucence. If poetry is a medium *through* which one arrives at a final vision, or through which one arrives at an ultimate philosophic attitude, it must not hold too tightly to the objects of the earth. At least, the modern poets who declare their transcendental intention reject sensory richness and literalness:

> poetry standing naked in its bare bones, poetry so transparent that in reading it we are intent on what the poem *points at,* and not on the poetry, this seems to me the thing to try for. To get *beyond* poetry, as Beethoven, in his later works, strove to get *beyond music.*[17]

Eliot's way is necessarily different from that of Poe and of Mallarmé. Except in its most obvious aspects (the rhythmic structure and the repetitions in poems such as "The Raven"), it is unlikely that Poe's specific technique could be used by any other poet, for it depends on images from an inner landscape. Since the images through which one glimpses the absolute both reflect and limit the absolute that he sees, Poe's vision is different from Mallarmé's, so different that the two poets seem at first glance to be linked only in terms of theory—that is, the formal theory found in their statements on the purpose of poetry. In the poems themselves, we see immediately that Mallarmé's stock of imagery is more traditional; his figures come to his hand as conventionally beautiful ones—the swan, the fan, gems. Poe's imagery is bizarre, both the horrifying and the beautiful being strongly grotesque. Poe's glimpses of the absolute are different in kind from Mallarmé's. Nevertheless, these poets have in common, as Morice declared, an impulse to get beyond poetry, and the difference in detail, diction and imagery indicates a difference in temperament and experience. The poets are individual and original, but they are impelled by one desire and employ one essential technique. Poe formulated the technique and articulated the desire. So it is that Poe's influence on Mallarmé was through poetry. If the French poet was interested in the theory of the American, it was theory implicit in all his work—tales, criticism, and poetry.

Poe as a poet has received most attention from the French critics studying Mallarmé because he was the Frenchman most impressed by Poe's verse. For that very reason, however, there has been some misunderstanding about Mallarmé's estimate of Poe, and considerable effort on the part of friends of Mallarmé to disclaim any true relationship between the poets. T. S. Eliot judged that Mallarmé did not know English adequately. Joseph Chiari thought that Mallarmé did not know the English tradition of poetry.

The evidence of his translation of Poe's poetry is adequate to show that he understood English, Poe and standards of excellence in English literature. He omitted not only youthful poems that are unformed spurts of expression such as "Dreams" ("Oh! that my young life were a lasting dream!") and "Alone," but also poems that are highly imitative or derivative, such as "A Paean" and "Hymn." But even more interesting evidence of his exercise of critical judgment is the rearranging of the poems, consigning some of the titles appearing in the *Poems* to a minor section which he calls "Romances et vers d'album," and removing two of the poems from the section "Poems Written in Youth" for placement in the section of "masterpieces." Thus the twenty masterworks are, in this order, "The Raven," "To Helen," ("Helen, thy beauty is . . .") "The Haunted Palace," "Eulalie," "The Conqueror Worm," "Ulalume," "A Dream within a Dream," "To One in Paradise," "Bridal Ballad," "Lenore," "Annabel Lee," "The Sleeper," "The Bells," "The Happiest Day," "Dreamland," "To Helen," ("I saw thee once . . .") "For Annie," "Silence," "The Valley of Unrest" and "The City in the Sea." Most American critics would probably agree with his selection, with the exception perhaps of "Eulalie" and "The Happiest Day." Furthermore, Mallarmé's marked preference—descending from the translator's impassivity—for a particular poem, and not the one whose novelty usually impressed the French as strongly as it impresses English-speaking readers, can reveal a great deal about his view of Poe. The poem is "For Annie":

> The realization of such a poetic miracle has been considered by experts to be a challenge the poet gave himself. If I dared, just once before ending these notes, to make a judgment on my own account, I would say that Poe's poetry perhaps never went so far beyond all that we know, with stilled and distant rhythm, as in this lyric, where the state of a spirit in its first hours of death is revealed in the light of convalescence. Triumph of deliverance, with the need of resuming something at once, even the gentle terrestrial paradise regretted; lulling by soaring and dearer hesitations.

Mallarmé's spiritual biography very readily suggests the symbolic aspect of "For Annie," which must have touched him deeply, for the poem has an analogy in one of Mallarmé's early crises of consciousness. He had undergone a period of spiritual extinction and rebirth; a fragmentary expression of it occurs in a letter to Cazalis in 1869:

> . . . my brain, invaded by the Dream, refusing its exterior functions which no longer importuned it, was about to perish in its permanent insomnia; I implored ·great Night, who heeded and extended her darkness. The first phase of my life was ended. Consciousness, overcome by shadows, awakens slowly, forming a new man. . . .[18]

The biographical comparison is justified because it illustrates the type of psychological subtlety that the Symbolists—and not Mallarmé alone—found in Poe. Even the specific acts of life, love and death were dramatizations of the life of the individual human consciousness, and consciousness itself was an absolute and a mystery.

Mallarmé's other specific comment on "For Annie" reveals that Emerson's "jingle man" seemed an artist in rhythm to Mallarmé. It is difficult to make any pronouncements about rhythm—its effect, its quality—with certainty, and a critic can do little but state an opinion. Nevertheless, it seems clear that the effect Mallarmé found was the one Poe sought. If it is less successful for an English or American reader, it is because his expectations are different and because he tends to read the poem too fast. If it is read at all expressively, it has both the hypnotic, obsessive effect of a psychological unwinding (the result of the repetitions) and a diminishing or distancing of mind into silence. In part, this is caused by the cumulative effect of the anapestic-iambic lines; in its completeness it is not so obviously mechanical, for the dominant tone is obtained partly by the progressive thinning of imagery and by the introduction toward the end of the poem of words, lines and stanzas intended to bring in the hypnotic serenity of a lullaby. At last, the demands of reason and sensibility having been lulled, the poem becomes a hynm of transfiguration. In bare, unornamented lines with an almost abstract vocabulary, the poem yields pure light:

> But my heart is brighter
> Than all of the many
> Stars in the sky,
> For it sparkles with Annie—

It glows with the light
     Of the love of my Annie—
With the thought of the light
     Of the eyes of my Annie.

Poe has sometimes been accused of sterility of imagination because of the kind of emptying of sense or sensuousness revealed in this poem. In French Symbolism, the tendency to decompose the wealth of affective experience in order to communicate an essential esthetic experience also resulted in adverse criticism, even though the purpose of the French poets was more thoroughly understood. The conclusion of Vielé-Griffin's sarcastic article on the Symbolist renaissance and its collectivist detractors suggests the same criticism:

> How much wiser the conduct of the champions of the materialistic civilization could be; they have apparently not guessed that by encouraging the pure cult of the Symbol and the Synthesis in these young Symbolists they could cause them to end by negating all literature: *the synthesis and the symbol being complete in the word,* the eminently suggestive reading of Littre's dictionary would have led to the decrepitude and death of these poets, dreamers, contemplatives, MUTES![19]

Distinctions must be made, of course, between the kind of inarticulateness Poe might be accused of and the kind referred to above, which is an apotheosis of the word. Neither in theory nor in practice did Poe give a Symbolist emphasis to the evocative power of the isolated word; the individual evocations were calculated for a final effect. His statement in "Philosophy of Composition," that he determined the effect of sadness before calculating how to achieve that effect can be credited. Yet here again the theory of conscious control impinges on metaphysics. The progress already traced in "For Annie" is calculated for the final moment in which the mind gradually departs from a concrete situation in order to hover momentarily in a state of spiritual exaltation detached from the sense impressions that conceived it. It is evident that the poet is not intoxicated with word or sound or sensation, but with the ineffable state. The tendency is toward annihilation of art in a mystic state, or, for the Symbolists, *dream.* This is, I think, what Mallarmé was implying in his obscure remark that Poe's ideas "occur in the space that isolates the stanzas and in the white spaces of the paper," and what Rimbaud attempted to define in saying, "I wrote silences."

In its ultimate transcendental intent, Symbolism undoubtedly failed, for a final mystic vision of the One has no need of words but takes place in silence. At its best, however, Symbolist poetry succeeds as art that communicates a sense of an absolute in inner experience and esthetic perception. Paul Valéry, in the poetry of his mature years, abandoned this transcendental goal. When the transcendental impulse took him, he refused at last: "one must try to live." Similarly, his essay on Poe's *Eureka,* written in 1923, reveals his departure from Symbolism, for he ceased to believe in the poetic mind's power to know an absolute reality. The work of imagination finally seemed a magnificent game. But in the days of his discipleship to Mallarmé, Valéry's aim was very much patterned on Poe's:

> I dream of a short poem—a sonnet—written by a subtle dreamer, a judicious architect, a clever algebrist, and an infallible calculator of the effect to be achieved. . . . Everything that he has imagined, felt, and thought will pass through the sieve, will be weighed, purified, submitted to the Form and condensed as much as possible in order to gain in power what it sacrifices in length. That sonnet will be a totality, carefully composed for its final, decisive thunderclap. . . .
>
> In short, the truly prodigious artist for me is the livid Edgar Poe, the great genius of intuition and masterly esthetics.[20]

NOTES

[1] Plowert, "Parenthèse et incidences," *Le Symboliste,* I (7 October 1886), 1. Some of the articles (those by Paul Bourde, Jean Moréas and Anatole France) can be found partially reproduced in Jean Moréas' *Curiosités littéraires; les premières armes du Symbolisme* (Paris, 1889).

[2] Gustave Kahn, "Réponse des Symbolistes," *L'Evénement,* 28 September 1886.

[3] Ferdinand Brunetière, "Le Symbolisme contemporain," *Revue des deux mondes,* CIV (1 April 1891), 681.

[4] Gustave Kahn, "Chronique de la littérature et de l'art," *Revue indépendante,* VIII (September 1888), 435-443.

[5] Mallarmé, Pléiade edition, p. 366.

[6] Mallarmé, *Propos sur la poésie,* ed. Henri Mondor (Monaco, 1946), p. 118.

[7] Mallarmé, Pléiade edition, p. 872.

[8] Paul Adam, "La Presse et le Symbolisme," *Le Symboliste,* I (7 October 1886), 2.

⁹ Paul Valéry, *Variété II*, p. 151.

¹⁰ Paul Verlaine, *Oeuvres posthumes*, II (Paris, 1927), 26.

¹¹ Kahn, "Réponse des Symbolistes."

¹² Charles Morice, *La Littérature de tout à l'heure* (Paris, 1889), pp. 332-333.

¹³ Arthur Rimbaud, *A Season in Hell*, trans. Louise Varèse (Norfolk, 1952), p. 51.

¹⁴ Mallarmé, Pléiade edition, p. 429.

¹⁵ Joseph Wood Krutch, *Edgar Allan Poe* (London, 1926), p. 232.

¹⁶ Charles de Moüy, "Etudes contemporaines; XX, Edgar Poe," 150.

¹⁷ T. S. Eliot, "English Letter Writers" (unpublished lecture delivered at New Haven in the winter of 1933). Quoted by F. O. Matthiessen, *The Achievement of T. S. Eliot* (London, 1935), p. 90.

¹⁸ Mallarmé, *Propos sur le poésie*, ed. Henri Mondor (Monaco, 1946), p. 87.

¹⁹ Francis Vielé-Griffin, "Inutilisations," *Entretiens politiques et littéraires*, I, no. 4 (1 July 1890), 132.

²⁰ Valéry, Ms letter to Pierre Louys, 2 June 1890. In the Bollingen Collection of Valériana.

AFTERWARD

Poe's symbolic role for the French ends with the superb essay on *Eureka* by Paul Valéry, for in that essay Valéry succeeded in reversing the tendency of earlier image-makers (and indeed his own early image) by rendering Poe respectable. The enormous prestige of Valéry the Academician (and the most formidable French intellectual of the twenties) had its influence in changing the critical perspective; but more important is the tenor of his essay which, philosophically disintegrating personality at the same time that it cast other conceptual systems in doubt, placed the mythic personality of Poe firmly in the nineteenth century while taking the philosophic and impersonal mind of Poe into a new literary and ethical context.

Part of that context is, of course, myth as a subject of serious investigation; but the emphasis changes from the poet as a figure of heroic myth to the poet as a consciousness making myths, like the creator James Joyce imagines in his *Portrait,* ". . . like the God of creation, within or behind or beyond or above his handiwork, invisible, refined out of existence. . . ." The new attitude to this function of creative consciousness tends to render irrelevant much of the argumentation of previous times about Poe's personal sincerity, his emotional impotence, and indeed the entire complex of *ad hominem* arguments.

Perhaps the most interesting aspect of Valéry's redirecting of attention to Poe is positive, however, rather than negative. The protean creative power of mind, as Valéry described it, links Poe to twentieth-century conceptions of mind, which break down previous distinctions between objective and subjective, mind and matter, and science and mysticism in order to recover a lost

human unity. Although there are suggested links to concepts
(such as Einsteinean relativity) which have been fruitful in the
very recent past, the emphasis is on ontology. One of the important twentieth-century tendencies, that of Jean-Paul Sartre's
Existentialism, is foreshadowed in Valéry's analysis of the action
of the creative mind:

> If we must have the idea of a nothingness, the idea
> of nothingness is nothing, or rather, it is already some
> thing: it is a deception of the mind that plays a comedy for
> itself, . . . I know that I am there, and have volition, and
> am indispensable in order to maintain, by a conscious act,
> the apparent nullity and the fragile absence of all images. . . .
> And if in the beginning I posit the idea of disorder pushed
> to extremity even in the smallest parts of what was, I
> perceive at once that this inconceivable chaos is arranged
> according to my conceptual design.

While it is true that Valéry uses Poe at the service of his own
conception and sees his conception demonstrated in *Eureka,* he
is quite clearly developing and emphasizing the theory of conscious creative control, which is present in Poe, and has
previously been taken up by the Symbolists on more esoteric
terms; and the conception on these new terms moves again into
the vanguard of thought, to merge again with a native literary
and philosophic movement.

The aspect of Poe's mind which remained outlawed—the
mystical, magical, occult powers of the Demiurgos—was to pre-
occupy Americans long after it had been placed and absorbed
in the tradition of Baudelaire in France. Moreover, the subterranean influence of Poe, working upon such writers as the
young Sartre, as on the young Yeats, cannot be defined with
such certitude as has been possible with earlier poets. In part
it is because Poe has been absorbed into a complex tradition; in
part because he still has the capacity to represent forbidden knowledge and forbidden attitudes: but less highly-nuanced images
have been found.

FRENCH CRITICISM

E. D. FORGUES

"STUDIES IN THE ENGLISH AND AMERICAN NOVEL: THE TALES OF EDGAR A. POE"*

The *Philosophic Essay on Probabilities* is one of the books in which the audacity of the human mind best reveals itself and goes to greatest lengths. Since Prometheus stole the unextinguishable flame from the alter of the gods, the world has hardly seen an undertaking as hazardous as that of the men who have tried to bring their calculations to bear on the changeable, uncertain, mysterious order of destiny; to penetrate the dark domain of the future; to reduce the accidents of luck to formula, and, in those myriad combinations which the single word *possible* embraces, to introduce algebra armed with its rigorous formulas and inflexible deductions. So it is that Laplace's book has a real fascination for certain minds which the power of reason dominates and intoxicates, and on whom a new truth acts as an opium pipe would, or a spoonful of hashish. They make it their Gospel, devoting themselves to spreading it, and I know some who go through the world hawking this marvelous treatise just as the Protestants do the Bible and our devout Catholics do the dialogs with the *beloved* composed for men *who do not want to perish*. This is understandable. The *Philosophic Essay* is not simply the ambitious effort of an intelligence motivated by a vain desire for knowledge; it has its moral conclusions, leading man to the practice of good by the calculation of favorable probabilities which are constantly

---

* Taken from *Revue des deux mondes*, XVI (1846), 341–366.

dependent on observation of the eternal principles that form and maintain societies.

Without rising to such an elevated plane, leading to such a noble end or emanating such vigorous thought, the tales we are going to discuss have an obvious kinship with the serious work of the wise marquis. If you are attracted by the incoherent fictions of the popular novel, do not look for anything similar here. Poetry, invention, turns of style and the concatenations of the drama are subordinated to a bizarre preoccupation—we could almost say to a monomania of the author—that seems to know only one source of inspiration—reason; only one music—logic; only one method of affecting his readers—doubt. So many narratives, so many enigmas in various forms and costumes. Wearing the fantastic livery of Hoffman or the grave, magisterial costume of Godwin remodeled by Washington Irving or Dickens, it is always the same contrivance confronting Oedipus with the Sphinx, the hero with the logogriph. The mind chafes at obscure events and apparently impenetrable mysteries; it attacks the veil drawn in front of it, until, after incredible efforts told in minute detail, it emerges victorious from the struggle.

In fact, you will say to me, that is the basis of more than one novel and of almost all drama. If you suppress curiosity, doubt and fear, and if you dissipate uncertainty about the infallible outcome of the narrative, which hold the reader in breathless suspense and trouble the spectator, where will you find the interest necessary to this kind of composition? Agreed—every novel, every drama, implies a conflict in which the doubtful vicissitudes are, according to the talent of the writer, more or less linked together by a logical bond. The syllogism is at the basis of the most pathetic situations, and a certain apostrophe which moved an entire theater to applaud is only, at bottom, an eloquently disguised *sorites*. But in the drama and the novel, logic is the hidden pivot of the action. It hides under an infinite number of details, all intended to befuddle our minds when we might rush too quickly and too directly from the given point of departure to the denouement. And to assure yourself that the details dominate the basic action, you have only to disentangle the logical substratum from its envelope of a thousand brilliant colors and ingenious embroideries; you will see what a poor argument and miserable plot have woven that magnificent tissue.

In contrast, in the original narratives about to be introduced to you, which come to us from New York by the latest *packet-boat,* the logic is bare. It dominates everything; it is queen and mistress. Its function is no longer to shore up, like unseen carpentry, a monument with a rich exterior; it *is* that monument, borrowing nothing or almost nothing from the other resources of art. It no longer plays the role of the submissive slave who lends his strong shoulder to the master who is unsteady with wine, and leads him, not without difficulty, to some unseen doorway; it walks alone, strong with its own strength. It is the end and the means, the cause and the effect. Just as, yesterday, in the hands of a scholar, it undertook the most arduous problems of speculative philosophy, so today it becomes a novel in order to place itself within reach of the greatest number, while sacrificing as little as possible its scientific dignity.

What was Laplace looking for in his analysis of chance, or Buffon in his political arithmetic? Following a thousand illustrious predecessors, each tried to subdue a rebellious *unknown,* to conquer, by the power of induction, the resistance it offered to thought and to make moral consequences take on the certitude of mathematical consequences. Thus, with the same balance, Laplace weighs the periodic returns of a star, the luck of a lottery ticket and the value of historical testimony in a judicial decision. The same reasoning serves to assure him that the influence of the moon on the sea is more than twice as great as that of the sun, and that Pascal's niece, young Perrier, was not cured of her fistula by the direct and miraculous intervention of divine Providence. Thus for the past, the present and the future, he imposes systematic rules and establishes general laws of probability.

Poe also concerns himself with judging and classifying probabilities, but after his own fashion. Instead of uniform precepts, he employs instinct, or innate sagacity, which is more accurate with one than with another and varies in power as it does in purpose, according to the aptitudes and the trade of each person. The fundamental idea of his tales seems to have been borrowed from the first adventures of Zadig, where the young Babylonian philosopher displays such a marvelous perspicacity. Poe's favorite actor, an eccentric character whose subtle intelligence he puts to such rigorous tests, would also have guessed by the simple inspection of their tracks that the spaniel of the queen of Babylon had borne puppies shortly before escaping from the palace, and that the king's horse, lost by a rascally groom, had 23-carat gold studs in his bit.

Moreover, that character is none other than Poe himself, who scarcely takes the trouble to disguise himself and, in the narratives where he does not make the fictional character appear, substitutes himself boldly for him.

Who, other than this seeker of problems, would have set himself the task of imagining the posthumous sensations of a man, or rather a corpse, first stretched on his deathbed, then in a shroud under damp earth, listening to himself disintegrate, watching himself rot? Who whould have thought of relating in such a rationally convincing manner the final catastrophe which returned this terrestrial globe to nothingness? To touch on these great secrets of the death and end of the world seems the business of the most profound thinkers, the longest meditations and the most complete systems. For Poe, it is only a matter of adopting a hypothesis, positing a first act and making it produce, among its probable and possible consequences, those which the human mind links the most easily and most willingly.

Monos is dead; Una, his adored mistress, follows soon after to the shadowy kingdom of death. They meet. Una wants to know what her beloved has experienced, from the moment when grief-stricken beside him she saw him immobile, cold, disfigured, marked by the final seal. Had all thought disappeared when life went? Is the divorce of body and soul so brusque, so sudden and complete, that the soul escapes utterly with the last gasp, leaving behind only an inert mass? Most men reply affirmatively; our author, unafraid of shocking the world's opinion, writes false to that unproven hypothesis, and with the help of logic builds his tale of the hereafter on his lone negation.

To tell the truth, this is not the first time that imagination has violated the limits of life, those limits that are not to be passed by reason and before which all philosophy lowers its eyes, humiliated; but I do not believe that anyone has ever given this kind of exact definition and reasoned conviction to the *memoirs of a dead man*. Here it is not a question of fantastic adventures, arbitrary complications, dialogs more or less filled with *humor,* but, rather, of an authentic monograph, patient, methodical, which seems to aspire to take its place among the other documents of human knowledge. Poe has deduced the characteristics of the sensibility of a corpse from those of the dreamer; he

has taken seriously the kinship of sleep and death, which so many
poets have sung; he has made a philosophic dogma of it, and
from that dogma he proceeds to draw all possible truths. Ad-
mittedly, this is not an overworked idea.

I no longer breathed, says Monos; the circulation of
my blood had ceased, my heart had ceased to beat. The
faculty of volition remained, but powerless. My senses, however, stimulated by an extraordinary activity and given
over to a bizarre confusion, usurped one another's functions.
Taste and smell, by an inextricable amalgamation, had
united in one and the same faculty, completely abnormal
and extremely intense. The rosewater that your tender
hands had sprinkled on my lips at the final hour awakened
in me the idea of unknown flowers, with perfumes quite
new to me—ideal flowers, beautiful in an entirely different
way from those of the old earth, but whose graceful prototypes I will show you *here*. My eyelids, bloodless and
perfectly transparent, only half hindered me from discerning
objects. The failure of my will, for a time paralyzed, kept
my eyes from moving in their sockets, but everything that
was within range of the visual hemisphere was more or less
distinctly visible to me; moreover, the cornea had become
more sensitive than the retina, and the anomaly was so complete that visual impressions were translated into accoustical
phenomena, in harmonious or discordant sounds, according
to whether the object placed beside me was well or poorly
lighted, with curved lines or sharply cut angles. At the same
time, hearing functioned, even though hyperacutely, in a
sufficiently ordinary fashion; however, it judged sounds with
a precision, a sensitivity, which I would readily term excessive. The sense of touch had undergone an even more
peculiar modification: its impressions, tardily received, but
retained with an unaccustomed tenacity, caused a physical
pleasure exalted to the point of paroxysm. Thus, the contact
of your fingers, gently pressed on my eyelids, a contact
which I was not aware of at first except by sight, after a
certain time, and after your hand had been removed for
several minutes, filled my entire being with a delightful
sensation, impossible to describe in all its strength. Note
that the sensation was purely physical, all my perceptions
remaining limited to the material order; the images transmitted to my now passive brain by the senses did not
undergo any of the transformations which a living intelligence imposes. Thus I experienced little or no suffering,

while pleasures were numerous and extreme. Morally, neither
pleasure nor pain. Nothingness, in all its apathy etc.

We will not prolong this curious quotation, indispensable
for justifying what we previously said of the distinctive character
that Poe gives this anatomy of a self-dissected dead man.

The final ruin of the globe, the destruction of our planet,
is just as methodically treated in the dialog of Eiros and Charmion
as the decomposition of a human being was in Monos and Una.
The principle is similarly presented. Given the elementary fact
that respirable air is composed of 21 parts of oxygen, 79 parts
of nitrogen, plus a small part of carbon dioxide, and given the
fact that the earth is enveloped by an atmosphere almost fifteen
leagues thick, what would happen if the ellipses described
around the sun by a comet led the latter star into contact with
the terrestrial globe? It is the supposition of Trissotin in *Les
Femmes savantes*. Poe does not accept that way of looking at
things. He presents the comet, not as a massive, weighty body,
but as a whirlpool of rarefied matter whose nucleus is much
less dense than that of our lightest gases. The encounter, then,
does not have exactly the same danger as the crash of two
locomotives meeting on the same rails, and we will pass effort-
lessly through the enemy star. But what will happen to us during
that strange passage? Oxygen, the principle of combustion, will
increase to unnatural proportions. Nitrogen, on the other hand, will
be completely extracted from the earth's atmosphere. What consequence will this double phenomenon have? An irresistible
combustion that devours everything and prevails against everything *(all devouring, omni prevalent)*. From this premise, once
given, the punctiliously logical narrative follows, with its pitiless
consequences, the necessary deductions. Refute the major premise,
the point of departure, if you like; the rest is strictly invulnerable.

Thus, in the beginning we witness the stunning spectacle of
an entire world surprised by the signal of its destruction. From
the moment the astronomers declare that the comet will approach
the earth and a meeting has become almost inevitable, the terrible truth, greeted at first with doubt and irony, gains more profound and general credence each day. From scholars and men
able to understand their calculations, the fatal conviction soon
extends to ordinary people, to simple, credulous minds. In all
parts of the globe, eyes are fixed on the menacing star. People
note its progress, they ascertain the very slow but continuous

and unquestionable increase in its diameter; they examine its color and seek to comprehend its true nature. Placing faith in the learned, they admit that it is neither a flame nor a solid body. They do not expect, then, either fire or shock; but that luminous vapor, so tenuous and devoid of heat, must exercise some influence. What will it be, and when? That is what all the philosophers and academicians of every country try to guess. The optimists reject the idea of catastrophe, referring, to support their confidence, to the passage of several comets among the satellites of Jupiter without causing any sidereal upset. The theologians, piously alarmed, return to the Biblical prophecies and preach to the people with a fervor and strength of faith and persuasion that the approaching crisis makes very natural; however, they obtain only limited credence. They foretell the igniting of the globe, and its inhabitants know beyond doubt that the meeting with the comet cannot have that effect. If you are astonished at the confidence the masses have in the conclusions of human knowledge, which are always more or less speculative, the narrator explains to you that prejudices and popular errors concerning comets—the groundless fears of war and pestilence that were previously associated with the appearance of the wandering stars —have vanished in the face of a more certain and better known danger. "By a sort of convulsive effort, reason had cast down ancient superstition from its already shaken throne. A new preoccupation, a dominating interest, gave the weakest intelligences a certain vigor."

Faithful to their instinct to know all, and even to foresee all, the learned men set about debating the various changes, more or less essential, that the meeting of the earth and the comet could not fail to bring. Will climate and vegetation be modified, or not? Should they fear destruction caused by electricity? Will the mysterious power of magnetism show itself in some disaster? While they discuss these secondary points, the hairy star draws constantly nearer, grows, casts a more terrible glare.

The moment arrives when the people no longer lend their ears to such vain debates. The danger, until then remaining in the domain of phantoms, suddenly bears the signs of reality and certainty, which sends fear into the stoutest hearts. "The comet had ceased to be a phenomenon in the sky; it was an incubus in our breasts, a cloud in our brains. With an inconceivable rapidity it had taken on the appearance of a vast curtain of transparent flame extending from horizon to horizon."

Suddenly the universal fear, having reached its apogee, diminishes. Already, and evidently under the influence of the fatal meeting which is the object of so much terror, the living beings go on living. Moreover, their limbs have more energy, their spirits have more vivacity, more elasticity. The extreme tenuity of the impalpable comet is evident to everyone, for the celestial constellations remain visible through the new substance with which the atmosphere is filled. Vegetation undergoes incon- testable changes, but they are not at all threatening: they are revealed only by an unaccustomed exuberance of leafage on each tree and plant.

However, the final account of the test remains—the height of the crisis, the moment when the very nucleus of the comet, and not its encircling envelope, comes directly into contact with the earth. At its approach, men, disabused at last, feel the first touch of the unknown illness, and a cry of horror and anguish arises on all sides. The preliminary symptoms consist of a painful oppression in the chest, accompanied by a dryness of skin that causes acute suffering. From that time it is certain that the atmos- phere of the earth is noticeably tainted, and all attention focuses on that. The prophecies of the Holy Word come to everyone's mind, and all humanity is in the position of Macbeth, when the equivocal predictions of the bearded sisters, at first belied by events, are fulfilled in a totally unexpected fashion, when Birnam Wood marches against him and he finds himself face to face with the man "who is not of woman born."

> I pull in resolution; and begin
> To doubt the equivocation of the fiend
> That lies like Truth.

Likewise, the pale human creatures curse their blindness and understand at last the mysterious decrees of Providence. The fatal gases of the comet, instead of lightning from Sinai, are going to extinguish the over-stimulated life in every breast; but before dying, humankind becomes mad. A sort of delirium goads. the inhabitants of the globe to run here and there, panting, feverish, sometimes cursing and defying, sometimes crying and shouting, according to the way they translate the impetuous vigor of the blood which circulates more rapidly in their burning veins.

However, Eiros continues, the destructive nucleus was upon us. I still tremble at that memory, even here in the heart of Eden. At first it was a livid, wandering light whose rays penetrated from all directions; then—let us bow, Charmion, before the majesty of the great Creator—a noise arose, resounding and formidable, like a death-sentence pronounced by Him; that ethereal mass in whose heart we were living burst suddenly into flame, transformed into an intense flame whose unspeakable glare and concentrated heat not even the angels in heaven can express. Thus everything was consumed!

You see that this extraordinary narrative, this unprecedented flight of an imagination that nothing can stop, has all the appearance, if not all the reality, of severe logic. Few people would deny that a comet and the earth could collide in space. If this is posited, you must admit, at least as a great probability, this conflagration of gas, this atmospheric fire, this horrible end for the human race reduced to breathing nothing but flame.

When one has once undertaken such problems, he is soon tempted to consider all the others which seem to be forbidden to science to solve, leaving them to God. Poe is led, then, to seek a plausible explanation for the human soul and for divinity. This is the subject of a third narrative entitled "Mesmeric Revelation." The author imagines himself at the bedside of an unbeliever who, at the final stage of a mortal illness, has himself treated by magnetism. Mr. Van-Kirk has doubted the immortality of the soul all his life. But for several days, troubled by vague memories which his somnambulistic ecstasies leave him, he wonders whether a series of well placed questions while he is in the peculiar state could not illuminate metaphysical truths with a totally new light —truths guessed, perhaps, but badly explained and analyzed by philosophy, which is blocked by the inadequacy of its ordinary resources. In fact, from the moment when the mesmeric action permits man to supplement his imperfect finite organs and transports him, endowed with a miraculous clairvoyance, into the domain of creations which escape the senses, isn't it very natural that the somnambulist, more than another, should have the power to explain the hidden realities of the invisible world to us? This first point gained, entrust yourself to the storyteller who will give you, in question and answer form, a very plausible theory about all that concerns the separation of body and soul, the essence which constitutes the power and superior order known by the name of God, the unknown relationship between the human soul, which is an individualized particle of divinity, and that divinity from which it is forever separated. It goes without saying that we do not guarantee the system proposed by the American story-teller against the illustrious representatives of modern philosophy.

One might equally well revive and defend the theories of the Cardinal of Cusa (Nikolas Chrypffs) on comprehensible incomprehensibility—theories with which Edgar Poe's theory has some distant relationship; or one might become champion of Giordano Bruno, who also seems to have contributed his share to Poe's ingenious hypotheses. The condition that Bruno called Nature, both a principle and an element of what is (as a pilot can be at the same time a person and a part of the vessel that he steers), Poe calls God. He calls into question the separation that men have tried to establish between spirit and matter. All is matter, even God, who is composed of only the most subtle substance, the very substance which acts in us under the name of soul. It is a separate substance, sublimated beyond all that the human mind can conceive—one, indivisible and not formed, as the others are, of a mass of particles. It fills everything, moti-vates everything, is everything which is included in it, that is to say, the entire universe. In repose, this Substance-God is the universal soul; active, it is the creative faculty. The part of our-selves that we call our soul is a fragment of the universal soul, which, without ceasing to be a part of it, is incarnated and individ-ualized for a time. Incarnation itself, by giving that bit of divine substance a limited body, limits the omnipotence that would other-wise be its necessary attribute. Consequently, separated from his body, man would be God or would return into God. But that separation is not possible. Man is a creature; creatures are the thoughts of God. By its very nature, every thought is irrevocable.

Explain yourself, cries Mr. Van-Kirk's interlocutor. Do you mean to say that man will never be deprived of his body?

I said, the somnambulist replies, that he will never be bodiless. The fact is that there are two bodies: one is rudi-mentary, the other is complete; an analogy will make you see the difference. One of these bodies is the worm, the other is the butterfly. What we call death is nothing but the painful metamorphosis that marks the passage from the first to the second of these conditions. Our present incarnation is progressive, preparatory, ephemeral; our future incarnation will be perfect, ultimate, immortal.

But we know how the metamorphosis of the worm is accomplished; we follow all the phases, one by one.

We do, undoubtedly, but not the worm. The rudimentary body is a matter visible to itself; but the organs which serve·it are too imperfect, too gross, to capture the interior form which has developed little by little under that perishable envelope at the moment when it escapes.

Mr. Van-Kirk explains with remarkable lucidity what happens during the mesmeric ecstasy in which, the organs of the rudimentary body being paralyzed, the clairvoyant medium of the ultimate body (that body too subtle to have organs) functions freely. We will go no further into this purely hypothetical explanation in which several passages reminded us of the inspirations, or rather the aspirations, of some of our novelists who thought it charming fourteen or fifteen years ago to put the visions of Jacob Boehme, Saint Martin, Swedenborg, even Mme Guyon into madrigals. But one must confess that Poe's logic is much more precise, much more persistent, then that of Louis Lambert or Seraphitus, the angelic hermaphrodite. It is not satisfied with big cloudy words and formulas that are impenetrable in their affected compression. Once the principles are given, his logic rarely deviates and, always clear and intelligible, it takes hold of the reader although he may be resentful.

The time has come to return to earth and follow that inexorable logic over terrain less favorable to snares of style and artistic illusions.

In "The Gold Bug" we see all the conjectural faculties of man at grips with an apparently undecipherable *number;* the possession of a rich treasure, formerly buried by a pirate, depends on understanding it. Here, reasoning plays the part of a talisman which can enrich someone in a few hours. Further on, in the "Descent into the Maelstrom," Poe will tell us how a well-taken observation, an argument well followed, will save an unfortunate fisherman from the devouring Norwegian whirlpool which draws him toward the depths of its abyss. We do not claim that ordinary verisimilitude is completely respected here, nor that a theory of gravity has ever been improvised by a common peasant in a situation which seems to exclude all exercise of mental faculties— that of a man carried away by the force of a wind dragon—but if everything that is rigorously, strictly possible is conceivable by the human mind under the heading of exception, one can admit that, in extreme peril, certainty of death might give the man all his composure, a peculiar lucidity of mind and miraculous powers of observation. That is enough to make this story capture you as Lewis' Anacandaia does, or the novel of Frankenstein, both being assuredly very faintly credible.

Here is something easier to believe.

*   *   *   *

(Summary of "The Murders in the Rue Morgue")

Apply this surprising perspicacity, the result of a marvelous instinct and an almost superhuman alertness of mind, to a police investigation, and you have an admirable sleuth, an investigator whom nothing escapes, a district attorney such as you have never seen. Poe takes that situation and pushes its most extreme consequences to their conclusion with a completely American tenacity.

Three or four of these narratives rest on this contrivance, which is very simple but has a very sure effect. We are only sorry that the foreign storyteller tried to enhance its interest by choosing Paris, which he has no idea of, and our present society, which is very little known in the United States, as setting for his ingenious hypotheses. His intention was undoubtedly to increase the credibility of his little dramas in the eyes of his compatriots by those means. *Major e longinquo*. A certain detail, unacceptable in a narrative set in Baltimore or Philadelphia, becomes believable placed 2000 leagues away, and no longer upsets the voluntary credulity of the American reader. The marvelous, and even the extraordinary, need perspective. Make the Calif Haroun al Raschid pace about in the streets near the Tuileries, remove the astonishing adventures that constitute the charm of the *Alif-Laila* to the banks of the Yonne—the story of Aboul-Hassan and of Chemsel Nihar, for example—and you would tell us some real news. Poe was wise, then, to place his stories at a distance in order to disguise the artifice of his painting and to give it all the illusion of truth; but he should have foreseen that French readers, stopping in front of the same canvasses, would be completely astounded to find the capitol of France completely jumbled, the principal districts suddenly displaced, a blind alley Lamartine near the Palais Royal, a rue Morgue in the Saint-Roch quarter and the Barrière du Roule on the banks of the Seine, "on the opposite bank from the rue Pavée-Saint-André." And then he should not have imagined, applying the ideas of a much more equalitarian country to our social hierarchy, that the prefect of police, at the end of his rope and not knowing what saint to entreat in order to discover a mysterious paper, would come casually one evening to smoke a cigar or two with the young observer we have spoken of, and to ask him for advice, expose his doubts to him, and make a bet on the success of the steps proposed by that obliging advisor. We have not cited all the blunders, nor even the most glaring ones, that our red pencil has marked in the margin of these strange little novels. Those blunders are explained, moreover, by their foreign origin and by the method the author adopts for bringing us real events selected among the crimes that have occupied the magistrates in New York or Boston. Thus, the story of Marie Roget is a famous American case; only the names are frenchified; the events could not have been. The Hudson becomes the Seine; Weehawken, the Barrière du Roule; Nassau Street, the rue Pavée-Saint-André, and so on. Likewise, Marie Roget, the supposed Parisian grisette, is no other than Marcy-Cecylia Rogers, a tobacco seller (*cigar girl*) whose mysterious murder horrified the population of New York several years ago. We will recount the occurrence as it was told in the New York *Mercury* and in *Brother Jonathan*. There will be time to return to fiction when we have an exact idea of the reality.

*   *   *   *

Such was the problem the New York papers seized upon, and it became the subject of a heated debate.

Poe seized it in turn, and threw his unusual actor (the living syllogism we have spoken of) into the war of opinions. Chevalier Dupin—such is the name that Poe has forged for him, a name typical of Poe and quite remarkably odd and unlikely— attentive to all the contradictory versions, argues them closely and submits them to mathematical analysis. We see that he has read the chapter devoted to *probability in judicial decisions* in Laplace's *Philosophical Essay*. Laplace says in effect that one must postpone judgment if, in order to pass a definite judgment in criminal cases, mathematical evidence is rigorously required. While seeking this evidence, Poe's agent seems to give up hope. But his calculation of probabilities is striking and curious. That is all that we should ask.

*   *   *   *

Now that you have an idea of the American author in his favorite habits, we must try to introduce him to you under a new guise. We have studied him as logician, as pursuer of abstract truth, as lover of the most eccentric hypotheses and the strictest calculations; now it is fair to judge him as poet, inventor of idle fantasies and purely literary caprices. For that, we have reserved two tales: "The Black Cat" and "The Man of the Crowd."

"The Black Cat" reminds us of the most somber inspirations of Theodore Hoffmann. The Serapion Club never listened to anything more fantastic than the story of this man, this unfortunate maniac, whose drink-inflamed brain harbored a monstrous hatred for his poor cat. He had previously loved it very much; but on a certain evening when he returned drunk, and Pluto (the name of the poor animal) wanted to escape his brutal caresses, he seized it in such a way as to hurt it. Pluto defended himself and bit his master slightly. The latter, in a black fit of rage, drew a knife from his pocket and, taking the unfortunate beast by the neck, unhesitatingly gouged out an eye.

The next day, when the alcoholic fumes had dissipated, the one-eyed cat seemed the incarnation of remorse, a living reproach to his master for his cowardly violence and insane cruelty. Besides, resentful and fearful, Pluto avoided the caresses of the man who had so mutilated him. Thus, little by little, the strange antipathy we have mentioned took root—the atrocious hate, which seemed to grow under the irritating influence of liquor. Finally, giving in to an impulse no less diabolic than the first one, the man hanged his cat, the poor black cat which had already lost an eye because of him.

By a strange fatality, his house burned down the following day. The fire destroyed every wall except one that had been freshly plastered. On this wall, which provided a perfectly smooth white surface, the curious crowd saw in astonishment—and the owner in horror—the image of a black cat sketched, so to speak, in relief. The cat could only have been Pluto, as the rope around its neck proved; it was reproduced on that fantastic medallion.

Undoubtedly, since we no longer believe in miracles, the cat had been taken from the tree where it was hanging and cast into the house by some malicious practical joker, when the fire began; a falling plank had pasted it against the new wall, and it had remained there while the house was burning. Something of this sort, at least, would have to explain that extraordinary tracery.

At any rate, after that fatal scene Pluto's phantom haunted the deranged mind of his killer, who sought an opportunity to expiate his crime. One evening in a cabaret where he spent the night, he found another cat, as black as Pluto, which seemed to receive the caresses he showered on it with singular pleasure. By buying this cat, which followed him very willingly, the poor madman tried to appease the shade of his victim. Next day, when he examined his new pet by daylight, the unfortunate man saw that, like Pluto, this cat was one-eyed. This almost inexplicable coincidence and the cat's similarity to the first one in all respects gave him a very natural aversion for the animal, an aversion that gathered, grew and poisoned each day.

In order to make this more comprehensible, one must add that there was a whitish spot on the black fur of the miserable cat—the only thing that distinguished it from its predecessor—and this spot, at first indefinite in contour, had finally assumed the very distinct and precise form of a gallows; at least the drunkard saw it thus. It was, for a sick imagination, an ominous forecast.

In spite of all these causes for hate, the man, his wife and the cat lived for some time without quarrels; the woman singularly loved the cat; the cat loved the man. The man feared the cat and scarcely liked the woman. Add to these unfortunate tendencies the evil influence of penury—*malesuada fames*—and the violent chimeras that drunkenness creates in a diseased mind, and you will understand what followed.

The man went down to the cellar one day with his wife and his cat. The latter, which always hovered around his master, got under his feet and made him fall. Then, forgetting his fears, heeding only his resentment, the man lifted a hatchet that he held in his hand; the wife intervened at an untimely moment to save the cat; the hatchet—we will not attempt to explain this error—went astray and hit the woman's head.

Once the crime had been committed, it was only a question of disposing of the body. After having reviewed all the usual means in such cases—from chopping the body into small pieces to bundling it into a trunk to be sent to an unknown address a thousand leagues away—the man hit upon the method adopted by monks in their *in pace,* that is, hiding it in the thickness of a wall. This fine plan was immediately put into execution; the murderer took away the bricks which had hidden the front of a condemned fireplace and placed the dead woman's body in the empty space. Then, in front of the body he replaced the partition, which was thus perfectly even with the rest of the wall. It is unnecessary to add that he had carefully stained the mortar that he used for that delicate operation, and mixed enough yellowish hair into the plaster to take away its indiscreet whiteness. In short, the work was well done, and the deception was executed in a very reassuring manner.

With this finished, the man returned to the idea of killing the cat, the only witness to the murder, once and for all; but to his great surprise and joy, he could not discover it anywhere. The wise animal had undoubtedly fled the blood stained house. His departure should have been a good omen.

Nevertheless, after four or five days the police were notified that the woman had disappeared, and put their agents to work. Suspecting the husband of having obtained the comfort of widowhood by some illicit procedure, they made a visit to his house. They searched it carefully. The master himself led the crestfallen officers from the attic to the cellar. With a sort of savage triumph, he led them to the very spot where the thing they sought was hidden. He took an evil pleasure in boasting of the thickness and solidity of the walls; his audacity was so great and his security so complete that he went so far as to strike the partition that hid the proof of the crime from their eyes. But then from that very wall came a long howl, an inhuman plaint that seemed like the voice of an accusing demon. The man fainted on the spot. The police pulled down the wall, dug, and found the big black cat crouching inside on the corpse of the murdered woman. Its single eye, glowing with hunger and fury, lighted the darkness of the cellar. The man had walled it in, too, without noticing it.

"The Man of the Crowd" is not a story; it is a study—a simple idea conveyed with energy. The author imagines that, in a moment when his eyes wander aimlessly over the crowd of people who pass and pass again in front of the windows of a cafe where he sits, he notices a face whose aspect strikes him with unutterable curiosity. It is the face of a thin, pale old man whose features indicate an uneasy conscience and the anguish of remorse with exceptional vividness.

*   *   *   *

We have already compared Poe's talent to that of Washington Irving, who is more genial, more varied and less ambitious, and to that of William Godwin, whose "somber and unwholesome popularity" has been so severely censured by Hazlitt. However, one must recognize a truer philosophic knowledge and a much less marked tendency toward purely literary paradox in the author of Saint-Leon and Caleb Williams. And if one wants to point out, in America itself, a predecessor for Mr. Edgar Poe, he could be compared to Charles Brockden Brown without forcing the analogy too much; the latter also sincerely sought the solution to some intellectual problem, even in the most frivolous fiction; he delighted, as Poe does, in portraying these inner tortures, obsessions of the soul and diseases of the mind which offer such a vast field for observation and so many curious phenomena to the thoughtful builders of metaphysical systems.

Brockden Brown wrote novels, it is true, and we know only very short stories by Poe—some have no more than six or seven pages—but it would be foolish, it seems to me, to class compositions of this type according to length. It is very easy to extend a series of events indefinitely, and very difficult, on the other hand, to condense an entire abstract theory, all the elements of an original conception, into a few words in the form of a narrative. Today, when the most insignificant scribbler gets to melodrama in ten or twenty volumes at the first leap, Richardson himself, if he returned to the world, would have to summarize his characters for the sake of his reputation, to prune his interminable dialogs and to divide the many figures in his vast tableaux into finely worked medallions. Yesterday, victory went to great batallions; tomorrow it will go to storm troops. From the big novels that amused Mme de Sévigné, people turned to the tales of Voltaire and Diderot. A whim of fashion has placed the Clélie and Astrée of the seventeenth century in the place of honor again, but people have not forgotten Candide or Les Amis de Bourbonne just because of that, and time, which has taken away nothing from these classic narratives, will bring back the taste for simple, laconic, skillfully concentrated form. Diamonds are never very large, attar never fills huge casks and one story like these of Poe offers more substance to the mind and opens more new horizons to the imagination than twenty volumes like those which were once manufactured by the hundreds by Sandraz de Courtils, Darnaud-Baculard and de Lussan, the precursors and prototypes of many contemporary feuilletonists. Between these last and the American author we will avoid establishing a definite parallel. It will be appropriate and useful to compare them when time has consolidated the budding reputation of the foreign writer and—who knows?—has shaken that of our fertile novelists a little.

CHARLES BAUDELAIRE

"MESMERIC REVELATION"*

There has been much talk lately of Edgar Poe. The truth is that he deserves it. With one volume of stories his fame has crossed the ocean. Instead of touching the emotions or arousing enthusiasm, he has astonished us. Above all, he is astonishing. It is generally so with novelists who depend entirely on methods created by themselves, methods that are the exact consequence of their temperaments. I do not believe it possible to find a good writer who has not deliberately created his method or, rather, whose primary sensibility has not been meditated upon and transformed into sure art. Thus, original writers are all philosophers to some extent—Diderot, Laclos, Hoffmann, Goethe, Jean Paul, Maturin, Honoré de Balzac, Edgar Poe. Notice that I cite authors of all tempers, the greatest contrasts. It is true of all of them, even Diderot, the most daring and adventurous, who set about analyzing improvisation and making rules for it. First he accepted his enthusiastic, sanguine, blustering nature and then—his mind made up—he used it. Consider Sterne: the phenomenon is evidently different and praiseworthy in its own way. That man also made his method. With tireless will and good faith, all these men imitate nature, pure nature. And what nature? Their own. Thus they are imaginative men who totally lack the philosophic spirit, but instead generally much more surprising and original than the simple

---

* Taken from *La Liberté de penser,* July 1848, pp. 176-178.

heap up and align consequences without classifying them or explaining their mysterious meaning. I said that these men were astonishing; I will go further and say that they generally *aim* for astonishment. In the work of several of them we find an endless preoccupation with supernaturalism. As I indicated, this is related to the inborn spirit of *quest-hood*—if I may be pardoned the barbarism—with the inquisitorial spirit of a district attorney, which perhaps has its roots in the remotest impressions of child-hood. Others, fanatical naturalists, examine the tumorous soul as doctors examine the body, and put out their eyes looking for the source. Still others try to blend these two systems into a mysterious unity—animal unity, fluid unity, the unity of primordial matter. By a strange accident, all these recent theories have fallen into the minds of poets at the same time that they occurred to scholars. Then, at last, there comes a time when novelists of the sort I speak of become jealous of the philosophers, and then they too propound their systems of natural order, sometimes with a lack of modesty that has its own charm and innocence. We know *Seraphitus, Louis Lambert* and a host of passages from other books in which Balzac, that great mind devoured by the legitimate pride of the encyclo-pedist, tried to weld various ideas taken from Swedenborg, Mesmer, Marat, Goethe and Geoffroy Saint-Hilaire into a definitive, unified system. The idea of unity also pursued Edgar Poe, and he expanded no less effort than Balzac on that fond dream. Certainly these special literary minds ride, when they set about it, some strange courses through philosophy. They open sudden breaches and make swift inroads by routes that are entirely their own.

To summarize my argument, I will say that the three charac-teristics of the *strange* novelists are (1) a personal method, (2) the astonishing, (3) a passion for philosophy. These three charac-teristics constitute their superiority. The selection by Edgar Poe which you are about to read is at times too closely reasoned, at other times obscure and, occasionally, strangely daring. One must accept his attitude and take the thing as it is. It has been particu-larly necessary to try to follow the text literally. Certain things would have become obscure in a different way if I had attempted to paraphrase the author instead of holding faithfully to the text. I preferred to write an awkward and sometimes baroque French and to give the philosophic method of Edgar Poe in all its integrity.

CHARLES BAUDELAIRE

"EDGAR ALLAN POE, HIS LIFE AND WORKS" (1852)*

Some destinies are fatal. In the literature of every country there are men who bear the word *unlucky* written with mysterious letters in the sinuous folds of their foreheads. Some time ago a wretch with the strange tattoo *no luck* on his forehead was led before the court. He carried the label of his life with him everywhere, as a book bears its title, and the questioning proved that his existence conformed to his advertisement. In literary history there are similar fates. One might say that the blind Angel of Expiation, seizing certain men, whips them with all his might for the edification of the others. Yet if we study their lives attentively we find they have talent, virtue and grace. Society pronounces a special anathema and condemns them for the very vices of character that its persecution has given them. What did Hoffman fail to do to disarm destiny? What did Balzac fail to do to exorcize fortune? Hoffmann was obliged to destroy himself at the very moment, so long desired, when he began to be safe from necessity, when bookstores fought over his tales, when at last he possessed his beloved library. Balzac had three dreams: a well-organized, complete edition of his works; the settling of his debts; and a marriage long savored in the depths of his heart. Thanks to an amount of labor which stuns the most ambitious and painstaking imagination the edition was made, the debts were paid and the

---

* Taken from *Revue de Paris,* **VII** (March-April, 1852), 90–110. The first pages of the revised version (1856) are appended to this essay.

marriage accomplished. Balzac was happy, no doubt. But male-volent destiny, having permitted him to put one foot on the promised land, wrenched it away at once. Balzac experienced a horrible agony worthy of his strength.

Is there a Providence preparing men for misfortune from the cradle? These men whose somber and desolate talent awes us have been cast *with premeditation* into a hostile milieu. A tender and delicate spirit, a Vauvenargues, slowly unfolds its frail leaves in the gross atmosphere of a garrison. A mind that loves the open air and adores free nature struggles for a long time behind the stifling wall of a seminary. This ironic and ultragrotesque comic talent, whose laugh sometimes resembles a gasp or a sob, has been imprisoned in vast offices with green boxes and men with gold spectacles. Are there then some souls dedicated to the altar, *sanctified,* so to speak, who must march to their death and glory through perpetual self-immolation? Will the nightmare of *Tenebrae* always envelop these chosen spirits? They defend themselves in vain, they take all precautions, they perfect prudence. Let us block all the exits, close the door with a double lock, stop up the chinks in the windows. Oh! we forgot the keyhole; the Devil has already entered.

> Leur chien même les mord et leur donne la rage.
> Un ami jurera qu'ils ont trahi le roi.

Alfred de Vigny has written a book demonstrating that the poet's place is in neither a republic, nor an absolute monarchy, nor a constitutional monarchy; and no one has answered him.

The life of Edgar Poe is a wretched tragedy, and the horror of its ending is increased by its triviality. The various documents that I have just read have persuaded me that the United States was a vast cage for Poe, a great accounting establishment. All his life he made grim efforts to escape the influence of that anti-pathetic atmosphere. One of his biographers says that if Poe had wanted to regularize his genius and apply his creative faculties in a way more appropriate to the American soil he could have been an author with money, *a making-money author.** He said that after all, the times were not so hard for a talented man; he always found enough to live on, provided that he behaved with order and economy and used material wealth with moderation. Elsewhere, a critic shamelessly declares that however fine the genius of Poe might be, it would have been better to have merely had talent because talent is more easily turned to cash than genius is. A note written by one of his friends states that Poe was difficult to employ on a magazine, and he had to be paid less than the others because he wrote in a style too far above the ordinary. All of that reminds me of the odious paternal proverb, *"Make money, my son, honestly, if you can,* BUT MAKE MONEY."* *What a smell of department stores,* as J. de Maistre said concerning Locke.

If you talk to an American and speak to him of Poe, he will admit Poe's genius, willingly even; perhaps he will be proud, but he will end by saying, in his superior tone, "But I am a practical man." Then, with a sardonic air, he will speak to you of the great minds that cannot retain anything; he will speak to you of Poe's loose life—his alcoholic breath, which would have caught fire by a candle's flame, his nomadic habits. He will tell you that he was an erratic creature, a planet out of orbit, that he roved from New York to Philadelphia, from Boston to Baltimore, from Baltimore to Richmond. And if, your heart already moved by these signs of a calamitous existence, you remind him that Democracy certainly has it defects—in spite of its benevolent mask of liberty, it does not always permit, perhaps, the growth of individuality; it is often very difficult to think and write in a country where there are twenty or thirty million sovereigns; moreover, *you have heard it said* that there was a tyranny much more cruel and inexorable than that of a monarchy, in the United States (that of opinion)—then you will see his eyes open wide and cast off sparks. The froth of wounded patriotism mounts to his lips, and America, by his mouth, will heap insults on metaphysics and on Europe, its old mother. America is a practical creature, vain about its industrial power and a little jealous of the old continent. It does not have time to have compassion for a poet who could be maddened by pain and isolation. It is so proud of its young immensity, so naively trusting in the omnipotence of industry, so convinced that it will finally devour the Devil, that it has a certain pity for all these incoherent dreams. Onward it says; onward and ignore the dead. It would gladly walk over solitary, free spirits and trample them as lightheartedly as the immense railways overrun the leveled forests and the monster ships overrun the debris of a ship burned the previous evening. It is in a hurry to arrive. Time and money are everything.

Some time before Balzac descended into the final abyss while

---

* In English in the original.

uttering the noble plaints of a hero who still has great things to do, Edgar Poe, who is similar to him in many ways, was stricken by a frightful death. France lost one of her greatest geniuses and America lost a novelist, critic and philosopher scarcely made for her. Many people here are ignorant of the death of Edgar Poe; many others believe that he was a rich young gentleman, writing little, producing his strange and terrible creations in the most agreeable leisure, and knowing literary life only through rare and striking successes. The reality was quite the opposite.

Poe's family was one of the most respectable in Baltimore. His grandfather was quartermaster-general in the revolution and Lafayette held him in high esteem and affection. The last time that he went to visit that country, Lafayette begged the widow of the quartermaster to accept his solemn testimony of gratitude for the services her husband had rendered. Moreover, Poe's great-grandfather married a daughter of the English admiral McBride, and through him the Poe family was related to the most illustrious houses of England. Edgar's father received a distinguished education. Having fallen violently in love with a beautiful young actress, he eloped with her and married her. In order to share her destiny more completely, he tried to enter the theater also. But neither one had talent for the trade, and they lived in a very poor, precarious fashion. The young woman managed to attract crowds by her beauty, and the bewitched public endured her mediocre acting. On one of their circuits, they went to Richmond and died there within several weeks of one another, both by the same cause: hunger, lack of clothing, poverty.

Thus the poor child who was naturally endowed with charm was abandoned to chance, without bread, without a roof and without a friend. A rich merchant, a Mr. Allan, was moved to pity and was charmed by the good-looking boy. Since he had no children, he adopted him. Edgar Poe was therefore raised in elegant and easy circumstances and received a full education. In 1816, he accompanied his adopted parents on a voyage to England, Scotland and Ireland. Before returning to their country, they left him with Dr. Brandsby, who kept a famous boarding-school at Stoke-Newington, near London, where Poe spent five years.

Those who think about their own lives often look back to compare the past with the present; those who have the habit of ready self-analysis know what an immense part adolescence plays in a man's final temperament. At that time, impressions are deeply stamped in the tender, receptive mind; colors are vivid then, and sounds speak a mysterious tongue. The character, temper and style of a man are formed by the apparently ordinary circumstances of his first youth. If all the men who have occupied the world's stage had made note of their childhood impressions, what an excellent psychological dictionary we would save! The color and course of Poe's mind contrast violently with the tendency of American literature. His compatriots scarcely found him American, yet he is not English. For this reason we are fortunate to glean a singular account of his life at the school in Stoke-Newington in one of his stories, the little-known tale "William Wilson." All of Poe's tales are, in a sense, biographical, and we find the man in his work. The characters and incidents are the framework and trappings of his memory.

*　*　*　*

[Translation of pars. 5-13 of "William Wilson"]

What do you think of this passage? The nature of this strange man begins to reveal itself. It seems to me that this school portrait breathes a black fragrance. I feel the cold shiver of dark years of seclusion pervading it. The prison hours, the unease of a meager, abandoned childhood, the terror of our enemy the teacher, the hate of tyrannical comrades, the loneliness of heart—Edgar Poe has experienced all these tortures of youth, but those melancholy matters have not vanquished him. In his youth he loved solitude or rather, he did not feel that he was alone; he loved his passions. The *prolific brain of childhood* illuminating everything made everything bearable. We see at once that the exercise of his will and his solitary pride were to play an important part in his life. Besides, we might say that he was attached to pain; he foresaw the future campaign, which was to be inseparable from his life, and he called for it with a hungry harshness, like a young gladiator. The poor child had neither father nor mother, but he was happy; he exulted in being deeply marked, like a Carthaginian medallion.

Poe returned to Richmond from Dr. Brandsby's school in 1822, and continued his studies under the best teachers. At that time, he was remarkable for his physical ability and his feats of agility; a marvelous poetic power of memory and a precocious talent for improvising tales were added to the charm of his strange beauty. In 1825, he entered the University of Virginia, which was then an establishment ruled by the greatest dissipation. Poe distinguished himself among his fellow students by an even hotter ardor for pleasure. He was already a highly commendable student and made incredible progress in mathematics; he had an uncommon aptitude for physics and the natural sciences—a fact worthy of passing comment, for we find a great scientific preoccupation in several of his works—but at the same time he already drank, gambled and played so many pranks that he was finally expelled. When Mr. Allan refused to pay some gambling debts Poe lost his temper, broke with him and fled to Greece. It was the era of Botzaris and the Greek revolution. By the time he arrived in Saint Petersburg, his wallet and his enthusiasm were somewhat exhausted. He began a malicious quarrel (motive unknown) with the Russian authorities. The matter went so far, it is said, that Poe nearly added the knowledge of Siberian brutality to the rest of his precocious knowledge of men and things. In the end he was very happy to accept the intervention and help of the American consul, Henry Middleton, in order to return home. In 1829, he entered the military school of West Point. In the interval, Mr. Allan, whose first wife had died, married a woman several years younger than he. Poe was then 25 years old. It is said that he behaved dishonorably toward the woman and that he mocked the marriage. The old gentleman wrote him a very harsh letter, to which Poe replied even more bitterly. The rift was irreparable and soon afterward Mr. Allan died without leaving a cent to his adopted son.

Here in the biographical notes I find very mysterious words and highly obscure and peculiar allusions to the conduct of the future writer. Quite hypocritically, by swearing that he intends to say absolutely nothing about things that must always remain hidden, that in certain atrocious circumstances silence must take precedence over history, the biographer casts very serious aspersions on Poe. The blow is all the more dangerous because it is struck in the dark. What on earth does he mean? Is he insinuating that Poe tried to seduce the wife of his adopted father? It is quite impossible to guess. However, I believe I have already put the reader sufficiently on guard against American biographers who are too democratic not to hate their great men. The malevolence that pursued Poe after the agonizing end of his pitiful existence recalls the British hatred that persecuted Byron.

Poe left West Point without receiving his commission and began his ill-fated struggle for life. In 1831, he published a small

volume of poetry which was favorably received by the reviewers;
but no one bought it. This is the eternal history of the first book.
Mr. Lowell, an American critic, says that one of these poems, addressed to Helen, has "a perfume of ambrosia," and that it would
not disgrace the Greek Anthology. The poem is a thing of Nicean
barques, Naiades, Greek beauty and glory, and Psyche's lamp. We
note in passing the weakness of the immature American literature
for pastiche. In its harmonious rhythm and sonorous rhymes (five
lines, two masculine and three feminine), the poem reminds us of
some successful attempts in French Romanticism, but we see that
Edgar Poe was then very far from his eccentric and electric
literary destiny.

However, the luckless poet wrote for the newspapers, com-
piled and translated for the book-trade and wrote brilliant articles
and some tales for the magazines. The editors printed them gladly,
but paid the poor young man so badly that he fell into dreadful
misery. He fell so low that he could hear the *creaking hinges of
the doors of death*. One day a Baltimore newspaper offered two
prizes for the best poem and the best prose tale. A committee of
literary men, among them Mr. John Kennedy, was charged with
judging the productions. However, they hardly bothered to read
them; the sanction of their names was all that the editor wanted.
While chatting about this and that, one of them was attracted by
a manuscript that was notable for the beauty, clarity and neatness
of its handwriting. To the end of his life, Edgar Poe still had an
incomparably fine script. (I find this remark thoroughly American.) Mr. Kennedy glanced through one page, and having been
struck by the style, he then read the entire composition aloud.
The committee gave the prize by acclamation to the first genius
who knew how to write legibly. The secret envelope was opened,
revealing the unknown name of Poe.

The editor spoke to Mr. Kennedy about the young author in
terms that made him want to know him. Cruel fortune had given
Poe the classic physiognomy of a fasting poet; it had made him
up as well as possible for the role. Mr. Kennedy tells that he found
a young man whom privation had reduced to a skeleton, dressed
in a threadbare redingote which was, by a well-known tactic,
buttoned to the chin, ragged trousers, boots in shreds and apparently no stockings; and with all that, a proud air, fine manners
and eyes flashing with intelligence. Kennedy spoke to him as to
a friend and put him at ease. Poe opened his heart to him and

told his story, his ambition and his great plans. Kennedy immediately took Poe to a clothing store (an old-clothes vendor, Lesage
would have said) and gave him suitable clothing; then he introduced him to society.

At this time, Mr. Thomas White, who had bought the
Southern Literary Messenger, chose Mr. Poe to manage it and
gave him 2500 francs a year. Poe immediately married a girl
without a cent. (That phrase is not mine. I beg the reader to note
the slight tone of disdain in that *immediately*—the wretch thought
himself rich, then!—and in the laconic, dry announcement of an
important event; but also, *a girl without a cent!*) It is said that
intemperance already played a certain part in his life, but, in fact,
he found time to write a great number of articles and fine critical
pieces for the *Messenger.* After having managed it for a year and
a half, he went to Philadelphia and edited the *Gentleman's Magazine.* This periodical was absorbed by *Graham's Magazine,* and
Poe continued to write for the latter. In 1840, he published *The
Tales of the Grotesque and Arabesque.* In 1844, we find him in
New York directing the *Broadway Journal.* In 1845, Wiley and
Putnam's well known little edition appeared, containing a section
of poetry and a series of tales. From this edition the French
translators have taken almost all the specimens of Poe's talent
that have appeared in the Paris newspapers. As late as 1847, he
published in rapid succession various works we will discuss later.
We learn that his wife died in utter destitution in a town called
Fordham, near New York. A subscription was gathered among
the literary people of New York to assist Edgar Poe. Soon after,
the newspapers spoke of him again as a man on the brink of death.
But this time it was a grave matter; he had delirium tremens. A
cruel note in a newspaper of that period indicates his scorn for all
those who called themselves his friends, and his distaste for the
world in general. Nevertheless, he earned money and his literary
work nearly supported him. However, I have found proof in some
admissions of his biographers that he had to surmount revolting
difficulties. Apparently, during the last two years when he was
occasionally seen in Richmond, he scandalized people by his
drunkenness. To hear the everlasting recriminations on this subject, one might think that all the writers of the United States were
models of sobriety. But on his last visit, which lasted nearly two
months, he suddenly appeared neat, elegant, correct, with charming manners and lofty as genius. Obviously, I lack adequate

information, and the notes I have at hand are not intelligent enough for these extraordinary transformations. Perhaps we could find the explanation in an admirable maternal protection which enfolded the somber writer and opposed his evil demon of heredity and previous sorrow with its angelic arms.

On this last visit to Richmond, he gave two public readings. A word must be said about readings, which play a major part in the literary life of the United States. No law forbids a writer, philosopher, poet, or anyone who can speak, to announce a *lecture,* a public dissertation on a literary or philosophic subject. He hires a hall. Everyone pays a fee for the pleasure of hearing ordinary ideas and phrasing phrases. The public comes or does not come. In the latter case, the speculation is a failure, like any other hazardous commercial enterprise. When the lecture is to be given by a famous writer, however, there is a crowd, and the lecture is a literary event. Evidently, it is as though the chairs of the Collège de France were put at everyone's disposal. One is reminded of Andrieux, La Harpe, Baou-Lormain and the type of literary revival that occurred in the schools, athenaeums and clubs after the abating of the French Revolution.

As subject for his discourse, Edgar Poe chose a perpetually fascinating theme which has been hotly debated here. He announced that he would speak on the *poetic principle.* For a long time there has been a utilitarian movement in the United States which wants to sweep poetry along with everything else. There are humanitarian poets, poets of universal suffrage, poets to abolish grain-laws and poets who want to have workhouses built. I assure you I intend no innuendos about the people of this country. It is not my fault if the same disputes and the same theories trouble various nations. In his lectures, Poe declared war on them. He did not insist, like some senseless, fanatical disciples of Goethe and other marmorean and anti-human poets, that everything beautiful is essentially useless; but the goal he set himself was to refute what he wittily called *the great poetic heresy of modern times.* This heresy is the idea of direct utility. We see that from a certain point of view Poe sided with the French Romantic movement. He said that the mind possesses basic faculties whose functions are different: some are concerned with satisfying rationality, others with perceiving color and form and still others with filling the function of construction. Logic, painting and mechanics are the products of these faculties. Just as we have nerves for scenting good odors, for savoring beautiful colors and for giving us pleasure in the contact of smooth bodies, we also have a primary faculty for the perception of the beautiful. It is intended for the sense of beauty and for no other. *To submit it to the criteria of other faculties is to wrong it.* It should never be applied to matters other than those which are necessarily the food of the intellectual organ which gives it birth. Undoubtedly, poetry may subsequently and consequently be useful, but that is not its aim; it is a bonus. No one is astonished if a market, a wharf or any other industrial construction satisfies the conditions of beauty, although that was not the principal aim nor the first ambition of the engineer or the architect. Poe *illustrated* his thesis by various bits of criticism applied to poets of his country and by recitations from English poetry. People asked him to read his "Raven," a poem that the American critics make much of. They consider it a very remarkable piece of versification, for its vast and complicated rhythm, its masterly interweaving of rhymes tickles their national pride, which is a little jealous of European feats of style. But apparently the audience was disappointed by the author, who did not know how to display his work. He had pure diction, but his hollow voice, monotonous delivery and great carelessness with the musical effects that his skillful pen had annotated only moderately satisfied those who had anticipated a good time in comparing the reader with the author. I am not at all surprised. I have often noticed that admirable poets are abominable actors. That often happens with serious and retiring minds. Fortunately, profound writers are not orators.

A huge audience filled the hall. People who had not seen Poe since his days of obscurity came in crowds to see their now-famous compatriot, and the fine reception filled his poor heart with joy. He was elated and very legitimately and excusably proud. He was so charmed that he spoke of establishing himself permanently in Richmond. The rumor spread that he was going to marry again. All eyes turned toward Poe's old love, a widow rich as she was beautiful, who was thought to be the original model of "Lenore." Nevertheless, Poe had to spend some time in New York in order to publish a new edition of his *Tales*. Besides, the husband of a very rich lady of that city wanted him to put his wife's poetry in order and to write some notes, a preface, etc.

Poe therefore left Richmond, but as he began his journey he complained of chills and faintness. Since he still felt weak on arriving in Baltimore, he drank a small quantity of alcohol to revive him. For the first time in several months the cursed alcohol touched his lips, and it was enough to awaken the Demon sleeping within. A day of debauchery brought on a new attack of delirium tremens, his old acquaintance. In the morning, policemen picked him up from the street in a state of stupor. Since he was without money, friends or dwelling, they took him to the hospital, and in one of its beds the author of "The Black Cat" and *Eureka* died on October 7, 1849, at the age of 37.

Edgar Poe left no relative except a sister who had remained in Richmond. His wife had died some time before him, and they had no children. She had been a young girl named Clemm, related to her husband in some way. Her mother, who was deeply attached to Poe and accompanied him through all his miseries, was terribly shocked by his premature death. The bond between them had not been loosened by the death of her daughter. Such great devotion, such a noble and resolute affection, does Poe the greatest honor. Certainly one who could inspire such boundless friendship had virtues, and his spiritual being must have been wholly compelling.

Mr. Willis has published a short note on Poe; I take the following excerpts from it.

*   *   *   *

How the poor woman worried about the reputation of her son! How beautiful and how noble she is! As freedom dominates fatality, and as the spirit is above the flesh, so the affection of this admirable creature rises above all human affection. I wish that our tears could cross the sea—the tears of all those who, like your poor Eddie, are unhappy and troubled and have often been dragged to debauchery by misery and pain; I wish that they could mingle in your heart! If only these lines, etched with the most sincere and respectful admiration, could delight your maternal eyes! Your quasi-divine image will hover forever over the martyrology of literature.

Poe's death caused real emotion in America. Authentic testimony of pain rose from various parts of the Union. Sometimes death causes many things to be forgiven. We are happy to mention a letter from Longfellow, which does him all the more honor because Poe had treated him badly: "What a melancholy end, that of Mr. Poe, a man so richly endowed with genius! I have never known him personally, but I have always had great esteem for his power as a prose writer and as a poet. His prose is remark-

ably vigorous and direct, yet copious, and his verse breathes a
special melodious charm, an atmosphere of true poetry, which is
all-pervasive. The harshness of his criticism I have never attributed
to anything but the irritability of an overly sensitive nature, exas-
perated by all manifestations of falseness."

The prolix author of *Evangeline* is amusing when he talks of
copiousness. Does he take Edgar Poe for a mirror?

Comparing the character of a great man with his works is a
very great and rewarding pleasure. A very legitimate curiosity has
always been stimulated by biographies, by notes on manners and
habits and by the physical appearance of artists and writers.
People seek Erasmus' acuity of style and precision of idea in the
cut of his profile; we examine the heads of Diderot and Mercier,
where a little swagger mingles with goodfellowship, to find the
warmth and show of their work. Voltaire's battle face reveals his
stubborn irony, and his horizon-searching eye reveals his power
of command or of prophecy. The solid countenance of Joseph de
Maistre is that of the eagle and the bull at the same time. And
who has not cudgeled his brains to decipher the *Human Comedy*
by means of the powerful and complex forehead and face of Balzac?

Edgar Poe was a little below average in stature, but his body
was solidly built; his feet and hands were small. Before his health
was undermined, he was capable of marvelous feats of strength.
I believe that it has often been noticed that Nature makes life very
hard for those of whom she expects great things. Although they
appear frail sometimes, they are built like athletes, and are as
good for pleasure as for suffering. Balzac corrected the proofs for
his books while attending the rehearsals of the *Resources de
Quinola* and directing and playing all the roles himself; he dined
with the actors, and when everyone was exhausted and had retired
to sleep, he returned to work with ease. Everyone knows that he
committed great excesses of insomnia and sobriety. Edgar Poe, in
his youth, distinguished himself in all exercises of skill and strength
and—as is revealed in his work—calculations and problems. One
day he made a bet that he could leave one of the Richmond docks,
swim upstream seven miles in the James River, and return on foot
the same day; and he did it. It was a boiling summer day, and he
did not carry it off badly. Expression of face, gestures, gait,
posture of head—everything singled him out, in his good days, as
a man of great distinction. He was *marked* by Nature as one of
those who, in a social circle, at a cafe, or in the street, *compel* the

eye of the observer and engross him. If ever the word *strange* (which has been much abused in modern descriptions) has been aptly applied to anything, it is certainly to Poe's type of beauty. His features were not large, but quite regular. His complexion was a light brunette, his expression sad, distraught, and, although neither angry nor insolent, somehow displeasing. His singularly fine eyes seemed at first glance to be dark grey, but on closer examination they appeared frosted with a light indefinable violet. His forehead was superb. It did not have the ridiculous proportions invented by bad artists when, in order to flatter a genius, they transform him into a hydrocephalic, but an overflowing inner force seemed to push forward the organs of reflection and construction. The parts to which phrenologists attribute the sense of the picturesque were not absent, however; they merely seemed disturbed, jostled by the haughty and usurping tyranny of comparison, construction and causation. The sense of ideality and absolute beauty, the esthetic sense par excellence, also reigned in this forehead with calm pride. In spite of all these qualities, the head did not present an agreeable and harmonious impression. Seen full-face, it was striking and commanded attention by the domineering and inquisitorial effect of the forehead, but the profile revealed certain lacks; there was an immense mass of brain in front and back, and a moderate amount in the middle. In short, there was enormous animal and intellectual power, but weakness in the area of veneration and the affections. The despairing echoes of melancholy running through the works of Poe have a penetrating tone, it is true, but one must also admit that it is a very solitary melancholy, uncongenial to the ordinary man. I cannot help laughing when I think of some lines that a writer highly esteemed in the United States wrote about Poe some time after his death. I quote from memory, but I will answer for the meaning. "I have just reread the works of the regrettable Poe. What an admirable poet! What an amazing storyteller! What a prodigious and superhuman mind! He was really the original mind of our country. Well, I would give all of his seventy mystic, analytic and grotesque tales, so brilliant and full of ideas, for the good little hearthside book, the family book, that he could have written with the marvelously pure style that gives him such superiority over us. How much greater Mr. Poe would be!" To ask a family book of Edgar Poe! It is true, then, that human folly is the same in all climates, and the critic always wants to tie gross vegetables to ornamental shrubs.

Poe had black hair, shot through with some white threads, and a bristling moustache which he neglected to trim and to comb properly. He dressed with good taste but was a little negligent, like a gentleman who has many other things to do. His manners were excellent, very polished and self-assured, but his conversation deserves special comment. The first time that I questioned an American about it, he answered me, laughing, "Oh! oh! His conversation was not at all coherent!" After some explanation, I understood that Mr. Poe took great leaps in the world of ideas, like a mathematician who demonstrates for very intelligent students, and that he often carried on monologs. In fact, it was an essentially meaty conversation. He was not a *fine talker*. Moreover, he had a horror of conventionality, in speaking as in writing, but his vast knowledge, acquaintance with several languages, profound studies and ideas gathered in several countries made his conversation an excellent instruction. In short, he was the proper man for people who measure friendship according to the spiritual profit that they can make. Yet it seems that Poe was very indiscriminate in his choice of listeners. He scarcely troubled to discover whether his hearers were capable of understanding his tenuous abstractions or admiring the glorious conceptions which constantly flashed through the somber sky of his mind. He sat in a tavern beside a sordid ruffian and gravely expounded the great lines of his terrible book *Eureka* with a relentless coolness, as though he were dictating to a secretary or disputing with Kepler, Bacon or Swedenborg. That is a special trait of his. No man has ever freed himself more completely from the rules of society, or troubled himself less about passersby; that is why, on certain days, he was received in low class cafes but was refused entrance to the places where *respectable people* drink. No society has ever forgiven such things, still less an English or American society. Besides, Poe already had to be forgiven his genius. In the *Messenger* he had ferociously pursued mediocrity; his criticism had been hard and disciplinary, like that of a superior, solitary man who is interested only in ideas. A moment of disgust for all things human had arrived, when only metaphysics mattered to him. Dazzling his young, unformed country with his intelligence and shocking men who thought themselves his equals with his manners, Poe inevitably became one of the most unfortunate of writers. Hostility came in crowds; solitude surrounded him. In Paris or Germany he would have found friends to give him understanding and solace.

In America he had to fight for his bread. In this way his intoxication and perpetual moving are explained. He traveled through life as though it were a Sahara, and he changed abodes like an Arab.

But there are other reasons—his deep domestic sorrows, for example. We have seen his precocious youth suddenly cast into the asperity of life. Poe was almost always alone; in addition, the terrible battle in his mind and the harshness of his work must have made him seek the delight of oblivion in wine and liquor. What fatigues others gave him solace. Finally, Poe escaped literary animosity, the vertigo of the infinite, domestic sorrows and the outrages of misery in the darkness of intoxication, like the darkness of the tomb. He did not drink like a glutton but like a barbarian. The alcohol had scarcely touched his lips before he rooted himself at the counter and drank glass after glass until his good Angel was drowned and his faculties were annihilated. It is a miraculous fact, verified by all who knew him, that neither the purity and perfection of his style, nor the precision of his thought, nor his eagerness for work and difficult study was disturbed by his terrible habit. The composition of most of the good pieces preceded or followed one of his attacks. After the appearance of *Eureka,* he gave himself over furiously to drink. The very morning when the *Whig Review* published 'The Raven" and the name of Poe was on every tongue, with everyone discussing his poem, he crossed Broadway in New York, stumbling and staggering against the buildings.

Literary intoxication is one of the most common and lamentable phenomena of modern life, but perhaps there are many extenuating circumstances. In the time of Saint-Amant, Chapelle and Colletet, literature was also intoxicated, but joyfully, in the company of nobles who were highly literate and who had no fear of the cabaret. Even certain ladies would not have blushed to have a taste for wine, as is proved by the adventure of one whose servant found her with Chapelle, both of them weeping hot tears after supper because of the death of poor Pindar, dead through the fault of ignorant doctors. In the eighteenth century the tradition continues, a little impaired. The school of Retif drinks, but it is already a school of pariahs, a subterranean world. Mercier, very old, is found in Cor-Honore Street. Napoleon has conquered the eighteenth century; Mercier is a little drunk, and he says that *he no longer lives except by curiosity.* Today, literary drunkenness has assumed a somber and sinister character. Now there is no particularly literate class that does itself the honor of associating with men of letters. Their absorbing work and aversion for schools hinders their uniting. As for women, their formless education and political and literary incompetence keep many authors from seeing anything in them but household utensils or objects of lust. Once dinner is digested and the animal satisfied, the poet enters the vast solitude of his thought; sometimes he is exhausted by his craft. What then? His mind grows accustomed to the idea of its invincible strength, and he can no longer resist the hope of finding again in drink the serene or terrible visions which are already his old friends. The same transformation of customs that makes the literate world a class apart is also undoubtedly responsible for the immense consumption of tobacco in the new literature.

I shall try to give an idea of the general character of the works of Edgar Poe. Giving an analysis of each work would be impossible without writing a book, for this singular man, in spite of his disordered and diabolic life, produced a great deal.

When he was appointed editor of the *Southern Literary Messenger,* it was stipulated that he receive 2500 francs a year. In exchange for this paltry salary, he was responsible for reading and selecting pieces for each month's issue and composing the part called *editorial*—that is to say, he evaluated all the works that appeared and weighed all of the literary events. In addition, he very often contributed a novella or a bit of poetry. He plied this trade for nearly two years. Thanks to his active direction and the originality of his criticism, the *Literary Messenger* soon attracted all eyes. Before me I have the issues of those two years. The editorial part is considerable, and the articles are very long. In the same issue, we often find reviews of a novel, a book of poetry, a medical book and a book on physics or history. All the reviews are written with the greatest care and indicate a knowledge of various literatures and a scientific aptitude reminiscent of French writers of the eighteenth century. Apparently Poe had put his time to good use during his previous misfortunes, and had turned over many ideas. He wrote a remarkable quantity of critical reviews of the principal English and American authors, and often of French memoirs. The source of an idea, its origin and end, the school to which it belonged, the salutary or noxious method of the author—all of these were neatly, clearly and rapidly explained. Although Poe attracted much attention, he also made many enemies. Profoundly absorbed in his opinions, he waged tireless war on false reasoning, stupid pastiches, solecisms, barbarisms and all the literary crimes daily committed in books and newspapers. Yet he could not be reproached, for he preached by example. His style is pure; it is adequate to his ideas and renders their precise impression. Poe is always correct. It is very remarkable that a man of such roving and ambitious imagination should at the same time be so fond of rules and so capable of careful analysis and patient research. He could be called an antithesis made flesh. But his fame as a critic damaged his literary future a great deal. Many wanted to be avenged, and every possible reproach was cast in his face as the number of his works increased. Everyone knows the long, banal litany: immorality, lack of tenderness, absence of conclusions, extravagance, useless literature. French criticism has never forgiven Balzac for *Le grand homme de province à Paris.*

In poetry, Edgar Poe is a solitary spirit. Almost alone on the other side of the ocean he represents the Romantic movement. Properly speaking, he is the first American to make his style a tool. His profound and plaintive poetry is nevertheless finely wrought, pure, correct and brilliant as a crystal jewel. In spite of the amazing qualities which have made soft, tender spirits adore them, Alfred de Musset and Alphonse de Lamartine would obviously not have been his friends if he had lived here. They do not have enough will and self-mastery. Although Edgar Poe loved complicated rhythms, he shaped them in a profound harmony no matter how complicated they were. One of his short poems, "The Bells," is a veritable literary curiosity, but it is totally untranslatable. "The Raven" had a huge success. In the judgment of Longfellow and Emerson, it is a marvel. The content is slight; it is a pure work of art.

*   *   *   *

The tone is grave and almost supernatural, like insomniac thoughts; the lines fall one by one, like monotonous tears. In "Dreamland," he tried to portray the series of dreams and fantastic images besieging the soul when the body's eye is closed. Other poems, such as "Ulalume" and "Annabel Lee" enjoy equal fame. But the poetic stock of Edgar Poe is slight. His condensed and finely-worked poetry undoubtedly cost much effort, and he was often in need of money in order to surrender himself to that delightful and fruitless pain.

As a novelist and storyteller, Edgar Poe is unique in his field, just as Maturin, Balzac and Hoffmann were in theirs. The various pieces scattered throughout the magazines have been gathered into two sheaves,· *Tales of the Grotesque and Arabesque* and *Edgar A. Poe's Tales* in the edition of Wiley and Putnam. There are approximately 72 pieces. Some are purely grotesque, some are preoccupied with magnetism, some are wild clownings, some are unleashed aspirations towards the infinite. The tiny volume of tales has had great success in Paris as well as in America because it contains stories that are highly dramatic, but dramatic in a special way.

I should like to characterize Poe's work very briefly and exactly, for it is a totally new creation. The qualities that essentially define it and distinguish it from others are (if I may be pardoned these strange words) conjecturism and probabilism. My assertions can be verified by examining some of his subjects.

"The Gold Bug": analysis of a succession of methods for deciphering a cryptogram which will help to disclose hidden treasure. I cannot help thinking regretfully that the unfortunate E. Poe must have dreamed more than once of means of discovering treasure. The explanation of this method, which becomes the odd literary specialty of certain police secretaries, is eminently logical and lucid. The description of the treasure is fine; what a good sense of warmth and dazzlement one has! For the treasure is found. *It was not a dream* as usually happens in novels—the author awakening us brutally after having aroused our spirits by whetting our hopes. This time it is a *real* treasure and the decipherer has truly won it. Here is the exact sum: in money, $450,000 (not an ounce of silver, but all gold and very ancient, enormous, weighty pieces with unreadable inscriptions), 110 diamonds, 18 rubies, 310 emeralds, 21 sapphires, one opal, 200 rings and massive earrings, some 30 chains, 83 crucifixes, 5 censors, an enormous punchbowl of gold with vine leaves and bacchantes, 2 sword-handles and 197 watches adorned with precious stones. The content of the coffer is first valued at a million and a half dollars, but the sale of the jewels brings the total above that. The description of this treasure makes one dizzy with largesse and ambitions of benevolence. The coffer hidden by the pirate Kidd contained enough, certainly, to ease many unknown desperations.

"The Maelstrom"· Would it not be possible to descend into

an abyss whose bottom has never been sounded, in studying the laws of gravity in a new way?

"The Murders in the Rue Morgue" could instruct prosecuting attorneys. A murder has been committed. How? By whom? This affair contains some inexplicable and contradictory facts, and the police have given up. A young man who is gathering evidence for the love of the art presents himself. Through extreme concentration of thought and successive analysis of all the phenomena of understanding, he happens upon the law of the generation of ideas. Between one word and the next, between two ideas which are apparently unrelated, he can establish a complete intermediary series before the dazzled eyes of the police, and fill in the lacuna of unexpressed and almost unconscious ideas. He has closely studied all the possibilities and all the probable associations. He has ascended from induction to induction until he succeeds in showing decisively that an ape has committed the crime.

"The Mesmeric Revelation": The author's point of departure has evidently been this question: With the help of the unknown power called magnetic fluid, could we discover the law that rules the ultimate worlds? The beginning is full of dignity and solemnity. The physician has put his patient to sleep simply to ease him. "What do you think about your illness?—I will die.—Will that cause you sorrow?—No." The patient complains that he is badly questioned. "Direct me, says the doctor.—Begin at the beginning.—What is the beginning?—(Very low) It is GOD.—Is God a spirit?—No.—Is he matter, then?—No." A vast theory of matter follows, of gradations of matter and the hierarchy of beings. I published this story in an issue of *Liberté de penser* in 1848.

Elsewhere there is an account of a spirit that had lived on an extinguished planet. This was the point of departure: Can one, by means of induction and analysis, determine what physical and moral phenomena would occur among the inhabitants of a world approached by a murderous comet?

At other times we find the purely fantastic modeled on nature, without explanation, in the manner of Hoffmann: "The Man of the Crowd" plunges endlessly into the heart of the crowd; he swims with delight in the human sea. When the shadowy twilight full of tremulous lights descends, he flies from the silenced districts and ardently seeks the places where human matter swarms busily. As the circle of light and life shrinks, he seeks the center uneasily. Like men in a flood, he clings desperately to the last culminating points of public movement. And that is all we know. Is he a criminal who has a horror of solitude? Is he an imbecile who cannot endure himself?

Is there an even slightly literate Parisian author who has not read "The Black Cat"? In it we find totally different qualities. This terrible poem of crime begins in a gentle, innocent manner.

* * * *

[Summary, and quotation of passage on perversity]

The burning curiosity of Poe was aroused not only by probabilities and possibilities, but also by spiritual maladies. "Berenice" is an admirable example of this type. However unlikely and outlandish my dry analysis may make it seem, I can state that nothing is more logical and possible than this frightful story.

* * * *

[2-page summary]

Poe usually suppresses the minor details or gives them a minimal value. Because of this harsh severity, the generating idea is more evident and the subject stands out vividly against the bare background. His method of narration is simple. He overuses the first person pronoun with cynical monotony. One might say that he is so sure of being interesting that he does not bother to vary his technique. His tales are nearly always the account or manuscript of the main character. As for his ardent exploration of the horrible, I have noticed it in various men, and it is often the result of a great unoccupied vital energy, of an obstinate chastity sometimes, and also of a profound sensibility which has been thwarted. The supernatural pleasure that a man can experience in seeing his own blood run—the brusque, useless movements, the cries almost involuntarily piercing the air—is a similar phenomenon. Pain is a release from pain, and action is a relaxation from repose.

Another peculiar trait of his work is that it is completely antifeminine. Let me explain. Women write and write in a swift overflow; their hearts prattle by the ream. Generally, they know neither art, nor measure, nor logic. Their style trains and coils like their garments. In spite of her superiority, the very great and justly famous George Sand has not entirely escaped this law of temperament; she throws her masterpieces into the mail as though they were letters. It is said that she writes her books on letter paper.

In Poe's books the style is condensed, tightly linked. The ill will or laziness of the reader cannot slip through the mesh of this logically woven net. All ideas, like obedient arrows, fly to the same target.

I have followed a long trail of tales without finding one love story. This man is so intoxicating that I did not think about it until the end. Without claiming to extol the ascetic system of an ambitious mind absolutely, I think that such an austere literature would be a useful weapon against the invading fatuity of women, who are more and more stimulated by the disgusting idolatry of men. And I am very lenient toward Voltaire, who thought it well in the preface to his womanless tragedy, *La Mort de Cesar,* to emphasize his glorious tour de force by feigning excuses for his impertinence.

In Edgar Poe there are no enervating whines, but always a tireless ardor for the ideal. Like Balzac, who died perhaps saddened because he was not a pure scholar, Poe is enchanted by science. He wrote a *Manual for the Conchologist,* which I have forgotten to mention. Like conquerors and philosophers, he has a compelling aspiration toward unity and he assimilates morality into physical things. It could be said that he attempts to apply the procedures of philosophy to literature, and the methods of algebra to philosophy. In the constant ascent toward the infinite, one loses his breath. In this literature the air is rarefied as in a laboratory. We endlessly contemplate the glorification of will applied to induction and analysis. Poe seems to intend to wrench language from the prophets and to monopolize rational explanation. Thus, the landscapes which sometimes serve as background for his feverish fictions are pale as ghosts. Poe scarcely shared the passions of other men; he sketched trees and clouds that seem to be the dream of clouds and trees, or strange characters shaken by a supernatural, galvanic shiver.

Once, however, he set himself to write a purely human book. *The Narrative of Arthur Gordon Pym,* which has had no great success, is a story of sailors who, after severe damage to the ship, have been becalmed in the South Seas. The author's genius delights in these terrible scenes and in the amazing sketches of tribes and islands which are not indicated on the maps. The style of this book is extremely simple and detailed.

*   *   *   *

[2½-page description of the charnel-ship]

Although *Eureka* was undoubtedly the long-cherished dream of Edgar Poe, I cannot write a precise account of it here, for it is a book that requires a special article. Whoever has read the "Mesmeric Revelation" knows the metaphysical tendencies of the author. *Eureka* attempts to develop the process and show the law by which the universe assumed its present visible form and organization. It shows that the same law which began creation will act to destroy the world and absorb it. One readily comprehends why I do not care to engage lightly in discussion of such an ambitious attempt. I would be afraid of erring and slandering an author for whom I have the deepest respect. Edgar Poe has already been accused of pantheism, and although I may be forced to agree that appearances lead to such a conclusion, I can assert that, like many other great men bewitched by logic, he sometimes contradicts himself. It is to his credit. Thus his pantheism is counteracted by his ideas on the hierarchy of beings and by many passages that obviously affirm the permanence of personality.

Edgar Poe was very proud of this book, which naturally did not have the same success as his tales. One must read it cautiously and verify his strange ideas by checking them against similar and opposite systems.

I had a friend who was also a metaphysician in his fashion, obsessed and absolute, with the air of a Saint Just. He often said to me, taking an example from the world and looking at me from the corner of his eye, "Every mystic has a hidden vice." And I continued his thought: Then he must be destroyed. But I laughed, because I did not understand. One day, as I was chatting with a well-known, busy bookseller whose specialty is to cater to the enthusiasms of all the mystical band and the obscure courtesans of occult sciences, I asked for information on his clientele. He said to me, "Remember that every mystic has a hidden vice, often a very material one—drunkenness, gormandizing, lewdness. One will be avaricious, the other cruel, etc."

Good Lord! I said to myself. Then what is the fatal law that binds us, dominates us, and avenges the violation of its insufferable despotism by degrading and sapping our moral being? The visionaries have been the greatest of men. Why must they be punished for their greatness? Hasn't their ambition been the most noble? Will man eternally be so limited that one of his faculties cannot expand except at the expense of the others? If wanting to know the truth at all costs is a great crime, or if it can lead to great error, if stupidity and indifference are virtues and guarantees of balance, I think we should be very forbearing towards these illustrious criminals, for we children of the eighteenth and nineteenth centuries can all be accused of the same vice.

I say this shamelessly, because I feel it comes from a profound feeling of pity and tenderness: Edgar Poe—drunkard, pauper, oppressed, pariah—pleases me more than do the calm and virtuous Goethe and W. Scott. I would readily say of him and of a particular class of men what the catechism says of our Lord: "He has suffered much for us."

We could write on his tomb, "All you who have passionately sought to discover the laws of your being, who have aspired to infinity, you whose rebuffed feelings have had to seek a frightful relief in the wine of debauchery, pray for him. His corporeal being, now purified, floats among the beings whose existence he glimpsed. Pray for him who sees and knows: he will intercede for you."

CHARLES BAUDELAIRE

"EDGAR ALLAN POE, HIS LIFE AND WORKS" (1856)*

Some destinies are fatal. In the literature of every country there are men who bear the word *unlucky* written with mysterious letters in the sinuous folds of their foreheads. Some time ago, a wretch with the strange tattoo *no luck* on his forehead was led before the court. He carried the label of his life with him everywhere, as a book bears its title, and the questioning proved that his existence conformed to his advertisement. In literary history there are similar fates. One might say that the blind Angel of Expiation, seizing certain men, whips them with all his might for the edification of the others. Yet if we study their lives attentively, we find they have talent, virtue and grace. Society pronounces a special anathema and condemns them for the very vices of character that its persecution has given them. What did Hoffman fail to do to disarm destiny? What did Balzac fail to do to exorcize fortune?

Is there then a Providence that with *premeditation* casts spiritual and angelic natures into a hostile milieu, like martyrs into the arena? Are there then some souls dedicated to the alter, sanctified, so to speak, who must march to their death and glory through perpetual self-immolation? Will the nightmare of *Tenebrae* always envelop these chosen spirits? They defend themselves in vain, they take all precautions, they perfect prudence. Let us block

---

* Revised version of 1852 essay.

all the exits, close the door with a double lock, stop up the chinks
in the windows, but the Devil will enter by a keyhole; a perfection
will be the weak place in their armor, and a superlative quality
will be the seed of their damnation:

> L'aigle, pour le briser, du haut du firmament,
> Sur leur front découvert, lâchera la tortue,
> Car ils doivent périr inévitablement.

Their destiny is written entirely in their own constitution: it shines
in their eyes with a sinister flash, and in their gestures; it circulates in their arteries with each of their corpuscles.

Alfred de Vigny has written a book demonstrating that the
poet's place is in neither a republic, nor an absolute monarchy,
nor a constitutional monarchy; and no one has answered him.
Today, I bring a new legend to the support of his thesis. I add
a new saint to the martyrology: I am to write the story of one
of the ill-fated great men, too rich in poetry and passion, who
came, like so many others, to undergo the rough apprenticeship
of genius among inferior souls in this base world.

The life of Edgar Poe is a wretched tragedy, and the horror
of its ending is increased by its triviality. The various documents
that I have just read have persuaded me that the United States
was a vast cage for Poe, a great accounting establishment. All
his life he made grim efforts to escape the influence of that anti-
pathetic atmosphere. The dictatorship of opinion is inexorable
in democratic societies; do not plead for charity, or indulgence,
or any elasticity in the application of its laws to the many-sided,
complex cases of moral life. One might say that a new tyranny
is born of the impious love of liberty—a tyranny of beasts, or
zoocracy that resembles the idol of the Juggernaut in its ferocious
insensibility. One of his biographers says that if Poe had wanted
to regularize his genius and apply his creative faculties in a
way more appropriate to the American soil, he could have been
an author with money, *a making-money author.** He said that
after all, the times were not so hard for a talented man; he always
found enough to live on, provided that he behaved with order
and economy and used material wealth with moderation. Elsewhere, a critic shamelessly declares that however fine the genius
of Poe might be it would have been better to have merely had
talent, because talent is more easily turned to cash than is genius.
A note written by one of his friends states that Poe was difficult

to employ on a magazine, and he had to be paid less than the others because he wrote in a style too far above the ordinary. *What a smell of department stores,* as J. de Maistre said concerning Locke.

Some have dared to do even more, and, uniting the grossest stupidity about his genius with the ferocity of bourgeois hypocrisy, have insulted him to their hearts' content; after his sudden disappearance, they rudely reprimanded the corpse— especially Mr. Rufus Griswold who, to recall the vengeful expression of Mr. George Graham, then committed an immortal infamy. Perhaps with a fatal presentiment of a sudden end, Poe had designated Griswold and Willis to put his works in order, write his life and establish his reputation. This pedagogue-vampire defamed his friend at great length in a monstrous, dull and hateful article placed at the very front of the posthumous edition of Poe's works. Is there no ordinance in America, then, forbidding dogs to enter the graveyards? Mr. Willis, in contrast, proved that benevolence and decency always accompany true wit, and that charity toward our colleagues, which is a moral duty, is also one of the commandments of good taste.

If you talk to an American and speak to him of Poe, he will admit Poe's genius, willingly even; perhaps he will be proud, but he will end by saying, in his superior tone, "But I am a practical man." Then, with a sardonic air, he will speak to you of the great minds that cannot retain anything; he will speak to you of Poe's loose life, his alcoholic breath which would have caught fire by a candle's flame, of his nomadic habits. He will tell you that he was an erratic creature, a planet out of orbit, that he roved from New York to Philadelphia, from Boston to Baltimore, from Baltimore to Richmond. And if, your heart already moved by these signs of a calamitous existence, you remind him that Democracy certainly has its defects—in spite of its benevolent mask of liberty. it does not always permit, perhaps, the growth of individuality; it is often very difficult to think and write in a country where there are twenty or thirty million sovereigns; moreover, *you have heard it said* that there is a tyranny much more cruel and inexorable than that of a monarchy, in the United States (that of opinion)—then you will see his eyes open wide and cast off sparks. The froth of wounded

---

* In English in the original.

patriotism mounts to his lips and America, by his mouth, will heap insults on metaphysics and on Europe, its old mother.

Again I say that Edgar Poe and his country were not on the same level. The United States is a giant infant country, naturally jealous of the old continent. Proud of its abnormal and almost monstrous material development, this newcomer in history has a naive faith in the omnipotence of industry; it is convinced, like some unfortunates among us, that it will end by eating the Devil. Time and money have such great value over there! Materialistic activity, exaggerated to the proportions of a national mania, leaves very little room for the things which are not earthly. Poe, who was of good stock and who declared, moreover, that the great misfortune of his country was in not having an aristocracy of race, thought that the cult of the Beautiful could not avoid being corrupted in a people without aristocracy. He charged his fellow citizens, even in their striking and costly luxuries, with all the symptoms of bad taste characteristic of parvenus; he considered Progress, the great modern idea, to be an ecstasy of simpletons, and he called the perfecting of human habitations scars and rectangular abominations. Poe was a singularly isolated mind. He believed only in the unchanging, the eternal, the *selfsame,** and he possessed—cruel privilege in a self-infatuated society—the great good sense of a Machiavel who marches before the sage like a column of fire across the desert of history.

What would he have thought or written if he had heard the theologian of sentiment do away with Hell through kindness for humanity, or the philosopher of ciphers propose a system of insurance, a subscription of a penny per head for the suppression of war (plus the abolition of the death penalty and orthography, those two correlated follies) and so many other sick people who write with their ears bent to the wind, spinning fantasies as soothing as the element that dictates them? If to this faultless vision of the true (a real handicap in certain circumstances), you add delicacy of perception so exquisite that a false note tortured it, a fineness of taste revolted by everything except precise proportion, and insatiable love of the Beautiful, which had acquired the power of a morbid passion, you will not be astonished that life became hell for such a man, and that he came to a bad end. You will wonder that he could *last* so long.

*　　*　　*　　*

* In English in the original.

ARMAND DE PONTMARTIN

"THE STORYTELLERS"*

I am ready to agree, if you insist: in this type of eccentric, isolated, exceptional literature, which is difficult to associate with any real literary group, nothing has appeared since Hoffmann's tales as original as these *Extraordinary Stories*. However, at the risk of recalling for the hundredth time the *laudator temporis acti,* permit me to note the difference in inspirations and eras. The dreams of Hoffmann—for his tales are only admirable dreams— reflect poetic and musical Germany, while exaggerating. In his excessive and hallucinated aspect, Edgar Poe reflects the calculating spirit of America. The content of Hoffmann's stories is art, love, music, the marvelous, astonishment and fear—all glimpsed through a sort of intoxication or ecstasy which magnifies the fantastic aspects and leads the imagination into a luminous night peopled with shadows and shades, stars and dark lanterns. The content of the stories of Edgar Poe is calculation, analysis and algebra, which desert their solid and positive ground and mingle, in a delirious or diseased mind, with the most subtle imagination. I cannot agree on this subject with Poe's very remarkable translator, Mr. Baudelaire, who sees Edgar Poe as a victim of the American spirit, and points out, in a strange prose as glittering as broken ice, the painful contrast between the beauty loving spirit who launches into the infinite spaces of the ideal and dream, and

---

* Taken from *L'Assemblée nationale,* 12 April 1856.

126

the country which is both giant and child, immense cog-wheel, implacable machine which grinds and pulverizes all the flowers of poetry under its wheels. It seems to me he confuses the fate of Edgar Poe with his talent. His fate was stormy, and no matter how little indulgence one may have for misfortune caused by disorder, one is seized by a profound pity in considering that short life stricken by such a cruel *jettatura*. One pities a man so gifted and so unsuccessful in spite of his rare good fortune (in the United States) in having a charming wife and an excellent mother-in-law—a man who died at 37 after a double agony of illness and misery. Yet beware: Do not give us, the old aristocrats of the old world, the pleasure of verifying a frivolous *non sequitur* from your pen. You accuse the young American democracy of having been a horribly harsh stepmother to Edgar Poe; you portray for us an exquisite, delicate nature deprived of air in that steaming factory and succumbing to the nostalgia of the artist in the midst of industrial fevers. But a certain literature that you well know levels these same accusations against our old European society; it is not necessary to cross the seas in order to find a constant series of Chattertons and Hégésippe Moreaus. Not very long ago this literature grew justly tender over the fate of gentle, enchanting Gérard de Nerval, dead also through lack of air, dew and sunshine in this dark Parisian cage where the cry of money-changing and machines so often muffles the voice of the nightingales. What is there to say? Over there as here, it is the eternal struggle, the eternal antagonism between the actual and the chimeric, between imagination and good sense. And if I concede that the actual is sometimes very harsh, and good sense thoroughly rigid, that societies both old and new have not always had maternal hearts for these children of fantasy and dream, won't you agree that the children frequently deserve the harshness, and that the orphans who complain about their abandonment begin by abandoning themselves? This question will be disputed for a long time; my discussion would fasten upon that, if I wanted to insist, and you would not resolve it by sentences such as these: "Alas! the one who attained the most difficult heights of esthetics and plunged into the least explored abysses of the human intellect, the one who, throughout a life resembling a tempest without calm, discovered new means, unknown ways of astonishing the imagination in order to captivate minds thirsting for the beautiful, has just died on a hospital bed. What a destiny! So much greatness and misfortune simply in order to raise a whirlwind of bourgeois comment, to become fodder for virtuous journalists!" At the,risk of being numbered among those virtuous journalists whom virtue and the newspapers rarely pay for their pains, I am compelled to tell Mr. Baudelaire that such a style is unworthy of him, that he has too much talent to be forgiven these neologistic sequins, and that neither the America of Edgar Poe nor the France of Gérard de Nerval is responsible for the grain of madness which, mixed with superior faculties in some men, mixed with mediocre faculties in many men, explains the disorder of some, the pretentions of others, and the misfortune of all.

This much decided, we can immediately state that "The Murders in Rue Morgue," "The Purloined Letter" and "The Gold Bug" are not three great dramas but three gripping stories in which the author arrives at irresistible, unbelievable effects by strange means previously unknown to the novel. Discover how two women have been killed by a monkey and not by a man; find a letter in an ambassador's home, which has been searched fruitlessly for three months by the finest police bloodhounds; follow the trail of a treasure from the hidden clue in which no one could guess that a meaning lay, to the last shovelful of dirt which, falling, yields the precious coffer: nothing there, you would say, can sustain interest or cause any very lively emotions. You would be mistaken. Induction, under the hand of Edgar Poe, becomes ingenious and impassioned. One notices such profundity of analysis, such powers of calculation, that curiosity grows from page to page, and imagination joins the game. The author takes us with him into space with its constellations of X's and figures, and his algebraic trail from the known to the unknown finally moves us as much as if it had been a question of real people and pathetic events.

That is the originality of Edgar Poe. It may define his literary physiognomy adequately, but it also has a bearing, in its most significant and striking aspect, on the very spirit of that active and inventive America which did not know how to understand, protect or support the life of Edgar Poe. I have mentioned Hoffmann and Gérard de Nerval; once more, could we not point out a kind of unhealthy alliance between these delightful talents (lacking the ballast necessary to highly intellectual people) and the environment where they have grown, the country whose proximity and influence they have endured in spite of themselves? Gérard de Nerval is French intelligence; Hoffmann is German reverie; Edgar Poe is American arithmetic. Everything in Poe is colored by the prism of the sorcerer's invention, but everything loses footing and soars into vague regions where light and darkness vie unceasingly. One more step toward the light and you would have genius; one more toward the shadows, and you would have madness. Between the two is something confused, compelling and disturbing, something like the lamps carried in subterranean passages or mines: the vacillating glimmer sketches capricious arabesques on the wall, until the light goes out, until the soul departs, giving up the struggle because it cannot win.

Such is the impression that the *Extraordinary Tales* leave with me; but I do not intend by that to belittle Edgar Poe, nor to excuse myself from pitying him, nor to question the merit of the translator, who sacrifices too much for the pleasure of not belonging to "the school of good sense," but has brilliance and a quick imagination. His translation, instead of being as flat and lifeless as a polyglot secretary's copy, is as alive and varied as an original work. As in all things, novelty is rare in literature, and in the novel more than in any other genre; 166 years ago La Bruyère could write, "Everything has been said." Today one is tempted to add, "Every story has been told." For this reason, we thank Edgar Poe for telling us something which has not yet been told, and for not relating what we already know by heart. No more sentimental adventures, no more marriages hindered by harrying circumstances or inflexible parents, no more misunderstood women struggling against their bonds, or unmated souls seeking and finding one another in the midst of the vulgarities of this lowly world; no more heroes and heroines, ingenues and traitors, love declarations, recognition scenes, lost children found, Alfred marrying Henriette, or Valentine sorrowing over not having married Arthur. None of that. Instead, a chain of reasoning, calculations of probability, a series of physiological, metaphysical and mathematical demonstrations become chapters in a novel and do not permit us to regret the absence of other sources of feeling or interest. And besides, what a difference from the point of view of morality! What security for the mothers who complain of not being able to permit their daughters to read the works of our storytellers. Ordinarily, they are afraid of seeing those young, tender imaginations transported by a tale of actions more interesting than real life, by a tableau of persons more appealing than ordinary men. Here, the danger is less. After reading Edgar Poe, the most romantic girl could only become impassioned over an algebrist; and, although love may be a great unknown X, it has never passed for a great calculator. Let us read Edgar Poe again, then, and render justice to his *Extraordinary Tales;* let us envy America and England for these stories that are so perfectly chaste, such innocent companions for a morning walk and for an evening at home. If Poe's procedure finds imitators, soon there will be no more men and women; that is the only sure way for both of them to avoid danger.

EUGENE DELACROIX

"NOTE ON POE"*

April 6, 1856. For several days I have been reading Baudelaire's translation of Edgar Poe with great interest. These really
extraordinary—that is, extra-human—conceptions have the attraction of the fantastic, which is an attribute of some northern
natures—or I don't know *what* kind of natures—but is denied,
certainly, to our French nature. These people take pleasure only
in what is outside of nature, or extra-natural; as for us, we cannot lose our balance to that extent: all our flights must be rational.
I have difficulty in imagining a debauch of that kind, but all the
stories are in the same tone. I am sure there is no German who
does not feel at home in them. Although there is a most remarkable talent in these conceptions, I think it is of an order inferior
to that which portrays the truth. I agree that reading *Gil Blas* or
Ariosto does not give impressions of that kind, and when it is only
a means of varying our pleasures, it has its merit in keeping the
imagination alert; but one cannot take large doses of it, and that
persistence in the horrible or the impossible made probable is for
us a freak of the mind. One must not think that those authors
have more imagination than those who are content to describe
things as they are; it is certainly easier to invent by means of
striking situations than by the road worn down by intelligent
minds of all the ages.

---

* Taken from his *Journal III* (Paris, 1895), 137-139.

LOUIS ETIENNE

"THE AMERICAN STORYTELLERS—EDGAR ALLAN POE"*

"Give me a geometrician to demonstrate the existence of God by A + B!" cries a character in the novel *Peau de chagrin,* during an orgy. The invasion of the novel and poetry by the spirit of mathematics was one of the traits of the strange, tormented literature of that era; except for some illustrious men who were saved from excess by a delicacy of taste foreign to numbers and quantities, there were more geometry and chemistry in French Romanticism than one might think. The peculiar combination of verse and geometric figures, of thought and the crucible, the pen and the compass, gave most of the works of that school their distinctive color. One novelist studies manners with the naturalist's microscope and analyzes the human soul by means of all kinds of acids, solvents and precipitates. Another novelist has the plumbline constantly in hand; his novels are full of trapezoids, ellipsoids and parallelograms. Hence, there is a certain heaviness of hand, drawing only strong and salient lines, intensifying what is characteristic and seizing ideas which are airy and fugitive by nature as though they were the solid principles of geometry mentioned by Pascal. The most famous poet of that school wrote these lines about himself: "His entire childhood was one long revery mingled with exact studies. That childhood has made his mind what it is. Moreover, there is no in-

---

* Taken from *Revue contemporaine,* XXXII (15 July 1857), 492-524.

132

compatibility between the exact and the poetic. Number is in art as in science. Algebra is in astronomy, and astronomy is related to poetry; algebra is in music, and music is related to poetry."

A second characteristic of Romanticism: "The Greek Eumenides are much less horrible and consequently much less true than the witches in Macbeth." So the author of the preface to *Cromwell* expresses himself. The degree of horror, then, becomes the measure of truth. It is the epoch when poets make "vampires, ogres, snake-charmers, ghouls, gnomes and black adders prowl hideously in our cemeteries." They left cold and uniform beauty to antiquity; they claimed the grotesque, the deformed and the horrible for modern genius—passions, vices and crimes. The beautiful, which is unique and unvarying, needs to be diversified, vitalized by the ugly and the terrible, which are varied, powerful, inexhaustible. Frightful vengeances, violent crimes, bloodthirsty subtleties run to the brim in these novels. There is no need to insist further; that aspect of Romanticism is so well known that it is a commonplace.

Those were two striking traits of our literature, and partly of all European literature, thirty years ago. Now suppose that a young poet came from America at that time and was lost in the crowd of young people among whom a famous school, the poly-technic school, gave the tone, launched reputations and alloted popularity to some extent. Imagine that he passed unperceived in the chaos of ideas and entirely literary passions, but that he took away with him the memory of some names, some books and especially the powerful impulse of newness increased by the prestige the Old World has for an American imagination. Having arrived in America, if he is forced to continue by himself and looks for a way, he will follow the impetus he has received in Europe. His imitation of the old world will be his originality in the new. In Europe, circumstances and revolutions will perhaps have changed the direction of the movement he once witnessed; since he has not met the same obstacles in his path, he will follow a straight course. This hypothetical poet is the storyteller who is the subject of this study. Edgar Poe is a Romantic of 1827 who has been forced to emigrate to the United States. He has always seemed eccentric to America, and it has never acknowledged him as its own. So it is for us: not only does he seem a ghost to us, but he has also lived in a country very different from our own.

*　*　*　*

[Attempt to prove that in the "lost year" after Poe's quarrel with Allan, he stopped in France and Italy on his way to Greece. Condemnation of America as a machine-society. Parts I and II.]

The Nature of His Tales

If we examine the tales of Edgar Poe closely, we notice that they do not all have the same source. If we compare them according to dates of publication, we recognize several periods in Poe's talent. Thus, his biography in hand, we find him first inspired by terror. The principle of his first works is to present the horrible with no other end than horror itself, in deliberate language, with the simple and naive conviction that the effect he produces is a superior one. This is followed by something more clever and more refined—a subtle and perverse ingeniousness joins the terrors. We find curiosity in the terrible, calculus and science applied to the dreams of the most somber imagination. At the same time, feats of complication laboriously unwind, accompanied by the play of wit of a mathematician, but always with sad, if not terrifying, overtones. Finally, his narratives and, in general, everything that comes from his pen take on a philosophic character. A certain morality emerges; the author is no longer simply an artist. He has complete awareness of himself, he reasons his fatalism and he is a confessed materialist and pantheist.

If he wanted to compete for a literary prize offered in America, a Romantic who disembarked after having been expelled from the military academy of West Point (then enlisting as Coleridge had done, and deserting), could only start by recounting a frightful and impossible sea voyage. The hero, a skeptical philosopher, is shipwrecked in the unknown regions of the South Pole and, at the moment of foundering, confides the history of the terrible things he has seen to a well-stopped bottle. Poe made his debut with the concentrated horror contained in that bottle; his fine handwriting caused the prize to be given to him; he was hired by a magazine; he was employed for marvelous and terrifying writing. Such was his beginning.

I will refrain from questioning the legitimacy of this kind of writing, and will readily concede that there are fine horrors, provided that in return it be granted that nature mingles beauty with ugliness and that the love of the latter should not become hate of the former. Let Edgar Poe and those who still want to be like him be the Salvator Rosas of literature; let them paint bandits and bohemians and dismal, frightful nature, but let them remember the avowals of Salvator Rosa in his satires. The taste of the time forced his brushes to be harsh and savage; the public wanted only rags, misery, cruelty and blood. Let them rely on the example of Shakespeare. If they like, they may gouge an eye from its socket, provided that in the same drama a Cordelia refreshes our spirits with her voice of filial piety.

The poetry of pure horror has furnished Poe with several tales. These are the stories that display hideous sights without purpose, funereal miseries without end, vices and crimes without resolution. The Red Death comes to strike Prince Prospero and his courtiers with a mysterious and sudden death in the luxurious retreat he has made. A phantom with purple-tinged face promenades through a festivity; the guests fall one by one. What does this fantasmagoria signify? I have no idea, except that there is a great deal of blood and a great many bodies. . . . An unfortunate madman who likes books, I cannot say why, entombs his living sister in the dungeon of his castle. She leaves it at the end of six days and comes to knock at his door in the midst of a fearful storm. The castle, destroyed by the wind, sinks in the middle of a lake. That is called "The Fall of the House of Usher." Another madman digs up his wife to pull out her thirty-two teeth, which are very beautiful. That bears the title "Berenice."

So far, no trace of real life. It begins to appear in the *Narrative of Arthur Gordon Pym,* and the American trademark is evident. The Americans have a certain literature which we can scarcely imagine, that of false voyages. This voyaging and seagoing nation does not find enough surprises and oddities in nature; it must also have fictitious ones. Our sea novels, imitated moreover from theirs, do not give an accurate idea of this genre. Ours are dramas like all the rest, played on the bridge of a ship by sailors, officers, passengers, one or two heroines (disguised or not), accompanied by shipwreck, disabled masts, mutiny and boardings. The sea is there merely for seasoning. It pleases by its novelty, as the odor of tar pleases the Parisian bourgeois who visits a three-master at the Havre or Saint-Malo for the first time in his life. But the false voyage is not a drama; there is no

hint of unity of interest. Its merit consists purely and simply in
lying well. Not everyone lies well. The mark of talent is revealed
in the fulfillment of two requirements: the size of the lies and
their credibility. The more completely one makes people believe
enormities, the more genius he has. In this matter the Americans
have a decided superiority. We have the gay lie, they have the
scientific. La Fontaine's voyager had to be French:

I saw, he said, a cabbage as big as a house.

If he had been American, he would have given the measurements
within half a yard; he would have shown a piece of its leaf
carefully pressed in his notebook; he would have measured it
before your eyes and would have succeeded, by calculations like
those of Cuvier with a fossil fragment, in reconstructing his colossal cabbage with its shape, size and three dimensions.

These reflections are a useful aid in explaining the entire
American aspect of Edgar Poe's talent. With his own naturally
somber imagination and its model in our new school, he was able
to combine laborious subtlety, genius for detail and the taste for
surprise which distinguish his country. In that way he approxi-
mates real life. For he is almost the only writer of our time who
tells us nothing of his country, its society and its manners. He
sees reality only as material to be molded, broken and twisted
in all ways in order to build marvelous and fearful structures.
His dual procedure is to carry hyperbole as far as possible, then
press the demonstration to the very brink of evidence. . . .

The hoaxing impulse produced several of his tales, among
them one of his most popular, "The Peerless Adventure of a
Certain Hans Pfaall." It is the very model of the "charlatan
genre." "The Ballon Hoax" is not unworthy of comparison.
Nothing is forgotten on this voyage of the English aerostat, not
even the coffeemaker for boiling coffee with lime in order to
dispense entirely with fire if that is judged prudent. Poe explains
in a footnote why the convexity of the earth disappears at a
great altitude and reappears at an even greater altitude. To what
lengths will science go? . . .

Fortunately, consulting good sense and dignity, the storyteller rises above scientific trickery and astronomy placed on the
level of humbug. "The Murders in the Rue Morgue," "Marie
Roget," "The Purloined Letter," "The Gold Bug," are masterpieces of ingenuity without making use of charlatanism. The

procedure is the same as that we have previously observed: complicate the difficulties to the extreme, and resolve them with entirely natural means. If there is anything unlikely in "The Gold Bug," it is not the cleverness of Legrand in discovering the treasure so much as the superfluous subtlety with which it has been hidden. One admires the writer's ability to undo Gordian knots less than his infinite skill in tangling them. The pirate's code that he analyzes is too complicated for the intelligence of a buccaneer. But the code is the body of the drama: the appeal is that of an algebraic equation. Undoubtedly, he abuses analysis and splits hairs in four, but he has talent for arousing extreme curiosity. He was very successful with some articles on codes and cryptography and in deciphering some very difficult puzzles of this kind. But can ingenuity pushed to such extremes be considered literature? If we were not in America, we would be tempted to reply, No! But literature is the mirror of a country, and in that country people easily confuse admiration and astonishment.

The Americans call this genre, tales of reasoning. Descartes invented the application of algebra to the geometry of curves; Edgar Poe, the application of algebra to the story and the novel. The poetics can be found in Laplace's book on probabilities. Edgar Poe throws facts into an urn, as Laplace threw his balls of various colors; he knows their number and he knows all the combinations in which they can emerge and be grouped. "The theory of probabilities," he says, "is the science to which human knowledge owes its most glorious conquests and its finest discoveries." He could have added, "and tales of reasoning such as mine." Like Laplace, he does not believe in chance because events, in multiplying, present a striking regularity. Like him, he does not believe in Providence because that regularity is the development of probability. Open the book of the famous mathematician and glance through his general principles. The second principle on the relative possibility of events is the line that leads Edgar Poe through the deciphering of the mysterious parchment in "The Gold Bug." In "The Murders in the Rue Morgue" a French witness declares that he has heard the harsh voice of a murderer who seemed to speak Spanish; another declares that he thought him Italian; a Dutch witness is very sure that the harsh voice belonged to a Frenchman; an English witness is certain that it came from a German; a Spanish witness does not doubt that it was English; an Italian witness offers to bet that it was

Russian. Six witnesses negate one another by proving that the harsh voice is neither Spanish, Italian, French, German, nor Russian. They corroborate one another by giving reason to suppose that it came from none of the known nations, that it was not the voice of a man. Pursue the reading of Laplace, and the mathematician will demonstrate for you that the murderer is an orang-outang.

One has only to glance through the work *Eureka* to be assured that Laplace is the most constant guide of Edgar Poe. It is a second French influence, but perhaps the one that could have the greatest attraction for an American. The appeal of a mathematician for a storyteller, a man of imagination, should not be surprising; Laplace has his moments of poetry, poetry in the manner of Lucretius, with a sense of the infinite but without eyes to see the light of God. He has above all the subtle spirit and the geometric spirit described by Pascal, qualities that our author also abundantly possesses. Nothing is better calculated to succeed among positivist readers than the union of the two—the premeditated dryness, the apparent rigor that wrests consent from you, so to speak, as does a mathematical demonstration. Just as Pascal, inventor of the calculation of probabilities, was tempted to apply it to the immortality of the soul, just as Laplace, who refuted Pascal, has transported that theory into moral sciences, so Edgar Poe (who can be compared to both only as talent can be compared to genius) submitted narrative fiction to the same calculation. For that reason he ought to please the inquisitive exactitude of his fellow citizens. He is the author of an Anglo-Saxon people, the people who invented whist, and his stories resemble that game. "The Gold Bug," "The Murders in the Rue Morgue," "The Purloined Letter," which pass for his masterpieces in America and England, are whist games admirably played. . . .

Edgar Poe owes his great celebrity to his analytic method. As for us, we find only a part of Poe in these ingenious involvements, and it is not the best part. The somber colors that his imagination has spread through the mass of his tales are of a higher order than the subtleties and cleverness. He overuses horror, and the sad hue of his talent is uniform; but the horror itself is poetry. When this mature talent found a way to fuse terror and reality, his tales were dramas; he produced emotion, which is more valuable than curiosity. It seems to us that the real merit of this storyteller is in a terror almost bordering on the marvelous, without ceasing to be credible.

Here the reader will not fail to recall "The Imp of the Perverse," "The Black Cat," "The Tell-Tale Heart"—fearful pictures of remorse which no one has surpassed. Strangely enough, Edgar Poe had no gift of heart. Moral sentiment is absent from his tales, and yet he has powerfully described the tortures of conscience. For him, remorse is fatality, a need to ruin oneself by running to meet punishment, a crime against personal interest. The author calls it perversity. The murderer first enjoys his crime in a profound peace, but wants to add another diabolic pleasure to the pleasure of crime, that of revealing it; the unrepenting heart is forced by some hidden power to speak in order to satisfy the blood that cries for vengeance. That is one of the favorite situations of the storyteller. . . .

Poe's masterpiece is the "Descent into the Maelstrom." In it he has developed a descriptive power that not only makes one tremble but also makes one think, and we see an imagination that takes pleasure in the mysterious recesses of the soul as much as in the dark terrors of physical nature. Romantic in its horror, American in its peculiar detail—everything is there. Whether he sketches the tempest in which the boat runs straight toward the abyss; or crosses the frothy zone of the whirlwind whose shrill clamor resembles the whistles of thousands of ships releasing their steam at once; or the boat, plunging into the abyss, seems suspended by magic on the inner surface of an immense funnel whose walls would have resembled ebony had it not been for the stunning rapidity of their turning and the rays of the full moon which streamed down the black sides of the whirlpool and penetrated far into its depths; there is a peculiar variety even in the uniformity of his colors. Although his paintings are always black or livid, he very skillfully varies the nuances. This admirable tale recalls the "Manuscript in a Bottle": the author has taken up the same idea, but placed it in real life. His spirit of observation and detail plays its part, but no longer for the sake of horror itself. There is masterful construction and calculation; the author is proving something. He himself has said that he does not believe one can attain truth without being both poet and mathematician. He is even a philosopher, and studies psychology in the very depths of the Maelstrom. . . . I imagine that an American reader, a man who likes to make the best of a situation, is delighted to learn how to escape even from the heart of the Maelstrom. The French reader, more fond of imagination than of know-how, especially admires the vigorous brush-strokes, without neglecting verisimilitude and illusion. Less sensitive to the practical results, he will be more aware, I think, of the lack of elevation that pursues Edgar Poe's talent everywhere. . . .

What is lacking in the best of these tales must also be lacking in the others. No loftiness, not even sensibility; merely passions that resemble fits of madness. . . .

The spirit! The spirit! That is what these chilling horrors lack. It is not because of the horror that they fall in the critic's judgment, but because they stir no more than the nerves, because they disturb only the head. They indicate a rare power, who can doubt it? They chill the flesh, they speed the blood, they give fever, but they do not reach the spirit. True, the horrible can be beautiful, original, admirable; that is one of the truths which are the finest heritage of Romanticism. The principle is good, although almost all the examples to support it are bad. True, the horrible is often the beautiful, but on one condition, and that condition is sovereign everywhere: the spirit must have a part in it. . . .

The Writer's Philosophy

The final characteristic, and the most striking, deserves separate discussion. In Edgar Poe there is an entire philosophy, and it was produced toward the end of his career. . . .

Poe seriously thought himself a great philosopher. In New York, on February 9, 1848, he read a cosmogonic treatise or theory of the creation of the universe. The writer was deeply convinced that he had divined the great secret—the title *Eureka* written on his work gave the measure of his confidence. He spoke of it with enthusiasm, with the tone of a person inspired. He dedicated it to *those who love me and whom I love,* to those who *feel* rather than to those who *think,* to those who *believe in dreams* as the sole realities. He offered them this book *whose truth consisted in its beauty.* He announced it not as a scientific treatise, but as a *work of art,* and gave it the title of *poem in prose.* "What' I propose here," he added, "is truth; that is why it cannot die. If anyone should succeed in killing it by trampling it underfoot, it will be reborn for eternity!" We might be tempted to believe that the great mystifier still wants to serve us a dish of his concoction. But no, this is serious. Although the author begins by ridiculing transcendentalism and Scottish philosophy, he believes in his work, his good fortune, his genius. He is not far from comparing himself to Kepler, and feels a sacred fire in his veins when he repeats the famous words of the German philosopher: "I care not whether my work be read now or by posterity. I can afford to wait a century for readers when God himself has waited six thousand years for an observer. I triumph. I have stolen the golden secret of the Egyptians. I will indulge my sacred fury."

Since the author of *Eureka* attempts to explain the world by intuition, his book should not seem alien to us, and we should be able to add it to the storyteller's baggage. The reader may put his mind at ease—the author of "The Gold Bug" has tried to be so profound this time that we would tremble to venture into that deep night, crossed here and there by flashes of lightning. It is enough to say that this very obscure little book, which we are perhaps the first to mention, explains the origin and the end of Newton's theory of gravitation, and confirms Laplace's theory of nebula—nothing more than that. Quite simply, Laplace and Newton prepared the way for a storyteller full of wit and imagination who, after having storied everything, set himself one day to tell how the universe commenced and how it would end. Add to his precursors the head of the positivist school, Comte, whose fame shone in the United States before an incisive pen (I will not say an intelligent pen, for that is too little), an eloquent pen, brought it to the attention of his own country, which was ungrateful enough not to have suspected it. So much for the importance of the work. . . .

Magnetism, or as the English and the Americans say, mesmerism, was bound to attract Poe's curious mind; it provides the material for several of his tales. Faithful to his method of apparent seriousness, he made some of his fiction pass for scientific accounts. "The Facts in the Case of M. Valdemar," having appeared in the *Whig Review,* deceived some innocent English philosophers who took the story for the account of a real phenomenon. The case was indeed curious: magnetic passes had retained life in a dying man for seven months, at the end of which the subject had enough strength to say "I am dead," and it was necessary to awaken him in order to let him die entirely. The "Mesmeric Revelation" is a sketch of the metaphysics of *Eureka* put into a novella. A hypnotizer questions a dying somnambulist about God and the immortality of the soul, and the replies reveal the materiality of God and of thought. . . . The matter-spirit is so infinitely rarefied, and its interstices so infinitely small, that it has no weight and no interstices. It is neither divisible, nor composed of parts: it is *unparticled*. What strikes us most in these tales, which are as learned as they are puerile, is not their material- ism, but their air of spirituality. Everything is spiritualist today, even matter and its partisans. Our era considers itself the century of spirituality because it has the language of spirtualism. But when it consults magnetism and table-rapping, what does it do but seek material proof for the existence of the soul? It wants to attain the spirit, and it interrogates matter! The revery of the somnambulist has more authority than Plato; a rising table leg is worth more than all the arguments of Leibnitz. . . .

We stated recently that American literature, thoroughly penetrated with puritanism, excelled in the portrayal of evil and that, in particular, we find a conviction that crime attracts man, a belief in the fascination of perversity, and mysticism in evil even when there is no longer any belief in good. Edgar Poe is an ·impressive illustration. With the philosophy that we have just extracted from his works, he must have been a fatalist; but in what somber colors that doctrine broods in him! Often one is tempted to think that, not believing in God, he believes in the devil. What is the archdemon he often invokes, the one who impels his heroes of crime and wickedness? He knows the demon of intemperance—the alcohol which he makes a new Beelzebub —who seizes his victim and makes him more irritable, more egotistical and more somber, and one might think that his invective is a reprisal on the enemy who is ruining him and will soon kill him. Yet he has no rancor against wine; drunkenness does not produce wickedness, but reveals it. Man himself is bad; wine does nothing but tear away the mask and let the demon emerge. The gin-saturated monster who seizes a cat and gouges out an eye with his penknife, as in "The Black Cat," commits that damnable atrocity because he is a man and has a diabolic nature. The devil exists; he is in the depths of the human heart. In the form of a hundred narratives the author argues that man is contemptible and wicked. Others are pantheists because they want to adore everything in man. Determined admirers of all his passions, feigning not to see anything weak or shameful in him, they make him divine; they are consistent. Through a peculiar inconsistency, Edgar Poe, scorning or even hating man, takes refuge in pantheism. What he detests in man seems tolerable to him only if it is divine. Not understanding evil, and seeing nothing but evil in nature, he justifies it by saying it is God.

Consequently, he refuses to impute evil to weakness. It is neither a misfortune nor a failure in human nature, but the exercise of a faculty. We have a fatal need to do wrong, as to eat or sleep. The author calls it perversity. He regards that faculty of *perversity* as a discovery he has made in the human soul. You philosophers, moralists, phrenologists believe that man does evil through interest, or passion, or pleasure; you are wrong, for it is through a desire for evil itself. . . .

A vigorous imagination evoking the terror at the heart of real life and a sense of poetry joined to a taste for science and mathematics—these are the gifts for which Edgar Poe has deserved popularity on this side of the Atlantic. As for the laborious subtlety of his constructions and the charlatanism in his ingenuity, we will leave them to America to enjoy. That kind of literary work is like the limitless number of boxes that fit into one another, against all laws of mechanics, or rings threaded on little ivory sticks on silk cords, which must be disengaged one after the other—a task that seems as difficult as to make a camel pass through the eye of a needle. In short, it is like all the other delicate games that make patience and good sense rebel. Their merit consists in an ingenious impossibility. Poe's stories are the Chinese puzzles of literature. We do not fear the contagion of these difficult inanities in our country; we consider them very odd little exotic monsters. The general spirit of Edgar Poe's stories is another question, and less innocent. A rare and audacious scorn of human nature flows through all these tales which do not move us, but startle us. The characters form a vast gallery of drunkards, murderers, madman, egoists, misers, misanthropes and vindictive men. I seek and do not find even one agreeable passion. Here and there, some hints of the love of poetry and beauty reassure us but leave us cold. All the others are violent passions, I would almost say bestial instincts—all that makes man resemble an animal. "It is dangerous to let man see how like the beasts he is," said Pascal, another mathematician. It is to be feared that Poe has been admired from that point of view, and people have seen only energy in the violence, freedom in the audacity and power in the crudity. People are highly shocked by the excess of horror, by disgusting scenes, by corpses. They are much less shocked by the intense materialism that animates these compositions, but that is where the danger lies. Realism is much talked about today. We are not frightened by words and willingly lend our ears to all the sounds coming from youth, that is, from the hope of the future. If realism is the animated image of human life, and loves lively colors and warm portraiture, it will be welcome. If it prefers what is true, real and sincere, to all other things, we will acquiesce to it. But it should bear in mind that life does not exist merely in the blood and the nerves; man has a soul, and forgetting it brings misfortune. The source of poetry is in the soul; the rest is arid. The soul constitutes life, the life which is so much spoken of but lacking in all our present novels. In vain you will make your narratives painfully anatomical, a physiology, a pathology, a Dupuyrian museum. The human soul is not there. Neither is it in Edgar Poe, in spite of all his talent. . . .

J. BARBEY d'AUREVILLY

"THE KING OF THE BOHEMIANS, OR EDGAR POE"*

He is really their king. His work is the first and the best, in
its way, of that unruly and solitary literature without tradition or
ancestors—*prolem sine matre creatum*—which has been labeled
"Bohemian," a name it has given itself and one that will remain
as its punishment. Edgar Poe, the American poet and storyteller whose works are now being published, is the perfect
Bohemian, Bohemianism raised to its greatest power. Born in
that whirlpool of dust that is called, by a mockery of history,
the United States; returned, after having left it, to that inn of
nations which will be a cut-throat tomorrow, and where 500,000
riff-raff alight year in year out, characters more or less bas-
tard, more or less evicted from the countries that they have
endangered or disturbed: Edgar Poe is certainly the finest literary product of that cream of the scum of the world. It is
logical and just that the most formidable of all the contemporary
Bohemians should be born in the heart of the Bohemia of
asylum, the potpouri of all revolts!

Although an individualist, like all Americans, never having
seen more than the *I* by which he perished, as they will also
perish, yet among his democratic compatriots Edgar Poe was
an aristocratically inclined Bohemian. In that most cynically
utilitarian country he saw nothing but beauty—beauty for its

---

* Taken from *Le Reveil,* 15 May 1858, pp. 231-233.

own sake, idle, fruitless beauty, art for art's sake. Nothing could be compared to the violent love he had for it. As he aged, Mr. Victor Hugo, traitor to that art for art's sake which was never more for him than a prefatory religion, gave over his Muse to very different preoccupations; yet even in the hottest years of his youth he was quite lukewarm and restrained in his love of form and beauty in comparison to Edgar Poe, the poet and inventor who has a patient frenzy when giving his work the finished form that is, alas, his only infinite. Decidedly, we are combating no doctrines, but rather the absence of doctrines. Egoism which is sensual, proud and profound; immorality in fact, even when it does not show in description or indecent details; deliberate scorn of all learning; the search for emotion that is excessive and all-consuming; and the smacking of lips over form itself: these have not had an expression at once more concentrated and more striking in any man of our time, no matter where we look.

To study the Bohemian in this man, his works and his techniques, then, is to study the malady in the most powerful organism that it has ruined in a long time. What good would it do to study it in some impotent and stunted creature? We will examine the greatest havoc it created. In order to demonstrate the baseness of literary Bohemia more clearly, we choose its finest corpse. In that devastated nobility we will see the causes of the ruin more vividly. In fact, this is almost a mourning, for Edgar Poe could have been great, and he is merely curious. Sadder than the stricken talent are the talent that has gone astray and the man who dies of having lost his way.

II

Edgar Poe was born a poet. The books that M. Baudelaire's translations have made known to us—such as they are, abortive but showing the signs of extraordinary capacity on every page—leave no doubt. He was by nature a true poet with an incontestable superiority of imagination made for ravishing inspiration from the greatest sources; but the Holy Word has said that it is not good for a man to be alone, and Poe, that Bohemian Byron, lived his life alone and died as he had lived—drunk and alone. The drunkenness of the unfortunate man had become the vice of his solitude. Although married (his biographer does not tell us at what altar), and married to a woman he loved, they say (but we know too well how poets love), a family did not create a sustaining atmosphere around him. Now since talent, we must repeat, is always molded by life and echoes it, the isolated Edgar Poe cultivated the abominable dramas of isolation during his entire life. In all forms which art (that comedy one plays for himself) seeks to vary but which it never varies definitively, Edgar Poe, author of the *Extraordinary Tales,* was never more than the insistent parabolist of the hell he had in his heart. For him America was only a frightful spiritual nightmare in which he sensed the void—and it killed him.

In the midst of the panting interests of that materialist country, Poe, the Robinson Crusoe of poetry, lost, shipwrecked in the vast desert of men, dreamed while awake, at the same time deliberating over the dose of opium to take in order to have true dreams at least, honest lies, a supportable unreality; and all the energy of his talent, as of his life, was absorbed in an enraged and constantly recommenced analysis of the tortures of his solitude. Obviously, if he had been another man, he would have been able to overcome, with strong affections or domestic virtues, the solitude that did worse than devour (for it depraved) his genius. But to overcome it, he would have needed the support and advantage of some moral education, and one asks himself pityingly what his was; what was the education of the son of an actress and *chance* in a society that one morning awoke to find the Mormons in the depths of its morality.

One asks but cannot answer. The biographer of Edgar Poe does not say and perhaps does not care. But two things tell us. He is silent on the question of moral education, a thing necessary even to the genius if he is really to be a genius—a kind of education that Poe undoubtedly lacked; in addition, the small space the human heart and its sentiments have in the body of work of this singular poet and storywriter informs us sufficiently concerning the rational or intuitive morality of a man who, after all, with a superb sensibility, was accessible only to inferior emotions. His mind, in the most complicated of his inventions, never has more than two convulsive movements—curiosity and fear.

III

Was it worth the trouble, then, to have so many faculties potentially? Curiosity and fear! In these *Extraordinary Tales,*

which are extraordinary distinctly less because of the content
than because of the technique of the writer, which is in fact
extraordinary, there is no human sentiment more profound or
more beautiful than curiosity and fear, those two vulgar emotions. He has the curiosity of the uncertain man who wants to
know and who circles perpetually at the limits of two worlds,
the natural and the supernatural, moving away from the first to
strike endlessly at the door of the second, which will never
open, for it has no key. He knows fear—a pale terror of the
supernatural that attracts and frightens as much as it attracts;
there has been no genius since Pascal, perhaps, more terrified,
more given over to the pangs of fright and its mortal agony,
than the panic genius of Edgar Poe.

Such is the double character of the talent, the man and the
work that the excellent French translation has placed us in a
position to judge; fear and its trances, curiosity and its thirst,
fear and curiosity concerning the supernatural, which he distrusts,
and all the follies of an epoch and a materialistic country. All
of it is agitated, stormy, terrible, almost mad; it can cause a
shiver in the flesh and the soul, but it does not penetrate if one
has a solid belief, a religious faith, a certitude. All that—ogre
tales for children who believe themselves men—has only a
moment's sway over the reader's imagination and, as art, it
lacks profundity and true beauty. Such fear is not the revolted,
shattered, frozen fear of Pascal. Fear does not dishonor the
sublime, terrified Pascal. It comes from something great, from
faith that presents hell to his naked eye and from the sense of
unworthiness that tells him that he can fall; but the fear of
Edgar Poe is the fear of a child or a coward, fascinated by
what death (the guard of the other world's secret when religion
does not give it to us) has of the unknown, the shadowy, the
cold. It is the application of Bacon's remark, "Men are afraid
of death as children are afraid of the dark."

That fear coming from the revolted senses takes a thousand
forms in Poe's stories; but whether it is translated specifically in
the horror that he has of being buried alive, or in the immense
desire to fall, or some other hallucination of the same sort, it is
always the same nervous fear of the hallucinatory materialist.
Edgar Poe excels in creating hallucinations, and he savors them
and reflects upon them at the same time that he faints with
fright. Unquestionably, in that strange game that the author

plays in good faith and, like the actor, fascinates himself, there
is (and the critic ought to see it) a talent for dramatic poetry
that would have been magnificent, removed from all the usual
subjects of Poe's tales—somnambulism, magnetism, metempsy-
chosis, the displacement and transposition of life. But there is
also, one must admit, the Perrault. It is hidden in the depths
of the great poet, and because it is there, one can boldly say
that it is the Bohemian who has put it there because of a lack
of great moral subjects, lack of ideas, great beliefs or imposing
certitudes.

IV

Thus, at the very heart of his own talent, diminishing it and
making its task wearisome, we meet the Bohemian, that is to say
the man who lives intellectually by the whims of his ideas, his
sensations or his dreams, just as he lived socially in that mass
of solitary individuals that resembles an immense penitentiary—
the penitentiary of American labor and egoism. Edgar Poe, the
son of chance and an unfortunate accident, is also a trier of
unfortunate inventions, although some of his stories, if we allow
that sort of materialistic and febrile literature, seem successful.
Instead of placing himself above the ideas of his time, as original
thinkers do, he pirates them, and what he steals scarcely merits
stealing. Gifted with the strength of that race of Puritans which
descended from England like a flock of starved cormorants, he
shares contemporary preoccupations that are not worth the
effort he exerts to use them; here we arrive at what I think
dominates the effects obtained by Poe's style—that is, the application of his method.

V

And, in fact, the true originality of Edgar Poe which will hold
an obvious place in nineteenth-century literary history is the
method found everywhere in his work, in the novel *Arthur Gordon Pym,* as well as in the *Extraordinary Tales.* It makes the
American poet and storyteller what he is—the most forceful of
the self-willed artists, a most astonishingly persistent will that
chills inspiration in order to make it a part of the will. As has
already been suggested, with thin invention that exploits only

two or three situations of the same eccentric series, Poe makes
his drama of almost nothing.

But in order to make that drama, in order to enlarge that
atom while decomposing it, he uses an extraordinary analysis
pushed to absolute fatigue, with the the help of heaven knows
what prodigious microscope, on the very pulp of the brain.
Literally, the reader witnesses the surgeon's operation; literally,
he hears the cry of the steel instrument and he feels the pain.
Edgar Poe applies a watchmaker's skill to something we may
call *impatience in curiosity*. He establishes the clock's turning
hand of analysis on the pivot of his own internal movement. He
has a nerve-wracking patience, a fury of patience that reins
itself in and often sacrifices a month simply to prepare for making the public boil for an hour. The Machiavellian side to his
genius here fringes on the deep ruse of the mountebank. The
poet—the poet, that divine self-sparker—expires in the frightful
exhibitions of the American charlatan and laborer.

VI

For he is American, no matter what he does, this man who
detested America and whom America, mother of his vices and
his poverty, pushed to suicide. Fatal origin and race! One never
erases from his forehead the sign of his nationality or his birth.
Edgar Poe, the Bohemian genius, is after all no more or less
than an American, both the product and the antithesis of the
American society of the United States.

*   *   *

When one summarizes that curious and eccentric literary personality, that fantastic form of cruel reality in high relief, compared to whom Hoffmann is merely a vague shadow of pipe-smoke
on a smoking-room wall, it is evident that Edgar Poe was melancholy to a desperate degree, and that, watch in hand, he ferociously described the phases of his melancholy in the novels
which are its story.

In comparison with him, handsome, lymphatic Lord Byron
appears to be no more than a vaporous belle; for this colossal
splenetic, in spite of the morbidity of his madman's gaze, has
the phlegmatic and penetrating lucidities of the condemned man
who knows he is at the scaffold. He has a dark hate not only

for life but also for death. Spiritually speaking, the question of
the other world has always weighed strangely on this man of
the other world (geographically speaking). It is everywhere in
his books, and the great anxiety of the American Hamlet was
a revenge of the spiritual force of thought on the swampy
immorality of life. This is the only truth in his books, which are
constructed like immense lies. This is the only emotion that he
has not bartered. All the rest is willed, arranged, *lied* about in
his books, which are probably nothing but the product of his
wit, atrocious pamphlets in revenge on life. He poisoned his
poisoners.

In actual fact, he ended by poisoning himself. A suicide
long-prepared, Baudelaire accurately called it; a suicide, the
Bohemian death, ended the Bohemian life of Edgar Poe. "One
morning, in the shadows of daybreak," Baudelaire recounts bitterly, "a corpse was found on the street—is that what I should
say?—no, a body still living but marked by death's royal seal.
On that unknown body neither papers nor money were found,
and they carried it to a hospital. There Poe died on October 7,
1849, at 37 years of age, overcome by delirium tremens, that
terrible visitor who had already haunted his brain once or
twice. . . ." Alas, once or twice, that is not saying enough.
Poe not only died of delirium tremens, he had lived on it. The
entire life of that strong but sick genius, until his last hour,
was a delirium and a quaking.

VII

Cruel, wretched story! The translator who has recounted it
through the love or pity he has for the poet has made Edgar
Poe's story a terrible accusation, an imprecation against all
America. It is the old thesis, the protest of the individual and,
one must add (since it is the same thing), the Bohemian protest against society. We expected a more virile thesis from
M. Baudelaire, who sometimes has the cold lucidity of Poe.

He could have been the charitable brother, the enshrouder
of the remains of a man of genius, without throwing them in the
face of an entire country; in the final analysis, Poe's country did
not deliberately assassinate him. He performed that task himself; he assassinated himself. Morally, America and Edgar Poe
deserve one another. They have no reproaches to make; both

have the same illness, as monstrous and mortal in one as in the other—the illness of individualism. Edgar Poe alone, then, must answer for his destiny, and the weight of it can in no way be diminished. God had given him exceptionally fine faculties, rare and powerful ones. He did not use them as he should have. As we have said, with the power that could have made him mount to the stars, he lost his way.

We who do not believe that Art is the principal end of life nor that esthetics should one day rule the world do not think that the loss of a man of genius is a great deprivation. On the other hand, no man is excused from being a useful moral being, a man of social responsibility; *there* is a loss that cannot be redeemed. But Edgar Poe was not a moral being. However, in order to give man strength, God gave him domestic feelings, after genius, which is also a beacon for the heart. The Robinson Crusoe of poetry, on his island, America, had more than a Friday to sustain and share his life. He married a woman who brought her mother as dowry. Yet even that last mother's affection, which never failed him and which survived him, did not impede him in his long suicide by alcohol. That is what makes him, because of the superiority of his talents and his faults, more guilty than another of the sinister and fatal Bohemianism of which he is now the king.

CHARLES DE MOÜY

"CONTEMPORARY STUDIES—EDGAR POE"*

A strange life and work, those of Edgar Poe. From this distance one seems as fantastic as the other. Both offer us splendor and darkness: the first is rapid and brilliant renown, lugubrious hours and a grim end; the second is mysterious as night: the eye penetrates the dim turnings with difficulty and genius glimmers suddenly there like an unexpected flare. Few writers find themselves so faithfully represented by their work, and indeed it seems that a man of suffering—uneasy, morose—was predestined to write these weird, marvelous tales and create these supernatural events, these characters who feel their way in the shadows, ceaselessly tormented by a febrile curiosity, drawn toward some singular or ominous discovery, and disturbed by a kind of drunkenness of soul. The painter of these abysses whose gloomy depths one could not contemplate for long without vertigo had to be a fearless and desperate man dismayed by nothing. Such men look at everything with the eye of a fever, a fixed, burning, sometimes troubled gaze, and analyze certain madnesses, deviations from natural law and mysteries with the poise of the madman who recounts the delirium of others. I know nothing more compelling than that tranquil tone, that minute, almost scientific observation applied to some monstrous fact, some unprecedented hypothesis, sometimes to the pursuit of some childish secret. One suspects an extraordinary state of mind, a mixture of precision and vagueness, a subtle mind, vigorous

---

* Taken from *Revue française,* VI (1 October 1863), 145-158.

even in its aberrations, a strange certainty of movement in the realm of delirium. It seems that Edgar Poe resolved in himself, among many other obscure questions, a psychological problem whose proposition could be thus stated: *to give the logic of madness.* Everything fits into sequence and is linked in the delirium that he describes and, on seeing the perfect order of reasoning and the calm of that absurd dialectic, one would say that dementia is as wise as common sense. This mixture of excess and calculation is, in fact, the life of Edgar Poe, perhaps one of the most brilliant of those whose swift glory and sudden end our century has seen. It was unusual, as the life of the narrator of unusual aspects of the soul and the world should be; it was like a nightmare, and Edgar Poe's ideas drifted endlessly in the most terrible hallucinations. He was the poet and novelist of the mists through which his diseased intelligence and disturbed life struggled to their death, as in a painful dream.

I

In less than a century, America has had some great literary names. While Washington Irving imitated the fine style of the classic English writers in his charming tales, Cooper really founded the original literature of the new society. He disengaged himself, perhaps without knowing it—like the finest geniuses—from the previous tradition, and he founded one that was profoundly national. Young nations need a great poet to sing of their origins and to start them on their intellectual path, just as statesmen organize a political body for them. They need ancestors to serve as guides in every branch of thought, and the glory of those who open up vast literary horizons where their strength will develop and their youth expand is not less than the glory of the soldiers who have defended them with the sword or the administrators who have served them in the beginning and, so to speak, formed them with counsel. From the first days of the American Republic, Cooper initiated his fellow citizens, I will not say to literature, for America had read for a long time, but to a new idea and a new inspiration. Would this recent people, scarcely established on its base, determined to take its place separately in the family of nations, destined for a prodigious future and profoundly unlike all other societies, continue to write as though it had remained English? Would it, on the contrary, assume a character of its own in letters as well as in politics? That was the question. Cooper resolved it on the national side; his works are American before all else, and that is his glory.

He had opened the path by novels as elevated as poems, where the history of the newborn nation and memories of the heroic struggle of the past still stirred, by the beautiful descriptions of a nature unknown to Europe, and especially by those marvelous tales where the savage races defend the imposing solitude of the wilderness against invincible civilization. He had given America an idea of what it could do by itself, and, without imposing a form of composition or fixed style on those who followed, he had freed his country of English tutelage and shown it the resources of liberty. America understood, and from that day its literature was created. Undoubtedly, there is little similarity between the various writers who have adorned it since then and the imperishable works of the man who has been called the American Walter Scott and who was much greater than Walter Scott in invention, feeling and especially influence; but all stem from him in that they have used the freedom won by his genius, and they have variously and with unequal power interpreted, expressed, so to speak, America in their writing. The English tradition is in ruins across the ocean. American thought has its own life, its own genius and consciousness of self; a new literary form is added to the patrimony of universal literature. Cooper had created the historic novel and poetry in the young republic; Prescott gave history to it; eminent writers have composed exclusively American novels of manners: Mrs. Cummins, the Methodist novel; Mrs. Beecher-Stowe, the abolitionist novel; Hawthorne, the transcendentalist novel. Poets formed its language to harmonious rhythms and an immense intellectual movement arose in the field of criticism and politics. Edgar Poe, finally, gave his country the richest and most surprising imagination and the fantastic *sui generis* which borrows its weird effects from psychological phenomena independent of ordinary analysis and perceptible to the mystic sense of the initiated.

II

He was born in Baltimore, of good family; he received all the material advantages. His face, handsome in its regularity, was

one of those that attracts people's glances and immediately reveals ability of the first order. His forehead was wide and high and
his eyes were fiery. The pallor of his face was not sickly; one
sensed intense life beneath that opaque whiteness, and the features
as a whole indicated habitual melancholy. He seemed, in fact, to
have been destined to a romantic and sorrowful life from infancy.
His father, the son of an American general whom Lafayette liked
and esteemed, fell in love with an actress and married her after
having fled with her from his native city. The unfortunate David
Poe also entered the theater and, gradually abandoned by fortune,
no longer finding any resources in his slight talent, died in Richmond, miserable and unknown, at the same time as his wife. They
left three small children stripped of everything, even of that
supreme and infinitely tender love that infuses forgetfulness of
ills and troubles in the soul at the same time that the maternal
kiss falls on the lips. Edgar Poe, then, was thrust into life very
young, without help or family: his painful story was about to
begin.

It seems that before letting him become the toy of pitiless
fate, Providence wanted to give several days of tranquil joy, at
least, to the child who was to suffer greatly as a man. Alone and
abandoned, Edgar was adopted by a wealthy merchant of Richmond who gave him tutors and took him on voyages. He saw the
British Isles and spent several years in the most serious study, then
returned to America to enter the university. It was then that his
destiny became somber and the seeds of fatal passions grew with
frightful intensity. These passions were to envelop his fine intelligence with mysterious shadows, to trouble his life and cast him,
always revolted and always powerless, into the most shameful
disorders a man can fall into. Finally and prematurely, one sinister night they were to open the tomb whose abyss he had dreamed
about and whose terrible questions he, more than any other man,
had sounded.

We must say with profound pity that this highly gifted being
who was so energetic in the face of all the perils of life was powerless in the face of the temptation of drunkenness. Was it really an
ardent desire, or was it the impatient intent to escape depressing
reality through delirium? Who can say? This is the mystery of
his mind. There is nothing more painful to observe than the sinister passions that victimize great minds; but among these passions
none is as frightening as the one that causes high intelligences to

degrade and brutalize themselves, and to make the flame disappear. We see a fine young man, created to dominate by his genius, to embrace and fill the imagination of the crowd; we see him slowly weaken, his eyes sad, his hair thin, his limbs feeble, beside that table where he has finally dropped the lugubrious cup. In this dreadful annihilation we see him forgetting everything, even the most beautiful and holy things, his dreams, his future and his hopes. All this should impress us with a painful sense of our weakness; it should halt our anguished gaze on the most somber ruin and by the extent of its sadness give us a mysterious regret for its extinguished splendor and overthrown power.

Such is the heart-rending sight that Edgar Poe presents to those who admire him. Should we be indignant, or should we be compassionate? Will history be gentle or severe? If, in its high wisdom, it casts down the man who paid for his faults with his life, after having suffered a fate perhaps stronger than he, wouldn't it infringe on the rights of the judge who alone knows all the circumstances behind our errors? To claim to see that great and shadowy soul clearly is to imagine oneself worthy of knowing the unknown and of fathoming the unfathomable. Moved by the implacable judges who often err, let us prefer mildness. I do not know whether Edgar Poe was unfortunate or guilty. I believe human reason vacillates at certain times, that there is more insanity than crime, that natures which are both passionate and nervous are subject to incalculable hallucinations, and that sorrow and error exhaust moral vigor at last. More often than we ourselves believe, the supreme dispenser of eternal judgment in his infinite vision recognizes what the flesh, over-excited by strange fevers or nearly nullified in its weakness, has cost the soul in courage and virtue.

Then let us pity this unfortunate poet besieged by deadly temptations emanating from strong liquors whose abuse creates poison; he suffered from his defeat, suffered until he died of it. From the moment when he abandoned himself, he never had a day of repose or joy. He wandered through Europe like an exile. Cast out by his adopted father, he visited Greece and the Orient; he went from South to North, a wanderer rather than a voyager; he crossed Russia and returned to America. One might say that he was fleeing someone or something in that swift course, and indeed he was fleeing himself and his implacable passion. He wanted to exhaust his persecuting desires by movement and noise.

Perhaps, tormented by the impatience of his troubled genius, he also imagined that he could satisfy his burning aspirations toward the other world by the sight of external things. Perhaps like so many great poets of the century, he experienced the irresistible fascination of the Orient. No one knows. He himself left nothing to explain or account for this period of his life, but his voyages to the East evidently gave his talent a new splendor. He owes to those lands the admirable color that sparkles in his work like fireworks.

III

Edgar Poe's return to America coincides with his literary debut. First he published a volume of poetry. Like most great writers, he poured out his first dreams in that sacred language. Verse is the language of the fresh inspirations of youth. It expresses their desires, sorrows and joys better than prose because it has wings and youth is winged. Later, the man who has been roughly forced back to earth attaches himself to it; his trouble and his happiness well up with less vitality. He has lost many illusions and hopes; he is involved in worldly ambitions, not without a trace of disdain for everything he formerly preferred, and then he speaks a sober and austere prose, the language of human affairs, controlled emotion and reason put to the proof of life. Edgar Poe had not yet known the harshness of the highway, the mass of miserable details that force a man to lower himself to their level, the disillusionment that leaves so much disgust and lassitude in the heart. He instinctively chanted the harmonious rhythm dear to those who still see life through their first tears and their first smiles, through their imagination (the fairy of the young years who makes visible, there where only bare reality exists, so many rainbows and so much darkness). But that was only a thoughtless experience for Edgar Poe, for he yielded to an impulse of the heart rather than to an artistic vocation. The poems that people have praised were undoubtedly very promising and already showed expression, melancholy and lively colors. They did not, however, succeed in expressing everything that the precocious author wanted to say: they were not the true form of his mind, for Edgar Poe—this is still one of the mysteries of his mind—was one of the strange poets who did not know how to speak in verse. There are many whose intelligence is so constituted that they have all of poetry except the language; but poetry escapes in another form. It is like a torrent that finds another way when a dam has been built in its bed, hence, the works of enraptured and musical prose which are the ornament of literature. In Edgar Poe, it was not to reveal itself by form, but by idea, in a distinct genre. He succeeded only moderately in poetry, then, and I think I know the cause of his failure. It reflects a peculiar law of human language: poetry, which seems essentially destined to express the nebulous, cannot endure too much of it. There are some things that would be said too obscurely; if poetry adds its rhythm to their nebulous grace, the entire meaning it not conveyed. Then prose enters and its precision re-establishes balance, for the form counterbalances the ethereal subtlety of the idea. That is why Edgar Poe was a prose writer. On reading his poem, one feels that the tenuous, misty idea evaporates in the very harmony of the form. Edgar Poe realized this, and he thereafter preferred to circumscribe the floating dreams of his imagination and the prodigious audacity of his fancy by the solid lines of his beautiful prose.

Hence, the tales that are his glory. It has been said that his countrymen do not understand them. As for myself, I am convinced that they do. The young man's fame proves that he was read and that his talent was appreciated. Furthermore, he faithfully reflected an entire aspect of the American character in his writing: the passion for hypotheses, the bold pursuit of the impossible, the aspiration toward the unknown. Isn't that the genius of Edgar Poe, and the genius of the young America? Like his compatriots, he had in the intellectual realm the adventurous courage, scorn of time and a taste for the eccentric (with a touch of the colossal and sometimes the monstrous), which seem to belong to a people tormented by an excess of daring and given over to the oddest transports because of juvenile inexperience. It is ignorant of the rein and the rule in the formidable desires of its imagination, infatuated with the most incurable materialism and, if I may use the neologism, the vaguest religiosity, filling immense cities with tumult and noise and feeling the attraction of immeasurable deserts. Edgar Poe, for those who know how to understand him, reflects these passions and this delirium in his work: the tempest of the multitude is heard there; the hallucinations of the mystic and the precise calculations of the coldest materialism are found there. He plays with the horrible and

he studies, analyzes and comments on all emotions and all terrors; he creates impossible situations as though to give himself an
unprecedented spectacle; he sets up enoromous, superhumanly
grotesque characters and supernatural scenes as though to conform to his country's taste for boundless fancy. Fearlessly, he
throws himself into marvelous plots, the byways of psychology
or physics, which are both admirably reasoned and insane. In his
tales as a whole we find the bloody brutality of a people who
often use revolvers, and the vast and solemn emotion of the colo-
nist roving the plains. I dare say no American writer since Cooper
has expressed the new world so perfectly by his literary technique,
but Edgar Poe began when the author of *The Spy* was about to
die, and a new society had arisen whose ideas had to be reproduced in a form that captured their greatness, their folly and their
weakness.

IV

Although it is impossible to give a complete and absolutely
true definition of such a varied genius in a few words, it seems
to me that in considering Edgar Poe at his best and, so to speak,
at his summits, he presents himself to criticism as an impassioned
specator. Certainly he is a great artist; but his art, his invention,
his colors, his style—everything is put to the service of an immense
desire and need to penetrate the secrets of nature or the workings
of the mind. The more one studies him, the more dominant one
finds that tendency: there is an enigma at the bottom of every
story—a physical or moral enigma, accessible or insoluble, mourn-
ful or chillingly grotesque—a mystery in which his mind delights,
often an abyss whose bends and turns, darkness and horror are
familiar to his soul and satisfying to his mind. He makes his way
among these obscurities, here feeling his way, there proceeding
with the certainty of second sight. Sometimes one would think
him a man leaning over a precipice, describing the depths of the
abyss with sovereign calm, attacked by dizziness but, by a superhuman effort, succeeding in analyzing scientifically the sensations
he experiences and the terrible unknown into which his acute
gaze has penetrated.

Hidden powers are what attract and fascinate him—the
power of passion, the power of industry, the power of calculation,
magnetic power; all those forces we do not see and which, diffused

in the universe in both matter and thought, are sometimes manifested in visible effects or incomprehensible phenomena. This is his element. When he wrote the tale entitled "A Descent into the Maelstrom," he revealed the very fate of his genius without knowing it in the shipwrecked man drawn to the bottom of a gigantic whirlpool. He too descended endlessly into a pit. Like the shipwrecked man of the Maelstrom, he observed all its horrors with incredible presence of mind; his hero's hair turned white in that formidable struggle, and Poe's mind was more and more distraught through having haunted the dark regions so long and so tenaciously.

Always and everywhere he felt himself surrounded by bizarre secrets whose magic word he sought with a kind of burning fevor, and often with painful irony. When he approached the mysteries of nature, he had to seek the most unfathomable: the pole where no navigator could land, or outer space where no man could live. Then he created his own science, a *sui generis* instrument of reasoning; he applied the cleverest inductions and the most rigorous deductions to disordered hypotheses. He used all the techniques of the various methods, and one would think that he was relating a physics experiment whose facts he had been able to verify and whose truth he had been able to judge. In "The Peerless Adventure of a Certain Hans Pfaall," he calculates and reasons out an entire ballon voyage from the earth to the moon with marvelous precision. The effect of the rarefaction of air, the shape of our planet seen from the empyrean, the prodigious phenomena of space and the tricks of light are the objects of wonderful treatises formulated with the most audacious coolness, with all the scientific apparatus and in such a way as to give the illusion of the most crushing reality. When he relates the fantastic "Descent into the Maelstrom," he describes the situation as a scholar as well as an artist; he discusses the problem of energy and velocity at the same time that he, with his marvelous imagination, constructs the most fearful episodes of the shipwrecked man in the whirlpool. Moreover, when it is necessary for the grandeur of his drama and the horror that it should inspire, he knows how to put aside the baggage of paradoxical erudition in order to represent only the most frightful anguish of the fantastic. When he gives the words of a voyager swallowed up by the hypothetical mouth of the pole, he confides the strange adventure, the description of the legendary ship and its phantom sailors to the "Ms Found in a Bottle." It reveals an admirable feeling for the terrible and the lugubrious, and shows a wild and superhuman passion to know what no one has ever known and to grapple with the inaccessible. In this last narrative, which no writer of supernatural things has ever surpassed in sinister expression, there is an impression of mysticism and man's terror before a secret that destiny bars from his sacrilegious view. He must pay with his life for the fatal honor of having dimly glimpsed the approach. One might say it is the dream of Vasco de Gama before the Genius of Tempests. These are the great terrors of man vanquished by a jealous god.

Edgar Poe's curiosity often attacked less important secrets, and his somber mind rested from its fantastic voyages by solving some ingenious puzzle and explaining its tangled relationship with infinite finesse and sometimes with malice. "I wanted to set myself up as the Oedipus of the Rattleborough enigma," he says at the beginning of the *Accusing Corpse* ["Thou Art the Man"] at the point of telling by what inextricable knots and by what slander the real author of a crime persuaded the judges to condemn an innocent man. In "The Man That Was Used Up" he describes the bizarre apparatus that replaces all the parts he has lost, and he makes a joke of the problem of life preserved by mechanical means. Still elsewhere, in "The Murders in the Rue Morgue" and in "The Purloined Letter," he leads the reader from induction to induction by an admirably forged psychological chain, to the discovery of a murderer or a rogue; finally, in "The Gold Bug," he introduces a man of subtle wit who deciphers a code message by means of prodigiously precise calculations and thus provides a key for resolving the hermetic forms with which ideas are prudently concealed in writing. It is a new and curious chapter on the mysterious question of signs.

"The Gold Bug" is a masterpiece of its kind; reasoned perspicacity could be pushed no further. I know nothing stranger to follow than the series of hypotheses verified by a sequence of mathematical proofs, seizing conventional, unknown signs one by one and substituting the correct letters of the alphabet by a violent effort of reflection and the technique of analogy. If Edgar Poe's intellectual ingenuity and skill in a tour de force appear here, we must seek elsewhere than in these novelettes (the recreation of his troubled and morose mind) in order to understand what secrets atttracted him even more. We have seen his scholarly curiosity; let us look at his psychological curiosity, where the richness of his imagination and the profundity of his scrutiny are revealed in their full scope. The study of the chasms of the soul troubled him to the depths of his being and left an inexpressible agitation in his mind. No one else could descend so far into the mystic darkness of human nature, or try to analyze the forces developed in us by artificial means or raving passions or articulate the dramas that are played in a mind at the mercy of hallucinations. No one else could yield with the characters themselves to the disastrous spell of a psychology excessive in its problems and efforts and painful as a nightmare. No one could create such a work without being haunted by troubling visions and having these ceaselessly queried visions invade the intelligence that is hungering to understand them. The mind is all the more subjected to their despotism as the seduction of the delirium is soft. The more the mind loses its way, the more it loves the phantom that dominates it.

One must read the terrible story entitled "The Assignation" in order to see how far Edgar Poe could push passion in the drama, or to see all the fatality of love, the exaltation of the characters that he tried to portray and the vast horizons of the afterlife into which he precipitated heroes impatient to be reunited. One remains stunned after this swift, intoxicating reading; this no longer seems to belong to the earth. One might say that these strange lovers who kill themselves in order to meet again elsewhere are impelled by the incorporeal life of forms glimpsed in sleep. In this scarcely suggested sketch, a thick fog envelops creation, and rays of light escape fitfully. We can see the characters, but with an uncertain vision. The effect of color strikes the observer much more than the lines do; one might say that the scarlet and gold draperies are shaken by a storm. Edgar Poe is a painter in the Veronese style when he describes the marvelous interior of a Venetian palace, but his drama calls him and he hastens on. In a few words he reveals the looked-for secret word and the insane resolution that two despairing creatures have suddenly given to their lives. We see that like a true American he loves these brutal conclusions, and after having penetrated souls he likes to cast them violently into the abyss from which no one ever returns and in which they will perhaps reunite.

In other stories, "Ligeia" and "Morella," his mind strays

among problems he poses. In the latter it is the soul of a mother reappearing in her daughter, and in the former a forgotten first wife taking the place of the second wife where she in her turn lies on her death bed. Edgar Poe struggles with the impalpable and the imponderable, face to face. He lives among spectres and questions the tomb; he tries to penetrate the stone under which the dead lie and to discover the fate of our tormented souls. He evokes those who no longer exist and makes them survive and even retain a vague memory of a previous existence, as in "A Tale of the Ragged Mountains." In "Eleonora" he hears the harmonious voices of the dead, which calm the anguish and remorse of the second love, which is disquieted by the name of the former beloved —the former beloved!—a shade that forgives the faithless lover and blesses him across the barrier of death. Edgar Poe is content among these phantoms, for they have funereal smiles and sorrowful revelations for him. But this insatiable inquirer has not summoned them without purpose. He pursues their secret and wants them to give him the ultimate word. What they refuse him, he asks of the new science, magnetism. Perhaps there he will find the meaning he has most desired, the meaning of the unknown and the words he has dreamed—the words that will tell him all the secrets of creation and life. He went so far as to wonder if mesmerism could arrest death. He wrote "The Facts in the Case of M Valdemar" in order to treat that weird question at his ease, and he studied the facts with his usual patience, recounting them with all his phlegm and scholarly method. For seven months the man is dead but the body survives. They awaken it, but the body, scarcely emerged from the cataleptic state, falls, crumbles and putrefies. In one second nature has done its work.

At this point, Edgar Poe's thought had reached the frontiers of delirium. He staggered among impossibilities; his disordered imagination was fruitlessly distraught. Yet his artistic talent was so great that he gave extraordinary life—I nearly said credibility —to these hallucinations of a troubled mind. Even in his worst hours and least lucid days, when free invention and drunken fatality mingled their tumultuous images in his artificially overworked brain, Edgar Poe truly remained a writer and a poet. With even greater reason he could manipulate language when he was master of himself, and describe most intensely the marvels that he dreamed—yielding to the most exquisite harmony, accumulating luminous or dusky effects, mocking with a haughty

or sorrowful tone, giving an unexpected hue to his picture and
discovering with rare felicity the strange combinations of tones
and lines that made the horizon recede to infinity. And his work
does not owe its luster and brillance simply to his art. We feel
the beat of his heart—his desires, illusions and despair. Identify-
ing himself with his characters, he breathes in them and suffers
their anguish and their delirium. Their sadness and terror transfix
him. He is wrought upon by their puerile curiosity and he follows
them in their terrifying voyages across the unknown. Then does
he always speak in his own name? It is always himself that he
dramatizes. *I, myself,* he says in all his stories, as though he could
not be detached from his own intense personality even in fiction.
He could not help revealing that he analyzed himself first of all,
that he exposed what he had felt and suffered and that he intoned
the poem of his life.

His life—it is there in its entirety. I have previously said
that the very disorder of his work reflects all his painful and
vague preoccupations and expresses his fatal aberrations. Here
and there we find clear evidence of the events that troubled him,
especially the death of his wife, the beautiful, gentle Virginia
Clemm, whose love had been the joy and honor of Poe's heart.
He was never to forget her; he undoubtedly dreamed of her plaintive shade when he wrote "Ligeia" and "Eleonora." It is she
whom he imagined, light and diaphanous, bending over his sleep
and alive in his heart. How great and pure he could have been
if he had lived by that dear memory! But the fatal passion dominated him. "What a disease alcohol is!" he said somewhere, and
he was to be its victim. Once they thought that he was again going
to find a calm life in another marriage illuminated by blessed
tenderness. He was to have married a young American who
would have given him all possible worldly guarantees of happiness in exchange for his name. On the verge of consummating
this union that anyone else would have desired, an unexpected
delirium seized the unfortunate poet and, in order to halt the
arrangements with finality, he abolished all sense of human dignity in himself and came to visit his fiancée in a state of complete
intoxication.

Fate had offered him a means of elevating himself in the
world's opinion and becoming as noble in character as he was
great in genius. He chose not to accept it. There are certain mis-
takes that are fatal; one bears the penalty until the final day. His

fame had grown greater and greater, and perhaps he was on the verge of his hour of supreme triumph; his readings in Richmond on the *Principles of Poetry* had been a brilliant success. But the Old Man he had tried so hard to conquer was still alive in him. Edgar Poe left for New York, but he met some old friends in Baltimore; he went into a tavern. When he left it, his mind was confused. The next day they picked up an unidentified body in the street and carried it to a hospital. A few hours later, one of the most illustrious writers of the United States died there. He was only 37 years old. Delirium tremens, brought on by debauchery, had extinguished this fiery mind. His work survives for the amazement of the future, and his shade, in the name of his genius, asks stern posterity for pitying sympathy.

ARMAND RENAUD

"EDGAR POE ACCORDING TO HIS POETRY"*

In any art, it is fashionable to belong to a school, to detest Ingres because one admires Delacroix, to refuse to hear of Lamartine because one approves T. Gautier. Sometimes, also, one accepts each artist in part; he takes from each one the most ordinary qualities, those that are most banal, and he composes a monster with the wings of a bird, the legs of a quadruped and the fins of a fish, but without the power to fly, walk or swim well. All this comes from the fact that we generally tend to seek an absolute, exclusive type, whereas, for man, only relative types exist. Certainly, there must be, somewhere very far away, a place where everything is condensed into unity, where Raphael's line and Titian's color are no longer separate; but it exists at such a height that man is lost there. We certainly ought to have that ideal in mind, but we must understand that it is vast enough to house all esthetic systems side by side, and that trying to formulate it would be restricting it. Wisdom lies in admitting all schools, provided that they result in something beautiful; in attempting to reconcile nothing; in not becoming embarrassed by opposites; in admiring Racine, who contradicts Hugo; in admiring Lamartine, who contradicts Molière. These contradictions are aspects of the finite, incomplete nature in which we move; the diversity of all these fine works is only an apparent one, for they have their sublime parentage in the infinite.

* Taken from *Nouvelle Revue de Paris*, IV (1864), 537-553.

What would you think of an explorer who, wanting to combine the mountain and the chasm, climbed the mountain halfway, descended halfway into the chasm, and then said, "I know
what is best in nature; I have seen what it is reasonable to see: a
little height, a little depth, not too much." You would laugh at
him. Everyone knows that in order to have a glimpse of immense
valleys and silent, clear sky one must go to the summit of the
mountain; in the same way, in order to find pearls or to contemplate marvelous vegetation one must plunge to the bottom of the
abyss. Nevertheless, more than one critic follows that explorer's
course; he always stops in mid-journey, that is, where poetry
commences. That is called eclecticism. In matters of art it is not
eclecticism that one must adopt, but pantheism: adore everything,
heaven and earth, light and shade, provided that the seal of genius
is on it, and consider art in all its variations as a harmony in
which one must suppress nothing under penalty of destroying
everything. That requires flexibility of mind, but it is the way to
experience the liveliest intellectual pleasure. It is also the way to
make fruitful criticism—not the kind that sees faults before all
else, but the kind that sees beauty and admires inspiration rather
than correctness; the kind that has no severity, finally, except
for the false classicism in which all virtues are restrictive or
negative.

Thus, having to speak of a man who has had a-very great
influence on contemporary literature, a writer especially remarkable for originality, I intend to speak without prejudice or indecision. Admiring Edgar Poe, I want to shout my admiration, and
yet without seeming to imply censure or disdain for any contrary
genius—Longfellow, for example. Longfellow is gentle, tender
and melancholy; Edgar Poe is sinister and bitter. One invites us
to revery; the other gives us chills. While one has limpid phrases
that flow like water from a spring, the other is harsh and obscure.
They detested one another, like the true creators that they were.
What does it matter to us? Both created works with the seal of
beauty. Only that is important. We are not going to commit the
blasphemy of wishing that Longfellow had had Poe's energy or
that Poe had had Longfellow's gentleness. Some day when we
want to see the blue sky, and are thirsty for stars, we will go
straying in the perfumed meadows of *Evangeline* and *Hiawatha*.
Today we are concerned with habituating our eyes to dizzy
heights and our feet to rocky crags; we are going to taste the
more rugged delight of the abyss.

Thanks to Baudelaire's admirable translation, everyone knows Edgar Poe's stories. The success of the collection as a whole has been great, but for each story it has been somewhat in inverse ratio to its value. Thus, the most popular are "The Murders in the Rue Morgue" and "The Gold Bug." Certainly these are ingenious, but not worth the psychological profundity of "The Imp of the Perverse"; the lyricism of "The Island of the Fay" or that marvelous page of chills, vacillations and mystery, "Shadow"; the fantastic quality of "Berenice" and "The Fall of the House of Usher"; or, finally, the scientific ingenuity of "The Descent into the Maelstrom." And of these four characteristics united in Edgar Poe—psychology, lyricism, fantasy and ingenuity—the one that is least appreciated is perhaps the greatest of all, lyricism. "The Island of the Fay" and "Shadow," although translated and placed among the narratives, are scarcely known. Even there the lyricism is veiled, so to speak, by the prose. When it shows itself in full luminosity and splendor—when it is lyricism in verse—the masses draw away and no longer want to understand. However, the very essence of Edgar Poe's genius is contained in his poems. They are short, these poems. Putting them all together, one could scarcely make a small volume. But the terrors, the vertigo, the suffering of that strange writer are found united and in full intensity, with all the concentration that poetry gives to ideas, with all the science of words and rhythms that cadence permits.

If a century had passed since Edgar Poe's death, and the public remained indifferent to his poetic works, we would not attack the public: in that case it judges definitively and without appeal. In the end, works are created for humanity; if humanity does not accept them, the works are in error. But when a writer has just died, and that writer has introduced a totally new way of seeing art, the public first likes the works which are least original, the least creative. People need a certain length of time to become accustomed to his ideas and to explore their depth, and this time is what I would like to abridge.

In his poetry, Edgar Poe especially likes effects produced by repetition. Often, the same lines are introduced several times in the stanzas; there are also a great many double rhymes and assonances, not only at the end, but also in the middle of the lines, in the Arabic manner. From this piling up of similar sounds a sort of monotony results, but a monotony so artistic that instead

of causing boredom it becomes something strange which fascinates and lulls the reader. Usually, a person on whom one fixes
his gaze begins to laugh, yet the most powerful effects of the
gaze are through fixity. The outer form of Edgar Poe's poetry
corresponds precisely to the form of his ideas; with other poets,
it would be puerile and pretentious, but with him it is magic.
Certainly we do not find the regular, placid beauty of Greek art,
nor the holy fervor of Christian art. This is neither the sky of
Olympus, full of golden arrows, nor the sky of Paradise, full of
white wings; rather, it is an overcast sky where lightning flashes.
But how superbly this lightning crosses the darkness! From what
high distances it comes!

Edgar Poe personifies despair. Anacreon said to you: Life
is beautiful, the roses are sweet, the honey of Hymettus is perfumed. Tomorrow brings nothingness and ashes; live today!
Christ says to you: Whether life be sad or gay, it matters little
to you. Heaven must be your goal. Do not become attached to
anything except your will, which permits you to devote yourself
to others and thus to attain limitless happiness.

Happy are the reasonable creatures who have followed one
of these two paths: happy above all are those who have followed
the second, so lavish in offering the only true felicity, hope! But
there are some beings who find the present joy sterile and who
see only darkness in the future; they feel themselves led toward
the unknown by the fatal stride of time; they are afraid, and they
want to cast themselves again into oblivion, complete oblivion.
Nothing can give it to them. They do not want voluptuous
drunkenness, the intoxication of wine and flowers, for it is powerless to calm the uneasiness which gnaws at them; and they throw
themselves into the other drunkenness, which brings torpor, by
alcohol or opium. To exalt vices which really degrade man, as
some have tried to do, is the work of those who like to adore
fetishes, but to condemn Poe irremissibly for his errors is a
severity stemming from lack of intelligence in nervous natures.
Man has will. It ought to help him to avoid reefs, and one can
reproach Edgar Poe with not having sufficiently used his reason
against his imagination; but we must not believe that he succumbed without struggling, or that ,if there are censurable qualities in him, there are no aspects which deserve praise.

Some people who are preoccupied with the bizarre have
made themselves his disciples. They never fail, after dinner, to

bring a brownish vial to their mouths, affirming that it is full of laudanum. What touches us in Poe and will never be found in the others is, first, sincerity in suffering; then, aspiration toward purity. No one has made a more ardent cult of womanhood than he has. He truly loved. Thence the ray of light.

The life of the American poet is a succession of violent acts and disorders. He caused himself to be expelled from every school, from every position. Continually protected, he continually sent away his own protectors; at 38, he died of the effects of an excess of drunkenness. A man would deserve nothing but disgrace for having led such an existence if, along with these impulses (and attenuating them if not erasing them), there had not been the contrast of a good affectionate soul. Sensing that she was close to death and having herself held up by cushions in order to write, a distinguished woman who lived for some time in close relationship with him summarized thus her opinion of him:

> You ask me, my friend, to write for you my reminiscences of Edgar Poe. . . . For you, I will willingly do so. I think no one could know him, no one who *has* known him personally—certainly no woman—without feeling the same interest. I can sincerely say that, although I have frequently *heard* of aberrations on his part from the straight and narrow path, I have never *seen* him otherwise than gentle, generous, well-bred and fastidiously refined. To a sensitive and delicately-nurtured woman, there was a peculiar and irresistible charm in the chivalric, graceful, and almost tender reverence with which he invariably approached all women who won his respect. It was that which first commanded and always retained my regard for him. . . .*

In this quotation we have listened to Edgar Poe's wife, the gentle, consumptive Virginia whom he surrounded with so much affection and care. Little by little, he saw her die in the grip of consumption. During his wife's slow agony, misery had invaded his house. While he was the prey of the double suffering of poverty and death, he was great; he had the devotion of nobility. The least questionable proof of his exemplary behavior is the affection Virginia's mother continued to bear him after the death of her daughter. When Edgar Poe died, here is what that venerable lady wrote:

---

* Letter from Mrs. Osgood printed in Griswold's "Memoir" to 1856 edition of Works, pp. lii-liv. Renaud goes on to quote five more paragraphs.

I have this morning heard of the death of my darling
Eddie. . . . Can you give me any circumstances, or particu-
lars? . . . Oh! do not desert your poor friend in this bitter
affliction . . . . As Mr. * * * * to come, as I must deliver
a message to him from my poor Eddie. . . . I need not ask
you to notice his death and to speak well of him. I know
you will. But say what an affectionate son he was to me, his
poor desolate mother.

These notes were necessary at the beginning of a study of
Edgar Poe's poetry. If his prose were being examined, this study
would show the weight of the moral maladies that disturbed
him and were the subject of his profound analyses. Considering
him as a poet, I have primarily tried to record the beating of
his heart in order to explain the tenderness that mingles with the
most somber despondency in his poetry. The man who dug so
many pits and descended so often the infernal slopes of the human
soul does not have to reproach himself with having sullied a
woman's name. All the women he has sung are like white birds
that fly with plaintive cries over the sea in stormy times. They
are ghosts rather than living creatures, but exquisite ghosts of
love and sadness.

Lenore, Ulalume, Annabel Lee, Irene, Annie, Helen—these
are the dark, gentle figures who pass through his poetry. Each
one passes only once, then disappears like a shadow or nocturnal
mist over a lake. Edgar Poe is preoccupied above all with the
irrevocable, that which goes never to come again. His soul is
really the raven which he presented so marvelously in the most
popular of his poems, the raven which, at midnight, while Poe
dreams over an old volume, enters with a slight rustling of wings
and alights darkly on the white bust of Pallas, replying to all
questions with the single funereal word, "Nevermore." The poet
asks him if he is a balm for his suffering; the raven answers,
"Nevermore." If, in a distant Eden, he will see the sainted girl
whom the angels call Lenore: the raven replies, "Nevermore."
Seized with terror, he tries to chase the bird away. He says to it,
"Be that word our sign of parting, bird or fiend! Get thee back
into the tempest and the Night's Plutonian shore. Leave no black
plume as a token of that lie thy soul has spoken! Leave my loneliness unbroken! Quit the bust above my door!" And the raven
repeats, "Nevermore."

Edgar Poe is a colorful poet, but he has what only poets

of the first order have—the gift of evocative description. Whereas
we see men with remarkable talents constantly performing stylistic
arabesques and accumulating all the marvels of fairyland in their
work, but producing only boredom, Edgar Poe transports us
with a few stanzas into a land that awakens a hundred times
more dreams than all the stage setting of the others had done.
In that land he places the most artistic fantasy imaginable, and
his fantasy, his pure art and his description even make us shed
tears, proving that the obstacle to evoking emotion by artistic
means is not in the art, but in the artist. Neither emotion without
art nor art without emotion can live: they would be glass trinkets
or pottery, and we need diamonds. The latter are more difficult
to chisel, but no one would deny their superiority simply because
some instruments are powerless to make them shine.

"Annabel Lee" is a model for this type of poem in which
emotion is allied to fantasy.

*   *   *   *

The poem entitled "The Sleeper" has the effect of a serenade
sung not by a mortal, but by a spirit. Everything is lulled in a
mysterious sleep deeper than natural sleep.

*   *   *   *

Then [at the end of "The Sleeper"] he comes to his favorite
idea, the idea of the sleep which is the better as it resembles
death more. "My love, she sleeps! Oh, may her sleep,/As it is
lasting, so be deep!/Soft may the worms about her creep!" Let
no one believe that he desires the death of the one he loves
because of a refinement of cruelty. No, he wishes her death
because death seems to him the supreme rest, the supreme happiness. In a piece entitled "For Annie," he imagines himself
sleeping the indestructible sleep of death, and sings of the joy
he experiences in dreaming of his beloved without anything
henceforth to disturb his dreams.

*   *   *   *

[Summary of stanzas 9, 11–15]

The "Bridal Ballad" expresses the feeling that more than
one young girl must have had on being wed. She has had a first
love, the holy and confident love that blooms at sixteen; eternal
vows have been exchanged. Then death carried off the fiancé of
springtime. And since those who are absent are always wronged

as life sweeps us along, she loves another; she marries. Nevertheless, the memory of the one who is dead mingles with present joys. The new bridegroom is happy, and the bride is happy in her good fortune, but at the same time the idea comes to her that the other must be suffering in his tomb—a shiver of cypress joins the perfume of orange blossoms.

In reading Edgar Poe's ballad, which renders this double sentiment so well, we imagine that he has put his own impressions into the young girl's mind. After the death of his first wife, he had new loves. Perhaps more than once the memory of Virginia embittered the outpourings of his soul, as the memory of d'Elormie, the young man who fell in battle at the bottom of the valley, troubles the girl in the ballad. For he loved her, that tender Virginia, dead of consumption like so many beautiful English flowers; and when he mourned for her under the name of Ulalume, he found the most heartbreaking accents in all elegy.

He imagines himself in the month of October under a gray sky at night, near a dark bog in a wood with brittle sere leaves, haunted by vampires. There, he walks with Psyche, his soul. On the horizon he notices a star and wants to follow it, thinking that it has shown him the road to the Lethean peace of heaven. But Psyche urges him to fly quickly. "In terror she spoke," says the poet, "letting sink her wings till they trailed in the dust. In agony sobbed, letting sink her plumes till they trailed in the dust, till they sorrowfully trailed in the dust." But the poet has confidence in the star; he wants to follow it. He embraces Psyche and leads her to the end of the walk. There he is stopped by the door of a tomb; he tells Psyche to read the name written on the door of the tomb, and she answers him, "Ulalume! Ulalume! the one you have lost." Then the heart that had winged forward full of hope, wanting to bathe in the splendor of the crystalline night, becomes like the dry, sere leaves. And he remembers that a year before, on that same night, he had brought a solemn burden to the same spot.

However, cruel stars do not always lead him to a tomb. At one time all conversations associated his name with that of one of the most brilliant women in New England, and it was publicly announced that he was going to marry her. The marriage was about to take place when he himself caused a rupture with the family by arriving intoxicated at the home of his fiancée's parents. Whatever reproach he deserved for such an action, the woman from whom he broke in this way forgave him, and after his death she ranged herself among his most ardent defenders. In reading the lines he addressed to her after he had seen her for the first time, lines that must have left a deep impression in the soul of the woman who inspired them, one understands her forgiveness.

To Helen

* * * *

These lines should compensate for many aberrations in the American poet. My duty is *to be saved* by their blaze, he cries. One senses the man struggling against a terrible passion, the source of morbid hallucinations and mortal fevers, which, like gambling, dominate one's will all the more as they speed his fall. The wise avoid the first step; the first step taken, one is above all to be pitied.

The other poems of Edgar Poe are more like the kind popularized in France by the *Extraordinary Tales*. The thing that is superior in the ones we have just analyzed is the emotion of tenderness mingled with imaginative unrest, each quality doubling the charm and power of the other. Certain poems must be placed among the tales in which the fantastic dominates exclusively: "The Haunted Palace," "The Conqueror Worm," "The Valley of Unrest," "The City in the Sea," "The Land of Dream," "Eldorado." We put aside "The Bells"—a simple game of imitative harmony which makes the mistake of recalling, without equaling, one of the masterpieces of German poetry; but some lines entitled "Silence" deserve attention:

* * * *

"The City in the Sea" is a combination of the effects of the gigantic creations of Martynn and the frightful calm of the Dead Sea. Enormous, mysterious monuments, a confusion of stone and metal, rise from an immobile sea; they are silent, heavy and slowly sinking. The idea of damnation weighs on the entire work. The sky is closed, the waves are inert. Nothing moves. The city is swallowed up without show of anger or pain; nothing tries to save itself; nothing tries to speed the act. It happens because it is destined, and in the manner that is destined.

* * * *

"The Valley of Unrest" is still more successful fantasy, having both greater vagueness in its entirety and more originality in its detail.

* * * *

Edgar Poe has found the poetic secret that Goethe possessed to such a high degree—that of composing the poem so that no positive meaning results, but giving it a mystic form which lends itself to interpretation. What is this formerly smiling valley, now sad? Who inhabits it? Why that agitation of flowers and trees? What nameless tomb hides under the lilies spilling tears of dew? We do not know, but the images are beautiful, the poetry is sonorous and there is much more than beautiful imagery and sonorous poetry. We are charmed as by the unreadable eyes of the sphinx, and we try to solve the enigma; a thousand possibilities present themselves to the dreaming soul, and meditation draws us into its pit. An effect analogous to music is produced. No apparent idea has been stated, but the artist has awakened sensations that lead to ideas. The pitfall in this kind of poetry is that of making an empty, tiresome work, devoid of sense, in which the sublime borders on the absurd. One could easily cite a new French poet who, in seeking the first, succeeded perfectly in achieving the second. But it is useless to mortify anyone. It is better to let the attempts which have probably been sincere lie in shadow, and not to laugh at failures but to be content with applauding triumphs.

It remains to us to speak of the poem of "Al Aaraaf," whose appearance in the world brought Edgar Poe many enemies. He was to give a lecture in Boston. Boston is the center of the literature opposed to his—the calm, reasonable, gentle literature that disapproves of asperity and audacity; it is the city where criticism and erudition flourish. Edgar Poe first intended to compose a flawless poem and triumph over his enemies by forcing their admiration; but indolence kept him from completing his project, and he chose to read a youthful poem, very inferior to his other productions. The success in the town was immense, precisely because it was to his more recent productions what the seed is to the plant, and Boston society understood his talent better in a homeopathic dose. In this success Edgar Poe saw his opportunity for revenge and showered his imprudent admirers with sarcasm. The latter were even less able to defend themselves because he sacrificed himself in the holocaust and, like another Samson, buried himself with the Philistines under the debris of the temple. Edgar Poe has often been reproached for this hoax and, in general, for the tone of mockery which he adopted with the public. When he had shown signs of inspiration and people had taken him seriously, he took pleasure in dispelling the enthusiasm that he had aroused, bursting into laughter in the face of his admirers. The first explanation that occurs to us is that of the *Demon of Perversity,* which he described so marvelously—the temptation to do wrong to others or to oneself, which gives one no peace until he has yielded. But perhaps there is a profounder reason, having less to do with the nerves than with the soul. Edgar Poe's tormented nature imagined the public to be an enemy ready to deride the noblest feelings that he had in his heart, and, for fear of seeing others break or steal his treasures, he disguised them and pretended to laugh at them himself, saying, "This is dust." The fear of disillusion made him run before it. He behaved like those people who, in grave danger, persuaded that they are soon going to die, dare not wait, but kill themselves.

We have tried to show by the most faithful quotations possible, the poetic talent of Edgar Poe. Now that we have sought in the mysteries of his personal elegies the quality of emotion he rarely had, but had in such a pure and elevated manner, we are forced to consider the attacks that have been made and the grave question: Do certain artists owe the originality of their genius to their very vices?

To make light of darkness, to try to find the source of genius in evil, is to insult the human soul in its brightest manifestation. It is perhaps true to say that an artist should have not only the good instincts of man, but also the bad; he should know all temptations and be tormented by all fevers, but woe to him if he let himself be swept away. The more passions he has, the higher he will go if he masters them, and the lower he will fall if he is their slave. In the interests of art, we would not erase a single perverse tendency of Musset or Edgar Poe; but in the interests of art we must wish they had had more will and that they had never succumbed. Then nothing that is fine would have been lost; they would not have failed because of the weakening of their brains through excess; they would not have given this sad example of lack of dignity; in short, they would have been greater. Let no one protest that it is impossible. One man with the most dangerous vices had the strength to overcome them—the ancient demigod, Socrates. The names that shine throughout centuries are those of the righteous—Aeschylus, Tacitus, Dante, Michelangelo, Corneille, Beethoven. They are not pure because they cannot be otherwise, in the manner of innocents and children, but pure while

containing impurity, virtuous while containing crime, good but
with the instinct of cruelty; they are those, in short, whose soul
is neither a cabbage patch nor a thicket of nettles, but a virgin
field with all its wholesome and poisonous plants. Through will,
they have been able to make everything serve the triumph of the
beautiful and the good.

This is for the people who adore the brandy drinker in Edgar
Poe and the absinthe drinker in Musset, and for those who fly off
wildly, with long, disheveled hair, seeking originality in dress
because they cannot have originality of mind, throwing the little
heart they have to the four winds, scorning everything because
nothing wants to have anything to do with them. After having
talked about impossible esthetics for some twenty years, knowing
no other expression of admiration except "It's insane!" they finally
die. They have had some coterie success. They have never given
or felt an emotion in their lives or their works; they have posed
as incorruptible adorers of form; and they have really done an
immense wrong to authentic talent because their tiresome productions have inspired public hate for works of art.

But there is another kind of artist, equally deadly, who is
successful through a reaction against the noise of the others: they
speak endlessly of good sense as the others speak of delirium and
are designated *hacks* by literary slang. They are the born enemies of Edgar Poe. They smile when he is named, telling themselves, "I don't drink brandy or commit improprieties. I speak
calmly. I'm superior to that American drunkard. I write things
that everyone understands. Instead of searching far and wide for
extravagant things, I study the manner in which people take tea,
talk and dance in the salons I frequent, and I reproduce all that.
I remain within nature; I am the true artist. I don't make a business of it; I write so many lines a year, no more, no less. I have
order, care and correctness. I amuse, I instruct and I moralize.
What do I lack?"

Poor men! You are convinced that you are honorable. You
are photographers, and because you sincerely mistake your apparatus for a priesthood, attacking you is painful. However, it is
necessary because you have an influence through respectability.
People believe you and you would kill the arts if they were not
immortal. What you lack is inspiration. The ideas of others go
astray sometimes, but you have no ideas. Their passion draws
them towards evil; certainly it would be better, even from the

point of view of art, if they were not so drawn. You, on the other hand, have no passion. Do you know something astonishing? Full of good intentions, you create works on which you preach virtue, and yet those works are dangerous, for you have no ideal and you habituate men to having none.

People encourage you, for you are comfortable for everyone, for the State and for the public. You hurt nothing and disturb nothing. Not requiring thought, you do not fatigue the mind. Far from impassioned, flamboyant, warlike ideas, you coldly sit down to your desk and you hatch your works as a hen lays eggs. You have a position as artist, just as one has a position as employee, and you fill it conscientiously; like any employee, you could write that way for centuries without having had or having given anyone the idea of change, of progress. You do not understand the seekers; when they triumph, you bow your head; when they fail, you turn away. No sympathetic pity binds you to Icarus, who tried to rise to heaven, nor to Edgar Poe, who became drunk in order to forget the earth.

Icarus was a poet, and Edgar Poe was a poet. You rhyme your verses in vain; you are only scriveners.

ARTHUR ARNOULD

"EDGAR POE, THE MAN, THE ARTIST, AND THE WORK"*

Every study of the work of Edgar Poe should be preceded by a biographical note—a very short one—because it is indispensible to the understanding of this peculiar talent which is dominated and inundated by strangeness. In Edgar Poe, the man and the writer are bound together by ties so numerous and tight, and the genius of the one corresponds so closely to the acts and attitudes of the other, that *race, milieu* and *moment*—to employ the exact terminology of a distinguished critic who adds to his other merits that of arousing the pious scruples of the French Academy—have marked each product of his pen so deeply that trying to judge the American writer without heeding these particular factors would be condemning oneself to impotence or banality, probably both at once.

In fact, in saying that Edgar Poe is a poet "too rich in passion and poetry, one of the ill-fated great men who came, like so many others, to serve the rude apprenticeship of genius among inferior souls," one defines any Gilbert at all, or a Chatterton invented by Alfred de Vigny, or the Hégésippe Moreau of legend; one repeats a thesis that has been a little outmoded for some thirty years, but the author of "The Raven" has not been explained, nor has the author of *Eureka,* "Berenice" and "King Pest."

---

* Taken from *Revue moderne,* XXXIII (April 1865), 65-83; (June 1865), 476-492.

It can be proved that the man's life was sad and wretched, that he struggled against poverty without vanquishing it and that he found fools, envious men and exploiters along the way; but these are ordinary events that occur in the lives of most individuals and are not the special lot of certain "sacred" souls considering themselves "dedicated to the altar, condemned to march to their death and glory through their own ruin." Reciting ordinary events, the chronicler reveals his view of the destiny that people have agreed to attribute to the poet, the man of genius. He reveals nothing about Edgar Poe, and we are no better prepared than before to understand the nature of his talent or to judge the complex elements that formed it.

In the name of these theories, which are neither new nor consoling, we are presented with "spiritual and angelic natures like martyrs in the arena." The theories differ from Roland's donkey, which had only one defect, in that they have two very serious flaws. First, they are usually false; next, even if true, they would still err in being so vague and elastic that they could be applied to everybody and everything with equal ease, thus defining nothing. It is a frame as banal as a photograph album where every illustrious personage of the time is placed—Pius IX and Garibaldi, Rigolboche and the Queen of England. Today, criticism is more strict.

Edgar Poe is too individual, his work is too strange, the bent of his mind is too eccentric for us to be satisfied with categorizing him in a way equally applicable, I repeat, to Gilbert or Rousseau, Chatterton or Champfort, Hégésippe Moreau or de Musset.

With the author of the *Histoires Extraordinaires* we enter a strange country haunted by fantastic creatures of a sharply defined type that seldom varies but presents an interesting intellectual problem.

We could judge the country and its inhabitants by the solemn rules of ancient criticism, or use a purely literary criterion to appreciate this original and monotonous work. We might apply classic proportion or Romantic breadth in order to measure it and determine whether it complies with the rules of beauty and good taste. We might admire it as the exceptional. product of imagination carried to its ultimate power, or we might found a new esthetic on it. All of these would result in seeing and understanding only the superficial aspect of the work. We would bypass the following question without solving it: What is the essential nature of this unique inspiration, and what is its origin?

There are a few men, and they are the truly great ones, whose genius is revealed to us by a kind of natural intuition; there is no need to inquire *why* or *how*. Thus one need not know that Molière lived in the seventeenth century in the reign of Louis XIV, that he was inwardly miserable, that he traveled around France at the head of a troupe of actors. Likewise, one need not know that Cervantes was born in Spain in the sixteenth century, that he first served in the army, took part in the battle of Lepanto and became a slave of the Moors, that he remained poor all his life and that the hand holding the pen of the immortal author of *Don Quixote* was the hand of a hero.

Undoubtedly, these facts are not irrelevant in the eyes of the critic, the observer, the moralist, the scholar—the man, in short, who knows that nothing is the result of chance—and the indelible imprint of the circumstances of his life and the mark of his origin and his century can be found.

Undoubtedly, when one knows the society of Louis XIV thoroughly, when he knows what tears drenched the laughter of Molière and has studied the mind of the Gaul through the ages, he can distinguish in the author of *Tartufe, Le Misanthrope, Le Festin de pierre, Le Médecin malgré lui,* a combination of qualities, a certain way of conceiving life and painting it, which could only be produced in the form they have taken in that man and that epoch.

Undoubtedly, sixteenth-century Spain, the Spain of heroism and fanaticism, emitting its final brilliance before perishing under the double pressure of its kings and its inquisitors, Philip II and Torquemada, collaborated completely in *Don Quixote,* and that admirable work had to be born to a people whose quick imagination had no outlet but mysticism and chivalric fancies.

But once we have explained the details that make the individuality of the works of Molière and Cervantes (to cite only two generally popular names), details that tell us how the work took shape, there still remains a changeless, timeless, fully human core which the most ignorant man responds to.

These two writers are distinguished by a more lucid understanding of life and the sublime ability to reproduce it under our eyes in its entire truth. Take away the circumstantial labels of Molière's characters, their ribbons and their red heels; take away

Sancho's donkey and Don Quixote's buckler and his shaving-dish; under Alceste or Scapin, as under Don Quixote or Sancho Panza, you will find all of man. You will find life itself.

Those are men of genius. But what is genius but the result of the natural play of a magnificent combination of equal faculties, and *only those* which are to be found, although in a lesser degree and in broken balance, among all men who are healthy in body and spirit?

Far from thinking that genius is a disease, a kind of special madness, we believe that it must be called perfect health. Only the man who has one faculty excessively developed is diseased, for the other faculties atrophy in direct proportion to this abnormal development. Everything in him and around him becomes modified. Then he sees only one thing, or rather, only one side of things, and the vital powers of his brain, concentrated on a single point, lead him sometimes to unexpected discoveries of details that astonish us, exciting our admiration quite justly. In writers, as in men, external circumstances, deep and special conditions of race and environment have an importance not merely primary, but absolute.

They would remain inexplicable if we failed to go back to the origin of the disease and to inquire about all the causes influencing its development. Usually a long gestation of several generations has been necessary in order to cultivate the germ of the exuberant faculty that is transmitted at birth, just as a child inherits from his parents the germ of the incurable disease that must kill him. But disease is a blind force over which free will has little rein. It undergoes the counterattack of outer shocks (air, nourishment and the type of life modify the necessary progress infinitely); it may remain in a latent state or suddenly take an acute and terrible turn, according to the influence of the environment. Likewise, an exuberant faculty received at birth through a fatal law of heredity undergoes all the influences of education, of the era and its events. If the intellectual surroundings are favorable, it grows to excess; if obstacles block the way, it takes a more devious course or becomes repressed. Having in itself only one movement and one predisposition, fattening on foreign elements that it encounters, it must then be subjected to a sort of chemical analysis, and at the end the various elements it has carried in its course will be collected at the bottom of the retort. For that faculty is a simple force, a simple tendency of

the brain. It attracts; it acts by cohesion. It does not stamp what
it has received from the outside with the seal of *stability* and
generality which makes the work of the man of genius so readily
approachable by all people in all times.

An example will make the idea clearer. Let us suppose that
a man is born with a dominant faculty of observation. In itself
it is obviously no more than an aptitude for quick and thorough
perception of all the events that occur around us, however
negligible they may appear to be—the events that escape a man
in whom this aptitude is feeble or totally lacking. It is also evident that the aptitude, according to circumstances, will be
applied more specifically to a given type of fact or idea. Such a
man can become either a great chemist, a great physician or a
great astronomer. He can also become a writer, but on condition
that this primary faculty be joined to another more or less
highly developed faculty, the one we call imagination.

It must be observed that the imagination is not an ordering,
reasoned power, but a blind force like observation, and its role
is limited to combining facts and giving them the essential significance that they have lost in leaving reality to be classed in a
mental compartment.

Thus this man, marvelously endowed to produce literary or
artistic works, will nevertheless remain condemned to two completely passive operations. Like a mirror, he receives an impression and transmits it. His horizon will end where his gaze stops;
his imagination will act solely on what he has seen and felt. If
he is French, born in the nineteenth century in the middle class,
we will find in all his works, and will find *exclusively,* the France
of a certain moment and a certain environment. If he is reared
in Paris, the son of a Parisian, or if he is born in Saint-Malo, a
Breton gentleman, every word from his pen will inform us and
serve as his certificate of baptism. It would be quite impossible
to appreciate him justly without knowing the France of that
moment and milieu, or without knowing the climate and the
past of Brittany.

This is the man of talent, that is to say, the sick man, the
man with one or two faculties. If he should have three or four,
he will advance further on the road that leads to genius, to
lasting and complete greatness. But no matter how many creative
faculties he has, they are always *unequal.* They will follow one
another at a distance, with one preceding the others and, because

of its excess, limiting the normal development of the following one.

To judge this man, or even to understand him and place him in his true rank, we must study him thoroughly. To avoid building false literary theories and ridiculous esthetics on his works and to discover the origin of certain qualities and defects, tendencies and peculiarities, we must study him, his surroundings, his family and his country, No familiar or material detail is irrelevant or negligible.

Otherwise, it would be impossible to appreciate the value of characteristics that might easily be mistaken for the signs of genius. These characteristics are merely the happy accidents of a favorable conjunction of the dominant faculty with an environment exactly suited to it. Otherwise, how shall we escape the unthinking astonishment that such a writer inspires? How can we avoid marveling at him as an inexplicable phenomenon, a living miracle with no cause but the whim of a superior will outside the known laws of intelligence?

On the other hand, genius is the essence of health, and health is no more than the natural and complete play of the various functions of the human organism, whether physical or intellectual: thus, genius does not present anything extraordinary or unexpected to the eyes of the crowd. Without force or surprise, genius offers to us for our admiration the great spectacle of all the faculties composing the sound man, but in a superior degree of power. The man of genius is not different from other men; that is why he enchants and dominates them. The only thing that distinguishes him and separates him from them is a power to project, in a durable and perfect form, ideas that are not at all strange or abnormal, ideas that we find in ourselves as soon as the genius has marked them. We willingly admit that the man of talent has special gifts which are exclusively his. Because an extensive part of his brain is atrophied and another part, nourished at the expense of the rest, has acquired colossal proportions, he persuades the common man, ignorant of the price of the sacrifices producing this result, of his marvelous intellectual wealth. Far from having wealth, he has a plethora in one place, impoverishment everywhere else.

When we read Molière or Cervantes or another of the great writers the movement of his mind is so simple and logical, satisfying our reason and conforming to the normal play of our minds, that admiration is not immediately aroused. We almost believe that we could have written what they have written. Nothing warns us, from the first moment, of the distance that separates us from them; their harmonious power, without show or effort, does not force itself upon our attention or seize our enthusiasm by burglary.

The true sign of genius is supreme good sense united to courage and directive faculties which have been perfected. Thus, instead of letting ourselves be surprised by the glitter of some excessive literary gifts, we ought to see glitter as proof that the equilibrium of true greatness has been totally broken.

However, the equilibrium and completeness common to all men of genius subtract nothing from their originality. As the most complete and *successful* type of humanity—humanity considered from a general point of view as a species with distinctive characteristics—they belong to humanity of all ages and all countries, but they are also individuals, that is to say, special beings belonging to their own race and century, obeying the dictates of moral and physical forces which no creature escapes.

These forces decide the direction of their thought and the special use they will make of their power. Combined with the natural faculties in varying quantities, they will place a particular faculty in the foreground—always subservient to good sense— so that it simply plays the part of the executive power in a country where liberty reigns.

In defining the man of talent, we have spoken of Edgar Poe without naming him, for he is most appropriately classed among the unwholesome minds that are at least as pertinent to medicine as to criticism. For Molière and Cervantes, the work takes precedence over the worker and is distinguished by easily definable, general, lasting characteristics. For Edgar Poe the opposite is true: the man is everything, the work is nothing; it has merely reproduced and explained the worker himself. The essential madness (fixed ideas or monomania) is found in all his work to some degree, but especially in his *Tales* and, in another form, in his philosophic poem entitled *Eureka*. But monomania is only a symptom, a manifestation of a special state of mind: *it announces the shattering of equilibrium*. Either the mind has only one idea, or it refers everything to the single idea (which amounts to almost the same thing because its functions are neither regular nor *complete*). Sometimes through a defective structure in the cerebral machine, sometimes through moral or physical shock, one faculty acquires an incomparable power, for it continues to act in the midst of the general inaction. Reduced to this morbid condition, the writer cannot embrace the external world in its totality. He must approach it at a single point, absolutely ignorant of anything that is not himself or his illness. His nature becomes exclusive; he mutilates everything he touches.

The known life of Edgar Poe can be summarized in a few lines.

*   *   *   *

[skeleton summary, following Baudelaire, often quoting him]

We notice that this account contains many lacunae and many obscurities. Personal details are lacking. We are ignorant of the mysterious circumstances of the voyage to Greece, which ended in Saint Petersburg, and of the true reason for the final rupture between the young man and his adoptive father.

It is possible that the circumstances were not entirely to the writer's credit, and that Edgar Poe carried some gnawing memory or painful preoccupation on that distant trek.

It is also possible that Mr. Allan's second marriage to a young woman caused one of the conflicts of passion more frequent in real life than in drama and the novel, or that money problems arising from the fruitful marriage had led to the final separation of protector and protegé. In spite of their importance, however, these details are not essential to our subject. What we already know is quite sufficient for reconstructing the moral physiognomy of the man.

Four major facts emerge from the preceding account: (1) Edgar Poe was American, that is to say, of the Anglo-Saxon race; (2) *passion* and romance presided at his birth; (3) he had a remarkable aptitude for *the physical sciences and mathematics;* (4) he was a drunkard and died of delirium tremens.

We will not dwell on the first point, that of race. Authoritative speakers have already said everything on this subject. We simply recall that the essential traits of the Anglo-Saxon race are, on the one hand, pride, not the expansive kind (as in the Spaniard, openly declared and ostentatious to the point of naiveté) but the reserved kind, irritable, suffering from the constraint it endures; and, on the other hand, the excessive development of personality, or individuality if you like, from which a series of inevitable consequences springs.

Therefore, what impresses the Anglo-Saxon in the universe is man, and in man, the individual. In his eyes society is composed of a number of independent entities, and the particular play interests him more than the totality itself. What he sees, he sees thoroughly, but he rarely looks far or high. His most adventurous speculations have a closely-defined end, which is not at all hazardous. His power is that of concentration and analysis. He is powerful because he does not waste himself. Because of the narrow world in which they are developed, his passions gain intensity, muted violence and fearful tenacity they might not have had if they had dared to release themselves in constant use. Rarely revealed, turned back upon themselves, they are like sums of money that the investor does not touch; they bring in not only the usual interest, but also interest on the interest, and in a few years they are increased tenfold. Thwarted, sharing the energetic vitality of concentration, the passions of such men easily deviate and turn to disease. If the individual is naturally healthy, with faculties in true balance, the passion will communicate no more than a fortunate and fertile originality; if, on the contrary, other agents have already broken the balance, if some fatal germ has been placed in the child's cradle, it will carry him irresistibly toward monomania. Like a drop of acid, it will trace a painful path in his heart. Pride will make that painful and violent condition more somber and irreparable, for pride is as melancholy and tenacious as vanity is light and mobile.

For such men, a physical inferiority or the sense of some defect can reduce self-esteem and suffice to make them mingle absinthe with their words, to make life seem desolate—the world guilty, the creature miserable.

At birth, Edgar Poe had received a double dose of the passion we have just defined, for his father's marriage and his wandering life as a result of the union dominated exclusively by love (contrary to all the considerations that usually determine our decisions in such circumstances) are proof of the existence of an exceptional ardor of imagination and impetuosity of desire in the family.

Now we come to the third important factor—*the young man's aptitude for the physical sciences and mathematics.*

In fact, this poet who declared that poetry should have "no other end than itself," this partisan of art for art's sake, this strange storyteller who seemed gifted from the beginning with an exuberant and disordered imagination, passed almost his entire youth, as far as we know, in schools particularly designed for studies preparing for engineering and the army. Mathematics was his principal nourishment, and he soon distinguished himself by a remarkable aptitude. Mr. Baudelaire adds: "Later, he will make frequent use of it in his strange *Tales,* and will take surprising techniques from it." How could it have been otherwise? Edgar Poe was a *mathematical mind* par excellence, and, although it may at first seem unlikely, we intend to show in the following discussion that imagination and the poetic faculty must be placed in second rank in this young writer, immediately after the mathematical spirit and subjected to it.

Certainly, Poe did not have a practical nature—as his life eloquently illustrates—but his was an essentially practical mind, and the tendencies of his intelligence led him to mechanize the processes of art beyond reason, but without giving man an exact and proper sense of the daily necessities of existence.

People claim that they recognize the devil under all his disguises, by his cloven hoof. So it is with the Anglo-Saxon; the practical side of the race persists even in the literary theories where one would least expect to see it dominant.

But that is not the distinctive characteristic or guiding faculty of Edgar Poe. The one that compels all the others and marks them with its deep and distinctive imprint is the mathematical spirit alone.

If we are astonished to see mathematics, imagination and poetry compose a trinity in which mathematics plays the role of God the Father, it is because we confuse these faculties with the ordinary sciences such as chemistry and physics.

But mathematics is not, properly speaking, a science, and it serves nothing but itself. It teaches us a procedure for solving the problems that applied science poses for man's curiosity; considered in its essence, mathematics is above all a means of resolving abstract intellectual conceptions into palpable calculations and of measuring space, one of the two forms in which we glimpse infinity.

Relying on mathematics, imagination can expand its wings and feel its powers increased a hundredfold. It no longer taxes itself to *invent* impossible events or *create* extraordinary images.

Why should we bother with useless, exhausting work that is quickly halted by our inability to rise for long above the environment which gave us birth and gives us sustenance? Mathematics is the domain of the extraordinary and the impossible. Furthermore, it is the very language of the infinite. It alone penetrates the infinite through and through, and when we stop, it is because our minds vacillate, dazzled to dizziness. The unfaltering instrument of our minds would still be there to serve us if our strength were not exhausted.

Moreover, our imagination acquires a magnificent assurance and certainty from that precious company. Expressing itself always in a resolute, exact, concise language, it has forged a path undirected. The reality of calculations, the tight logic of deduction, have both intoxicated and sustained it. The world is still under its feet—the finite world within its reach—and yet it has traveled boundless space and limitless time.

Yet it is dangerous to apply this process to the speculations of the mind, rather than to an exact and definite science which serves as a counterweight to maintain the mind's balance. When, instead of analyzing material facts and solving limited problems, we use that uncircumscribed tool in dealing with abstract ideas, the mind loses the sense of the *real* truth, that is to say, the *human* truth. It no longer perceives the abyss into which it plunges, impossibility disappears before its eyes, and, because it proceeds by precise measure, it ceases to doubt that it measures the incommensurable.

Our own time has shown examples of the mathematical spirit and imagination which is its own dupe and the dupe of its technique, whether the men with such gifts wanted to reform the State, society or religion, or whether they strove to embrace and solve all three problems at once.

Other effects of that spirit are to be found applied to literary production by Edgar Poe. But we must remember that Poe, as an American, is the enemy of speculation that is too vague, too vast and, especially, too general. Minute and patient analysis would not know where to take hold in an unlimited situation, but needs a closed, narrow horizon.

However, the mathematical spirit has a fatal slope, and no one ventures there with impunity.

After having borrowed its most materialistic procedures for his poetry and its methodical analysis, steady and logical progress, and powerful reductions to unity for his *Tales,* he follows it at last through time and space and gives us, in

Eureka, a renovated if not new explanation of creation without abandoning for a moment the terms borrowed from mechanics, statics and other sciences with a similar goal. He remains convinced that he has not erred and cannot err, for his *calculation* is exact and his *operations* are correct.

When poetry (to return to our point of departure) is reduced to having no other end than itself—so reduced by both Poe and a certain French school whose representatives would be easy to name—it almost becomes transformed into a problem of pure mathematics in which the role of the imagination gradually disappears in the face of exclusively mechanical procedures. Restricted to two elements, harmony and measure, it becomes a branch of music and could be annotated like music. One could reckon it like any other arithmetic quantity. Later we will see, for example, that the poem "The Raven" is the product of a kind of algebraic equation.

Only the drunkenness and delirium tremens of the American author remain to be considered.

Let us begin by stating that we do not confront the problem from a moral point of view. We are not attempting to blame or condone Edgar Poe, to accuse or defend him. This sunspot obviously distresses Mr. Baudelaire. Not that he feels obliged to show severity toward a vice that is shameful or inoffensive, according to the degree to which it dominates its victim, but that he feels some embarrassment in anticipating public opinion. In particular, he fears that this innately vulgar weakness will drag poor Edgar Poe down (in the eyes of French readers) from the sublime heights where his translator, as one of the poetic brotherhood, would have placed him at all costs.

Mr. Baudelaire also attempts to establish extenuating circumstances for the crime and to emphasize carefully "the infinitely precious fact of premeditation as attested and proved"; he prefers that his hero be a little more guilty rather than a little less great. A poet does not joke about poets, and these "sanctified spirits" have mutual indulgence, reciprocal tenderness, for one another. Like the workers on ancient Babel, all these sons of the Muse are working on the same gigantic monument—their own pedestal. However, the confusion of tongues, dispersing them to the four corners of the earth, has not shattered their union; they understand one another perfectly in their various dialects, and each one continues to bring his stone to the edifice of their common glory.

From Mr. Baudelaire's plea we will take only two facts which seem important: the first, that Edgar Poe "did not drink like a glutton, but like a barbarian, with completely American energy and economy of time, as though accomplishing a homicidal function, *as though harboring a thing he had to kill.*" Second, that the greater number "of his excellent pieces" were "preceded or followed" by a spell of drunkenness.

Mr. Baudelaire adds, with reason, that the words *"preceded* or *followed* imply that intoxication could serve as *stimulant* as well as relaxation."

Again, the degree of Edgar Poe's responsibility or guilt does not matter, but the result is important—the effect alcoholic abuse has on the brain. The first effects of intoxication and its immediate action on the moral being vary according to the temperament and intellectual training of the *subject*. Thus, in a sanguine man, a period of gaiety and expansiveness is soon followed by a heavy torpor. If the attacks are frequent, a complete brutalization finally extinguishes all the powers of the unfortunate man.

In a lymphatic man, alcohol first creates a factitious vigor and energy. He seems to have more ideas; he has courage and vivacity. His mind, like a steed that feels the spur, suddenly begins to gallop. Once the crisis is past, the man becomes even more sluggish and impotent than before, and idiocy rapidly overtakes this easy prey.

Another spectacle awaits us in a nervous and bilious individual. His intoxication is feverish; it resembles an attack of nerves. Laughter and tears alternate, then mingle until irritability supplants them, to be displaced in turn by prostration. After excitement comes sadness; after anger, spleen and despair. Misanthropy, monomania and even madness are the inevitable conclusion of such a state if it is often repeated. The too-delicate nerves are crushed; bile embitters all the visions engenered by alcohol.

But in all imaginable cases and in all possible circumstances the first effect of intoxication is to bring about a momentary abdication of will—will considered a directing force and a pendulum intended to regulate the actions of our minds and the succession of our ideas or sentiments. At the moment of a drunken seizure, anarchy reigns. It is a steeplechase of all sensations, desires and passions. Law exists no longer, brutal force is in command and tyranny (that is to say, the fixed idea) is born of the disorder.

In fact, if sensations, desires and passions are left to themselves without rein, the liveliest sensation, the most burning desire and the most violent passion must necessarily take hold and rule despotically. Under social or civilized man, natural or instinctual man suddenly appears. He reveals himself as he is at heart, fully subjected to the fatality of his temperament. If he has a hidden, ceaseless preoccupation, it will emerge and absorb him utterly. If he has an ambition, if will flaunt itself. If he has a claim, he will state it. A regret, a sorrow will speak. If, finally, he has one highly developed faculty, a special bent of mind, a particular way of conceiving life and judging man, it will burst out, crushing and blotting out the rest.

Intoxication, then, could become, to some extent and at some times, "a method of work," to use the exact words of Mr. Baudelaire. By annihilating the will and bringing about momentary abdication and enforced silence of everything but the dominant faculty and the ceaseless preoccupation, intoxication fosters literary inspiration.

The imperfection and incompleteness of such a method are evident. It has more dash, it is true, and produces stranger works. It gives them the highest intensity, it transmits a fever and a startling audacity, but it condemns them to monotony and restricts them to the narrowest horizon. The mind goes far, but in only one direction. Forms and images are constantly reproduced with a fatiguing tenacity. We no longer see a play of many elements, a battle and truce of ideas, a conflict of feelings and passions—the representation of the life of humanity which each man summarizes in a small way, more or less completely. On the contrary, we find ourselves confronting a single element, idea, feeling or passion.

If the writer who has recourse to this "mnemonic technique, this method," has a nervous and bilious temperament all his work will assume a hue of dark sadness and acute despair. All joy, luster, expansiveness and active vitality will disappear from his view. His paintings will be desolate or horrible and his dreams will become nightmares. If intoxication increasingly subjugates him and delirium tremens develops, the diseased man will see nothing and recount nothing but disease. His perverted sensations will lead him to love only odd tastes and savage paintings; he will fall into an intellectual *perversity* that finds pleasure in pain, grace in epilepsy and "beauty in strangeness."

Delirium tremens will not dry up the source of literary production, but will poison it. If he were sanguine or lymphatic, brutalization or impotence would halt his pen, but he is nervous and bilious. He becomes a monomaniac, and madness threatens him. Neither monomania nor madness destroys the intellectual functions. Only their action is affected and their balance shattered.

This is the history of Edgar Poe. He was the drunkard, the writer, the poet and the diseased man.

Without arguing with Mr. Baudelaire about Poe's private virtues and his behavior toward his wife—admitting that he was not malicious—one refuses to believe that he made his companions happy. On this point there can be no argument. There are things that cannot be disputed, things that one can state without knowing them.

Edgar Poe, whatever he was, must have caused suffering in those who loved him. He belonged to a race fatal to others; we have encountered more than one specimen of it. Pride, nerves and the rupture of intellectual equilibrium cause an agonizing and endless struggle. Unfortunately, these men are not wicked; the fact makes them more formidable. They attract soft hearts and ecstatic imaginations, as the void attracts women and children. They have the fascination of the tempest and the temptation of the abyss. They suffer, and people are compassionate; they make others suffer, and people love them. They are ill, and you try to cure them; in their agony they strangle and kill you, only to weep bitterly afterward over their crime and your death.

If they were malicious one would fly or at least struggle, and hate would give him strength equal to their strength. But they are not malicious; they are sincere. Their tears and despair are sincere; everything is sincere, for everything rests on the love they have for themselves. That love, I assure you, is as sincere as it is deep and pitiless.

It matters little, then, if someone shows, paper in hand, that Edgar Poe was a difficult friend, an ungrateful son, a cruel husband, causing the death of the loving wife whom he loved; it matters little if someone insists on proving the contrary. Whoever loved Edgar Poe also wept.

All that is necessary for finding the key to this writer's work and for judging it is now known. All the essential elements of his talent have been noted, and it would be inexplicable if even one of them were missing.

This first analysis and reconstruction of the man can be summarized by saying now, with the certainty of being understood, that Edgar Poe, as writer, *is the product of alcohol and the mathematical spirit in a man of imagination of the American Anglo-Saxon race.* If one prefers a formula that is even more concise and directly applicable to the work itself, we can define it thus:

THE MATHEMATICAL MIND, IMAGINATION AND ALCOHOL IN AN AMERICAN BRAIN AFFECTED BY DELIRIUM TREMENS.

II

Before entering the study of Poe's works in order to seek the development and many combinations of the elements that have already been defined, it is useful to question the artist and learn his methods from him. Undoubtedly the work is the direct product of the man, but in order to be produced it must wear a certain form, adopt a certain gait and submit to more or less methodical and absolute rules. The artist is still a man, of course, but a man who applies his particular faculties to literary creation. There are many people in this world who are American by race, nervous and bilious by temperament and dominated by a passion for alcohol, yet none of them has ever thought of giving his nightmares the enduring life of art. Therefore, there had to be a special state of mind, a particular force that must not be neglected. Its characteristics and effect must be known.

In order for Edgar Poe, at a given moment, to feel the desire and the capacity to set his dreams to paper so that his sensations might become poems and stories, he had to divide into two selves —one passive, experiencing the dream and the sensation, the other active, analyzing them and submitting them to a veritable inquest. He had to proceed by a series of logical deductions destined to coordinate and systematize the dreams and the sensations.

Sensation always precedes sentiment, and impressions precede ideas. The second is always the child of the first, but a proud and argumentative child who always wants to establish his genealogy and legitimacy.

In the artist, then, we find only the theoretic guise of the natural, unconscious actions of the man himself. However, since the theory or systematic afterthought is called upon to give the work its literary stamp and original form, its structure and details must be thoroughly known. Particularly, in regard to Edgar Poe, it is important to know how he justified his own tendencies—the fatal inclination and necessity of his genius.

A literary work is the definitive and complete expression of the man and the artist, the supreme product of their collaboration. The work contains both, the man having provided his impressions, the artist having given them a language and having placed them in an environment favorable to the *effect*.

Thanks to the wisdom of Mr. Baudelaire, who had the idea of translating a remarkable and revealing fragment, a precious document for studying the artist in Poe is available.

This essay is Edgar Poe's own analysis of "the progressive steps" he has followed in composing one of his most famous poems, "The Raven." That fine and detailed analysis, like everything else coming from the pen of the author of the *Tales,* intends "to show that no aspect of the composition of the poem 'The Raven' can be attributed to chance or to intuition, and that the work moved step by step towards its solution, with the precision and the rigorous logic of a mathematical problem."

* * * *

[2-paragraph summary of "The Raven"]

This is all of the little poem. The effect is startling. The word "nevermore" ending each stanza creates an impression of growing sadness in the mind of the reader. We see doubt and despair embodied in the raven. Under the short, lively allegory, we delight in catching sight of a true feeling, a keen sorrow. We neither believe in the sage raven, nor concern ourselves with his questioner, but we imagine that the poet, hidden behind the fantastic stage setting, has revealed some of his secret suffering; he has given words to some of the deep anguish that troubles imaginative men when, coming upon a newly-opened grave, they confront the question of a future life. We think "The Raven" poetically expresses the struggle that takes place, in such a case, between our passionate desire to prolong love beyond death, and cool reason, which replies that everything has ended forever, and we will see one another "nevermore."

Not at all. "The Raven" contains nothing of that, at least not in the author's intention. He had another preoccupation and another goal. If he arrived at that effect, it was by a series of logical deductions and mathematical reasons.

*   *   *   *

[summary of "The Philosophy of Composition"]

These are the theories and the method of an American, with his marvelous faculty of analysis, his passion for detail, and his respect for *reality*. His practical mind needed to impose narrow and strictly defined rules even on imaginative flights and poetic inspiration.

Immense pride without vain ostentation is the solid basis and unchanging background of the Anglo-Saxon character; it animates the entire essay, yet never obtrudes. The author does not say, "I have written a masterpiece, and my poem is sublime; I am a great man, and all the other poets of the known world do not come up to my ankle." But coldly and determinedly he shows us that "The Raven" is the only poem that ever existed or could exist that is perfect and worthy of the name. It is the summit of art. Beyond, there is nothing.

We must remember his reasoning. He has found the MOST poetic and the MOST beautiful subject. He gave it the ONLY suitable length. He composed it in stanzas ending in a refrain, and the refrain itself is the MOST powerful means of achieving an effect. He has given this effect the GREATEST perfection by reducing it to a single word that admits various applications. That word is the MOST sonorous and the MOST melancholy in the English language and, thanks to this combination of circumstances, he has chanced to create the GREATEST emotional intensity possible.

"The Raven" is not only an excellent poem, one of the most remarkable, but it is THE poem, because it unites all the conditions of perfection—and the ONLY ones—to the highest degree.

To tell the truth, we do not believe that all this reasoning and fine calculation really preceded the composition of "The Raven." The poet has probably followed his inevitable tendencies more naively and naturally.

He chose a melancholy subject because his disorderly life, insatiable pride, unexpected reversal of fortune, the suffering and death of a beloved wife, his devouring passions and the ravages of drunkenness in a nervous and bilious temperament (joined to an analytic spirit that enlarged and emphasized all the painful details), as well as the ineffaceable nature of his race, impelled him toward bitter sadness and savage melancholy.

He chose a short subject because writing nearly always under the influence of the artificial nervous excitement of an attack of alcoholic fever whose length could not be prolonged beyond a certain rather limited time, the attack necessarily became the measure of the inspiration itself. He was preoccupied with himself, imprisoned in the circle of his own sensations, a sick man studying his malady; his environment was too confined and monotonous for his inspiration to enlarge and renew itself freely. Because his spirit of mathematical analysis impelled him to concentrate his gaze on a *single* point and to atomize and reduce everything to its simplest expression, he was not able to enrich his material with foreign elements and must soon have arrived at the supreme moment when nothing remained at the bottom of the retort but inert molecules without relationship to one another.

He stated that "beauty" was the sole legitimate domain of poetry. Truth and passion were excluded because his origin made him love palpable reality and mathematical exactness—which are only found in infinitely small details—and condemned him to giving art no other end than the production of an effect. That effect, setting aside general truth or vital passion, could only result in a sharp, violent emotion of the "soul" (to use his word), a sharp electric shock that makes the nerves vibrate.

He sought the maximum in everything—the maximum of sadness, sonority, beauty because, reduced to preoccupation with detail and pursuit of effect (and by purely material means), he knew instinctively that the effect ought to be the most powerful possible in order to stun the mind and justify itself by the power of its thunderclap. That power could only be found in the "totality or unity of effect" he assiduously pursued in "The Raven," in his *Tales,* in every work.

Later, after the fact, he constructed the theories we have just cited. Speech and inspiration have always preceded grammar and rhetoric, but grammar explains the genius of a language and rhetoric gathers the manners and *customs* of inspiration into a body of laws. Thus the man previously described is found almost in his entirety in the theories and methods of the writer.

We have spoken of the mathematical spirit, imagination and alcohol in an American brain affected by delirium tremens. The mathematical spirit flashes from every word of the curious analysis of "The Raven" we have just borrowed from Edgar Poe himself. Imagination is revealed in the choice of characters and scene and in the unusual creation of a raven that answers in one despairing word all the questions of a lover who mourns for his beloved.

The American brain is more than adequately indicated in the precision of detail and the exact realism in the fantastic, which are among the main features of the poem.

If alcohol and delirium tremens seem less evident at first glance, it is because they cannot play a direct and, so to speak, *external* role in literary theories. They have made their contribution to the general tendency of the theories; they have fortified and exaggerated the theories, but only at the moment of execution do we find them performing as active characters, their role sometimes becoming dominant. They influence the choice of subject and the color of the painting.

The method itself, apart from the moral and physiological causes that engendered it, can be reduced to two principal elements: minute and complete reality of detail and "unity or totality of effect."

These are the two poles, the alpha and omega of his inspiration. He has, therefore, a double purpose never lost from sight but continually pursued through all subjects with equal tenacity.

In regard to "The Raven," he tells us at the end of his analysis, triumphant about his own skill:

> So far, everything is within the limits of the *accountable*—of the *real*. A raven, having learned by rote the single word "Nevermore," and having escaped from the custody of its owner, is driven at midnight, through the violence of a storm, to seek admission at a window from which a light still gleams—the chamber-window of a student, occupied half in poring over a volume, half in dreaming of a beloved mistress deceased. The casement being thrown open at the fluttering of the bird's wings, the bird itself perches on the most convenient seat out of the immediate reach of the student, who, amused by the incident and the oddity of the visitor's demeanour, demands of it, in jest and without looking for a reply, its name. The raven addressed, answers with its customary word, "Nevermore"— a word which finds immediate echo in the melancholy heart of the student, who, giving utterance aloud to certain thoughts suggested by the occasion, is again startled by the fowl's repetition of "Nevermore." The student now guesses

the state of the case, but is impelled, as I have before explained, by *the human thirst for self-torture,* and in part by
superstition, to propound such queries to the bird as will
bring him, the lover, the most of the luxury of sorrow,
through the anticipated answer "Nevermore." With *the indulgence, to the extreme, of this self-torture,* the narration
in what I have termed its first or obvious phase, has a natural termination, and so far THERE HAS BEEN NO OVER-
STEPPING OF THE LIMITS OF THE REAL.

In a poetic, imaginative subject, fancy and feeling ought to
have first place, one would think, but in Poe the mathematical
spirit, geometric rectitude and cold analysis have dispossessed
them. This preoccupation with precise reality (*"Chance* and the
incomprehensible were the two great enemies" of Edgar Poe)
and the material possibility of events seems strange to a French
reader, to say the least, and it would never have obsessed the
mind of a writer of the Gallic, Latin race. However, this inces-
sant preoccupation gives Edgar Poe some of his power, and the
resolute and patient application of these methods, which seem
anti-artistic at first glance, brings the strange and startling results
that we are going to study.

Poe achieves unity or totality of effect by seeking and determining in advance the *maximum* possible effect to be produced;
according to the circumstances, it may be the word, situation or
event that contains the greatest possible amount of interest or
intensity of emotion. Once this point is found, he does not take
his eyes from it; he moves away from it and chooses the swiftest
and most direct route for reaching it from another given point,
which we will call the point of departure. His entire task, then,
consists of systematically removing all the obstacles separating
him from his goal and causing him to detour or merely to slow
his pace. He proceeds by successive eliminations, allowing only
the absolutely necessary distance to exist between the point of
departure and the point of destination so that he can cover the
distance in a single prodigious and thundering leap.

A comparison will throw this strange process of mind into
relief.

Everyone knows the tactics of the carnivorous birds that
describe a series of great concentric circles around their fascinated victim, progressively enclosing it more narrowly until the
moment when they suddenly drop on their prey in a straight line
and with the speed of lightning.

Poe, when he composes, follows precisely the same tactics. He does not take up his pen until he has described all those tightening circles, that is to say, until he has eliminated everything but a *single* emotion, goal, idea, style or development. He reveals himself to the public only at the moment when he leaps, in a straight line also, with dizzy speed and a terrible force of concentration toward that supreme *effect* that has been chosen after slow elaboration.

To these two primary and constitutional preoccupations of his talent we must add a third artistic preoccupation—originality —a preoccupation at least as American as realism and material verisimilitude of events.

Edgar Poe readily admitted that originality is a matter of apprenticeship. "The fact is that originality," he added, "except in minds of unheard-of power, is not at all a matter of enthusiasm or intuition, as some people suppose. Generally, in order to find it, one must consciously seek it and, although it is a positive merit of the highest order, in order to attain it we need the spirit of invention less than that of *negation*."

This laborious search for originality will astonish many people in France, where the great goal and supreme effort are to be like everyone else, where people almost never dare to be themselves. This search explains the extremes to which Poe nearly always pushed his methods and his effects. If he had been less intent on originality—and he could have ignored it, for he had it naturally —if he had willed less, he would not have over-charged his palette. But, as he himself reports, originality never ceased to be his fixed intention and violent prejudice, even in the slightest detail. As soon as he found the greatest and most original effect possible to his state of mind and faculties he fastened upon it and would not let go. Hence, in part, the monotony of his types and methods, which are always the same.

Now we know the man and the artist.

The product of their collaboration—the written work—remains to be studied. The trail of these various elements remains to be followed, and their combination and interplay must be considered.

From the union of such a man and such an artist—in short, from such a brain using such means—a strange and powerful but limited and incomplete work emerges. It is exact and abnormal, vigorous and unwholesome, precise and disordered, geometric and frenetic. It is lucid and rational madness finding savage pleasure in the horrors of its delirium and ecstasy in convulsion. We know the depraved enjoyment that certain fanatics have in the midst of physical suffering, at the sight of their spilled blood and gaping wounds. This enjoyment is Edgar Poe's ideal: delight in moral and physical disease, *"All the more delicious because it is insupportable."*

We must not forget that everything contributed to the creation of this unusual work—the man's temperament, his life, the composition of his brain and the literary theories emerging from that combination of facts. When truth and passion are banished from poetry and it is reduced to nothing but the most intense nervous excitement, a kind of ecstatic catalepsy like that produced by opium or hashish, poetic inspiration, like those two poisons, must finally ravage the brain subjected to such a dreadful, repeated orgy. It can join hands with alcohol.

JORIS-KARL HUYSMANS

"THE PATHOLOGY OF THE WILL"*

In exploring thoroughly, however, he [Des Esseintes] discovered first that, in order to attract him, a work had to wear the guise of strangeness that Edgar Poe demanded, but he willingly ventured farther on that road and called for Byzantine brain flowers and complicated deliquescence of language. He wished for an uneasy indecision around which he could dream until he had made it, according to the momentary state of mind, vaguer or clearer. In short, he wanted a work of art both for itself and for what it consented to lend him. He wanted to depart, as though sustained by an adjuvant or carried in a vehicle, into a sphere where sublimated sensations gave him an unexpected thrill whose cause he sought for a long time to analyze.

*　*　*　*

In order to enjoy a work that combined an incisive style and the penetrating and feline analysis he desired, he had to go to the master of induction, the strange, profound Edgar Poe, for whom his ardor had not declined when he read him once again.

More than any other, the latter corresponded by innate affinity to the postulates of Des Esseintes.

If, in the soul's hieroglyphics, Baudelaire had deciphered the coming of age of feelings and ideas, Poe, on the path of

---

* Taken from A *Rebours* (Paris, 1955), pp. 222-223 and 235-237.

morbid psychology, had more especially examined the realm of the will.

Under the emblematic title, "The Demon of Perversity" ["The Imp of the Perverse"], he was the first in literature to spy upon the irresistible impulses that the will is subject to without being aware of them, the impulses that cerebral pathology now explains almost with certainty. He was also the first to reveal, if not to notice, the effect of fear acting upon the will. It is as depressive as an anesthetic, which paralyzes the senses, or curare, which destroys the nerve impulse centers. He had made his studies converge on this point, the lethargy of will. He analyzed the effects of this moral poison and indicated the symptoms of its progress: the disturbance beginning with anxiety, continuing with anguish, finally exploding in terror that stuns the will while the intelligence, although shaken, does not break.

Death, abused so much by all the dramatists, he somehow sharpened. He altered it by introducing a superhuman, algebraic element. In reality, he did not describe the actual agony of the dying but, rather, the moral agony of the survivor beside the bed of mourning haunted by monstrous hallucinations engendered by sorrow and fatigue. With an atrocious fascination he emphasized the acts of terror, the snapping of the will; he reasoned coldly about them, pressing little by little on the throat of the reader who suffocates, panting, under these mechanically contrived nightmares of fever.

Convulsed by hereditary neuroses, maddened by moral St. Vitus' dance, his creatures merely lived on nerves. His women— the Morellas, the Ligeias—possessed immense erudition steeped in the fog of German philosophy and the cabalistic mysteries of the ancient Orient, and all had the inactive boyish breasts of angels; all were, so to speak, asexual.

Baudelaire and Poe, those two names so often linked because of their joint poetics and their shared inclination to examine mental disease, differed radically in the affective conceptions that played such a large role in their works. Baudelaire had a corrupt and evil love whose cruel disgust made one think of the reprisals of an inquisition. Poe had chaste, celestial loves for whom the senses did not exist; the brain alone had erection without correspondence in the organs which, if they existed, remained forever frozen and virgin.

As soon as his attention wandered, that spiritual surgeon

who vivisected in a stifling atmosphere became the prey of his imagination, which made somnambulatory and angelic apparitions rise like a delightful miasma. That cerebral clinic was for Des Esseintes a source of unwearying conjecture; but now that his neurosis was aggravated, there were days when such reading shattered him, days when he remained on the watch, with trembling hands, feeling overwhelmed by an irrational dread and a secret terror like that of the devastated Usher.

Thus he had to restrain himself, scarcely touching those fearful elixirs; for the same reason, he could no longer visit his red room without suffering for it, nor could he intoxicate himself with the gloom of Odilon Redon and the tortures of Jan Leyken.

Nevertheless, while he was in that state of mind, all literature seemed insipid after the terrible philtres imported from America. Then he turned to Villiers de L'Isle-Adam, in whose scant work he noticed observations that were still seditious, still spasmodic vibrations, but with the exception of his Claire Lenoir at least, did not shoot forth such a devastating horror.

ALBERT SAMAIN

"THE VERTIGINOUS BEYOND"*

Read Edgar Poe's *Eureka*—frightful feeling, especially when you are approaching the end. The grandeur of the hypothesis, the excessiveness of the concept, intoxicates me. I tried to read all of it in one evening, and that dizzy ride through the immeasurable dropped me on my bed, battered, my head broken. Having devoured the last chapters by candlelight in the deep silence of two in the morning, my cerebral activities were driven to such power that I feel unbalanced; the normalcy of my inner relationships is disrupted by the feeling that my mind does not want to return to my body, or that it cannot do so. The very routine of life, the little external phenomena which form a chain and make the routine, the daily preoccupations, even the setting of my ordinary life seem far away—far—as though I contemplated earthly things from the basket of a balloon floating at an enormous height. . . . And the reintegration of my normal perceptions is achieved very slowly, with an indefinable troubling of my being.

Decidedly, thought is weighty for the poor creature of flesh and blood! Tonight I have breathed an air too pure, too rarefied: my temples throb; asphyxiation has begun . . . and then, an indescribable anguish in my heart, an unease located nowhere precisely, but manifesting itself in something black in which I seem to bathe.

---

* Taken from *Carnets intimes*, (Paris, 1939), pp. 50-52 and 111-113.

A persistent feeling like the breathlessness of high places, where the constriction of breathing is accompanied by a lessening of the perception of light.

O Sphynx of Flaubert! I too have climbed the furrows of your brow and have looked into your eyes; and I have read there, in those implacable, sad eyes that you too would devour me.

In the weeks when I have sent my unbridled mind into the vast plains of speculation, why have I repeatedly felt that stifling, mounting bitterness . . . that breath of death?

Guyau consoles me, Poe terrifies me. I am crushed by these conceptions in which my humanity, my spiritual personality are lost without purpose and without return. In that law directed magnificently to my reason, exalting it, there is nothing left for my heart. . . . And my heart is chilled!

*   *   *   *

I have read Poe this week. He is definitely to be classed among the greatest. The power of his conception, the magnificence of his hypotheses and the marvelous originality of his imagination always contained and maintained by an extraordinary will compose a figure almost unique in the arts for its combination of faculties. If the word *perfection* has ever been appropriately spoken, it is in such a case as that.

What is particularly striking is the parallelism of two faculties usually possessed unequally—imagination and logic. Nothing could be more mathematically ordered than these stories that are built in the heart of dream. A work of a unique kind is born of this dual nature. The projections of a powerful mind in the most rarefied spheres of lofty thought give an impression of a very special essence made of a thorough mixture of elements that are ordinarily absolutely disparate. At the same time, the extreme spirituality of the conception gives the style something inexplicably airy, immaterial fluid. . . . Couldn't that sense of a language that is all soul, expressing itself in a sort of absolute, be compared to music—the music of certain great symphonic composers, Beethoven, for example? At least the impression given by various parts of the reading—an impression directed to the mind and the flesh at the same time, simultaneously piercing them with the same strange shiver—could scarcely find analogy except in music.

Isn't music also pure dream condensed by pure thought, formulating itself according to the complex rules of Order? All unconsciousness is strictly banished from that art where the Will rules. Now this is what makes it seem singular, since the unconscious has invaded us through every pore of our Romantic education.

On leaving the plumed tumults of the generation of Hugo we find will, order and logic in inspiration only in the studied architecture of Baudelaire's sonnets. They are the supreme, rarefied art, crystalized in impeccable form, their flashing and *incorruptible absoluteness* giving the impression of precious stones. Flaubert also offers us an example of that magnificent triumph of Will over Instinct.

In addition, we find in Poe a compelling and vertiginous beyond. From the height of certain phrases one breathes airs that have come from unknown depths and make the soul tremble. Space opens out, horizons enlarge. One advances forever, forever. . . . And, little by little, one feels remote, very remote, down there on the tip of an imperceptible tongue of land, which is Reality, and which is enveloped on all sides by the wide, fluid, luminous surges of the spiritual Sea.

GUSTAVE KAHN

"THE POEMS OF POE TRANSLATED BY
STEPHANE MALLARMÉ"*

The translation of Edgar Poe by artists devoted to the glory of his ideas has just been completed; only a few pages of esthetics and criticism remain. After Baudelaire, we now have Mr. Stéphane Mallarmé, whose translation of the poems, with notes, has appeared in a luxurious and fanciful typography, embellished by a spiritual portait by Manet and with a raven's profile as endplate. In a tracery of hieratic lines like ebony, here is a transposition of the rare poems, the rare poems in *verse*—for what should *Shadow* and *Silence* be, if not poems in prose—which the brief life of Poe has left us.

It would be odd to praise Mr. Mallarmé's virtues as a translator. For such an artist, translation is a homage rendered to a glorious memory; it is also a preventive measure to keep some businessman from contriving to betray one of the elect. The translation, a close imitation, is in a prose that forms lines like nocturnal horizons of the original; it is also supple enough to note the various ironic passages from one idea to another and to note the refrains in familiar terms that enmesh; one hears harmonies as if they were echoes of other, remote harmonies formulated in a different alphabet with different signs. The glory of this translation, in short, is that one can read it with the

---

* Taken from *Revue independante,* VIII (September, 1888), 435-443.

pleasure that an original work would give, feeling an almost direct communication with the creating artist.

On the threshold is the famous classic sonnet "Into Himself at last resolved by death . . ." that will be acknowledged as luminous when the mass of present works—whose reputation for intelligibility rests on a monstrous pact between reader and writer (that the reader believes he understands words to which he attaches no precise meaning, and that the author trusts the reader to give the words any meaning whatsoever)—when these works are dead and justly bear the stigma of "decadent books" with which every new writer in these times, and even others, has been branded.

Then came "The Raven," "Helen," "The Haunted Palace," "Ulalume," some romances already published (in this same translation) in issues of dead literary magazines and the unpublished *Notes,* whose erudition and truth one can only subscribe to.

Poetry—and English poetry has been freer than ours for a long time—had often tempted Poe. Somewhere he expresses regret at not having persisted in this kind of rhythmic translation, synthesized and pared of environmental details; the regret is like that of Nerval, who published his fine sonnets and then complained of being no more than a callous proser. He believed that poetry died in man after a certain autumn of life; perhaps, more exactly, the feeling came to him that it is difficult and useless for a man to think of making the ideas he wants to translate in their richness of setting and circumstantial interest conform to the rules of strict measure, which are always established by an individual without mandate, an individual all the more honored and autocratic because he is without mandate. In a theoretical passage Poe shows himself amazed that no one dared to alter the form of poetry. And, in the midst of the perpetual evolution of forms, ideas, frontiers, commerce, motives, hegemonies, in the midst of such a perpetual renewing of language that a grammarian entitles some essays *The Life of Words* (in the Horatian sense), isn't it quite astonishing that only verse remains generally immobile and unchangeable, and that popular cataclysms, barbarian invasions and ten thousand evils should be necessary before it change? Could it be that great minds like Poe and Nerval avoid the work of slaves, that true poets like Flaubert evade possible chains, that Baudelaire, hesitating, seeks a form of prose poem more musical and less a matter of carpentry than the poetry of

his time, from which he took all he could? Whatever the reason
for the successive ankylosis, nearly fifty years were necessary, after
the Romantic emancipation, before poets had the freedom of
their sensations and could herald themselves as comparative
heralds.

This complex problem (for freed verse is still not fully
used verse) has received attention from Poe in all its aspects.
First, the *Genesis of a Poem* (which he later declared a fantasy);
then a lecture on poetry and Anglo-American poets. From these
two texts—for, if Poe disavowed the dogmatic form of the first
essay, he nevertheless wrote it—the following concept emerges:

Poetry has little or nothing to do with truth; neither is it
concerned with passion—naturally, then, not with morality or
sentimentality. It has love as its essence. In order to differentiate
between passion and love, Poe evokes the images of the Uranian
Venus and the Dionysian Venus.

Further on, he indicates what the elements of poetry are; he
lists nocturnal calms, twilight dangers, the visible splendors of
woman, the life and perfume which her garments spread, the moments when one awakens on the brink of memory as at the limits
of dream, etc. All this indicates an attempt to translate pure sensation: love without the contingencies that might limit it to such
and such a person, but *with* the evocation of all curves and all
aspects pertaining to it, and, so to speak, completing its gamut
in true nature and in things called civilized. The poet's task would
consist in purifying his sensations of small passing rhythms—
anger, jealousy, pleasure, etc—that usually form the background
of little elegiacs; his task consists in purging his mind of the
idea of love as a necessary game, necessary at least to the exigen-
cies of life and the inclinations and vitality of man. He studies
love in its essential phase. It may be, as in "The Raven," its
most definitive and complete aspect—sorrow for the final loss
of a beloved woman; it may be in the new form that the woman
takes in the mind of the lover (Ulalume); it may be in the suggestion emanating from a landscape whose melancholy, uniting
with the immanent memory, imposes a more bitter mourning for
the lost one and causes a physical, cardiac anguish.

Two of these poems, "The Haunted Palace" and "The
Worm," are found set like jewels in the tales "The House of
Usher" and "Ligeia"; let us see how poetry is used as a facet
in a narrative.

We consider "The House of Usher" to be the dramatization of an internal psychic fact personal to Poe. In a setting saturated with gloomy and sulphurous sadness—a castle split by an imperceptible crevice, like a soul fallen into profound, contagious mourning, walled inside its existence of abnormal dreams—the visitor meets a very old friend whom he scarcely recognizes and whose inner phenomena he portrays (perception of silence and of consciousness) as of a second self; that creature who is both similar to the visitor and very different from him dwells in a chateau whose walls are ornamented with designs familiar to the visitor but a little altered by the strangeness of the circumstances, or perhaps by the rarity of the experience. A woman passes—tall, superhuman, MUTE—and one does not see her again. The soul that is incorporated into the soul of the visitor and evoked by the situation of the chateau, the atmosphere and the passing of the woman—that soul delimited by extraordinary, ecstatic faculties of perception and the genius for bizarre perversions of known musical themes—must be made to live completely and, so to speak, move. Here Poe places the poem "The Haunted Palace," making it the symbol of the exact state of that superior soul, formerly ruled by a noble, untroubled conscience, now the prey of a horde of evil impressions risings to the surface in futile pleasures. Then the memory of the woman imposes itself upon that haunted soul, upon some contemplation, some trifling book: the woman too soon walled up comes to die again on the lover's breast, and everything crumbles, and will crumble many times. The exact function here of "The Haunted Palace" is to make Poe's principal idea concrete and subtle: he makes it concrete by presenting it as a symbol, simpler and easier to recognize, since the introduction of these stanzas is a hint to the reader who has learned from tradition that lyricism is the translation of essential truths; he makes it subtle in that the truth of the narrative, the allegory and the complex symbol bearing the guise of an event is presented in this brief poem shorn of the laborious preparations in which truth is first revealed. I use the word truth here, after having previously said that Poe really excluded all that had the appearance of a didactic demonstration of truth, as well as all that might be the dry development of a scientific principle in which his contemporaries expected to find the truth. He used the term in a relative sense, as he did that of length, when he banished long poems and rightly said that *Paradise Lost* could not be read except in fragments. It is useless to construct long epics which the human brain cannot appreciate, for the effort made to absorb them blunts the mind after a few lines. But this term *truth* is essentially relative, and here it means didactic and instructive, for one can scarcely say that the author of *Eureka* was not sensitive to the appeal of authentic truth, even obsessed by the quest of it. If, incontestably, the poet is not concerned with making judgments on practical and social problems, or new and sound opinions on thermodynamics, at least he has to know his own personal mental truths in order to achieve what Poe meant by poetry—the elaboration of feeling in its essence, that is to say purified of the environment and the accidentals that are the cause of error. Now, to seek to isolate a sentiment from its causes of error, what is that but to pursue its exact and sincere evocation, to seek to know it in its truth? Likewise, for the morality of poetry, Poe forbade only the didactic, preaching characteristics of popular and philosophic morality; for whoever speaks truth speaks morality. The good, for the individual as for the species, consists simply in putting the momentary phases of life into logical and harmonious relation with his unchanging destination. To study these phenomena of conscience, as in "William Wilson," "The Telltale Heart," "The Man of the Crowd," "The Oblong Box," is to create a moral work. Examples taken from one of Poe's lectures, where he presents some selections from his favorite Anglo-American poets, prove it: Thomas Hood's young girl is like a social plea, but one founded on a human fact and ending in emotion; the same is true of the little poem by Willis and the ballad by Shelley which is cited as a sort of love serenade.

If we study "Ligeia," a construction analogous to that of "The House of Usher" appears; it is like a remote bazaar in a marvelous land with heavy draperies that do not hang from the walls and are not essential, heavy draperies of a precious metal on which arabesques form dissimilar interlaced patterns of monsters for the eye that sees them obliquely; sarcophagi of black granite form the corners of the room. And in that place occurs the phenomenon of the constantly recurrent presence of the unforgettable eyes of the Lady Ligeia. When the Lady Ligeia is about to die, after the circumstances of the meeting and their love have been made sufficiently enigmatic and the reader has been warned that a sum of precious, rare and extraordinary things is going to disappear, the horror increases as the poem makes the fact of disappearance so general, ordinary and human that the angels of hope can only veil their faces and lament when the ineluctable laws of destruction are fulfilled. Again, the symbol that serves as the theme for the tale "Ligeia" is made concrete and subtle.

Poe's life, if it had been longer and, thanks to an income, more homogeneous, would certainly have provided an evolution for poetry. With him, and conseqeuntly with Baudelaire, one finds what Baudelaire called felicitous moments, moments of heightened consciousness, of consciousness itself, the echo of passionate events, of consciousness accepting the influence of wayside impressions and adapting them to its momentary soul-hue—impressions stamped with pain, since these times and circumstances are such that they reduce all literature worthy of the name to being simply a pathology of passion. One finds in it a wisdom of art, wise in itself and not rich in previous models (which is the point in all poetic technique). There is neither teaching, nor bric-a-brac, nor use of unusual phrases; Poe's poems succeed in being pure poetry. But this special use of verse in the tales, which could be the beginning of a series of new forms, shows the artist to be very much preoccupied with the general tendencies of poetic rhythm. On this special point he is on the verge of discoveries that are buried. In the same way, we cannot help thinking that Baudelaire, with his poems in prose, had begun a serious revolt against the poetic uniformity of his contemporaries and their security in simple cadences to which they clung, declaring them the only good ones; in reality, they used them through lack of better cadences and through ignorance of their art, and even of their craft.

STEPHANE MALLARMÉ

"NOTES TO THE POEMS OF POE"*

Notes on the "Tombeau"

Beside the America that you and I hold in high esteem (it is, unfortunately, a country within a country), I know one forever blinded by that too-vivid light, Poe.

What can the race of the *spiritual prince of this age* (also superbly called somewhere *"one of the greatest literary heroes"*) claim against him except that he did not subjugate it, force it to admire him, and bind it to his triumph? Strange reproach, perhaps formed by human lips for the first time—yet not without point. His duty was to vanquish, for one part of genius is an ineluctable despotism. Poe had the power, as our present French admiration, which he has compelled, testifies. He was merely wrong not to be placed in the right milieu, the one that requires the poet to impose his power. The man that he was always suffered from that error of fate; and in the two phases at the extremes of his life—toward the beginning and the end—when he moistened his lips in an evil cup, who knows whether the congenital alcoholic capable of defending himself so nobly from the fatal hereditary vice whenever he lived or achieved his work did not at last welcome the illusion of liquor in order to combat the vacancy of an extraordinary destiny thwarted by circumstances. The glorious voluntary victim had early asked that same drug

---

* Taken from *Oeuvres complètes,* Pléiade ed. (Paris, 1945), pp. 228-230.

215

to give him a disease that a man can have the duty to contract, and to give him his only chance of arriving at certain required spiritual heights, which his nation confesses it cannot attain by legitimate means.

Arcana that wear such precision only in the absolute, but can nevertheless tinge the serenity of a people with subtle unease.

Thus I do not cease to wonder at the practical means these people, disturbed by so much insoluble mystery forever emanating from the bit of earth where the abandoned remains of Poe have been lying for a quarter-century, have used, in the guise of a tardy and useless tomb, to roll the immense, formless, heavy, deprecatory stone, as if to block completely the place that exhales toward heaven, like a pestilence, the just vindication of a Poet's universally banned existence.

Poe's biography has already been written in this country; the sublime tableau in the style of Delacroix, half real and half imagined, with which Baudelaire has illumined the translation of the *Tales* (that translated masterpiece of French intuition prefaces an English edition) rightly haunts our memories. The rapid notes you are going to leaf through, perhaps, treat only of occasional facts having some bearing on the conception or execution of the poems, without encroaching further on literary criticism.

However, for those who want to know the simple or monotonous existence of the man of letters that the poet really led (in a country where such a condition is above all a trade), I point out the excellent *Life of Poe* by Gill, which is rich in accurate details, and the necessary introduction to the *Tales* and *Poems* published in London—the noble Memoir placed before the first of his two English editions of the Work, durable as the work itself, by the wise and loyal critic John Ingram.

Note on Poe's preface to his poems

So few lines of poetry at such long intervals—but in which the poet affirmed his entire poetic vision—should we reduce them further? Yes, in order to give the new reader attracted by the title of these poems nothing but marvels. Thus, almost every one of the twenty poems is a unique masterpiece of its kind and produces in one of its facets glittering with strange fires, the thing that was always either flashing or translucent for Poe, pure as the diamond—poetry. Various intimate and occasional fragments with the lesser plays of fancy follow the first selections, and we entitle them (perhaps irreverently) *Romances and Sketch-Book Stanzas.*

We dared to prefer such a division of the work to the other, which was provided by the perspicacity of J. H. Ingram and indicated by Poe himself, *Poems of Manhood* and *Poems Written in Youth.* In our opinion, many of his juvenile poems take their place among the finest and fit into the places abandoned by certain pieces insufficiently striking to retain their luster in translation.

The lyric work entirely fills these pages, which are closed to narrative poems and long poems—essays of a mind before a supreme esthetic reigned with inevitable tyranny.

Note on "The Raven"

Nearly everyone has read that strange piece of prose in which Poe delights in analyzing his Raven, dismantling the poem stanza by stanza in order to explain the mysterious dread and the subtle mechanics of the imagination that seduces our spirits. The recollection of a quasi-sacrilegious examination of each effect now pursues the reader, even when he is carried along by the movement of the poem. What should we think of the article, translated under the title of *Genesis of a Poem* by Baudelaire, entitled *Philosophy of Composition* by Poe, except that it is a pure intellectual game (if one is to credit a letter recently brought to light). Here is an extract. "In discussing 'The Raven' " (writes Mrs. Suzan Achard Wirds to Mr. William Gill) "Mr. Poe assured me that the account he published of the method of composition of that work had no authenticity, and that he had not expected people to give it that character. The idea came to him, suggested by the commentaries and investigations of critics, that the poem could have been composed in that way. Consequently, he produced that account simply under the heading of ingenious experiment. It had amused and surprised him to see it so promptly accepted as a *bona fide* declaration."

Very interesting revelation when one remembers how much of our literary vitality was once, for a moment, spent in defending and attacking the very new poetic theory that had suddenly arrived from a distant America. Mistakenly, I think, for the subtle art of structure here revealed has been used in all times for the disposition of the parts in those literary forms that do not place the beauty of the word in the foreground, notably the theater. In a country that did not have a stage, properly speaking, Poe brought down, if I may so express it, his architectural and musical talents (identical in the man of genius) on lyric poetry, authentic daughter of the single inspiration. Nothing is extraordinary but the new application of procedures as old as Art. And from this special point of view is there mystification? No. What is thought, *is*: and a prodigious idea escapes the pages which, written afterward (and without foundation in fact—there it is) did not therefore become less congenial to Poe, less sincere. The idea is that all chance ought to be banished from the modern work, and if it is there it must be feigned. The eternal wing-thrust does not exclude a lucid gaze studying the space consumed by its flight. If one chooses to take a significant image from the poem, the Raven, black wanderer of wild nights, abjures his dim vagaries to alight at last in a room of beauty, sumptuously and judiciously arranged, and he resides there forever.

REMY DE GOURMONT

"MARGINALIA ON EDGAR POE AND BAUDELAIRE"*

I do not believe that the American surroundings were more hostile to Poe than the French milieu is to our contemporaries. He had enemies, but he also had literary friends and admirers; he lived with two women whom he adored, Mrs. Clemm and Virginia; he earned his living by work that seems not to have displeased him, for he took pleasure in writing articles as well as poems and stories: combative, delighting in polemics, he wants to have the last word although his insolence is ill-calculated to disarm an adversary.

They did not know his value, but they granted his relative superiority; it seems certain that his last years would have been those of a literary master if he had lived. He was destined to overshadow, even in the corroded minds of his compatriots, the reputation of Longfellow, who was cruelly treated by Poe and yet gave him justice.

In England, of course, he would have been more appreciated, for there is a public that is authentically intellectual and aristocratic, one that considers an original page a prize and knows how to show itself grateful in a pecuniary way. The Englishman pays for his pleasures.

In France, Poe would have suffered even more, perhaps. He would have been no more able to earn his living than were

---

* Taken from *Promenades littéraires* (Paris, 1904), pp. 348-382.

Baudelaire, Flaubert, Villiers, Verlaine and Mallarmé; his stories, thoroughly ideal like those of Villiers, would have been scorned by the mass of democratic readers, and no review or journal would have welcomed his violent, disdainful criticism, which suddenly stops attacking simply to discuss the most obscure problems in the expression of ideas in a style sometimes so precise as to seem a little hard.

A highly intelligent writer always judges his surroundings to be the worst of those in which he might have lived. The same contempt that Poe expressed for the Americans, Schopenhauer felt for the Germans, Carlyle for the English, Leopardi for the Italians, Flaubert for the French. Some know that all human flocks are alike: they do not long to graze in other meadows, for the grass everywhere is poisoned by the wickedness of man.

2

There is not always a logical relationship between the life of a writer and his work. Life goes by like the water of a swift stream, or a weary river, or a gay brook, and the flowers and works that grow on the banks have their own nature: the rivulet may be ornamented with the proudest iris and the rushing stream by the most insipid little flowers; the river flows through a monotony of grass. A tragic work does not imply a tormented life; the literature of revolutionary eras is often like the baaing of sheep; people try to explain Milton by examining Cromwell; Florian's fables appeared in 1793.

Poe's life contains nothing extraordinary. It was the life of a man of letters who was successively contributor to magazines and their editor. He divided his life wisely, as others have done; the great poet was also an active professional writer who often descended to pedantry because of an inborn need to preach to his contemporaries. It is absurd to represent Poe as an unhealthy dreamer; he was educated to the point of erudition, and his shrewd, precise intelligence had something of the quality Pascal called the spirit of geometry. We can assume that he was perfectly conscious of his fate and his genius.

3

Poe's family was of Irish origin. Can that and the stay in Baltimore explain the aura of Catholicism that surrounds his work? Sometimes he speaks like Tertullian and sometimes like Joseph de Maistre. He loves rules, he thinks he submits to rules —he whose eccentricity is so particular.

4

He resembled his mother enormously; it is the same face, one feminine, the other masculine; besides, something tomboyish in the attitude of the actress adds to the illusion. She could not have had more than a purely physical influence on him, for he lost her when he was two; his father was already dead. The eccentricity of Poe developed all the more freely because it was not hobbled by any loving authority. Many children who are too well brought up, too much loved and sheltered, model their young minds on those of their parents, thus receiving impressions so profound that they determine their mental activity forever and usually annul it. How many mediocre parents have crushed their children in this way!

5

Poe's life bears no traces of great friendships with men, but of deep affections for women: Mrs. Clemm, Frances Osgood. Moreover, he has no prejudice against women; in his criticism he never makes preliminary distinctions between the literature of men and of women. He sincerely admired Frances Osgood. Although he loved the society of women, their conversation, their wit, he never seems to have required more; the chastity of his writing was that of his life—a very rare harmony, for we know that there is a very unreliable relationship between men and their works. *Lasciva est nobis pagina* writes Ausonius to Paulin, sending him the Nuptial Centos, *vita proba,* and he cites all the authors of antiquity *quibus severa vita fuit et laeta materia.*

6

The contrast here between Poe and Baudelaire is very great, even though they are intelligences of the same type. An unpublished preface to the *Fleurs du mal* summarizes his esthetic:

> His reverend Vice displayed in silk
> And his laughable virtue—
> For I have taken the quintessence of each thing:
> You gave me filth and I have made gold of it.

Baudelaire scorns civilized woman because she is too uncivilized, too natural, too instinctual: "A woman is hungry and she wants to eat; thirsty, and she wants to drink. She is in heat, and she wants to be kissed: a fine attainment!" (My Heart Laid Bare) He treats her as an inferior because in demonstrations of love she never separates soul from body, sentiment from sensation. Indeed, one can see a weakness there, but on the day when women, like men, acquire the power of separating sentiment from sensation, they will have become creatures so different from the ones we know that they will need another name. It is also true that this is the price of their freedom; it is perhaps too dear.

7

Nowhere does Poe express his opinions on the masses.

The laboring proletariat did not exist in his time in the United States, any more than it existed in Europe at the time when there was free land; he saw no revolution.

For then is the time when one really sees the people, when they leave their lairs and come to get themselves killed for the profit of a handful of scoundrels. Baudelaire did not scorn the political role of rogues; he found honest folk too timid: "Only the rogues are sufficiently convinced to succeed." He extended the word's meaning rather far, even applying it to the serious bourgeois who is full of aphorisms: "A cold character, reasonable and common; constantly speaking of nothing but virtue and economy, he freely associates the two ideas; his intelligence is Franklin's kind. He is a rogue *à la Franklin*." (Sketch for The End of Don Juan) This hasty judgment is not without elegance.

8

Naturally, Poe defends poets. He declares that they are irritable because they have a very sharp perception of the beautiful and, as a result, of the ugly, of the true, the false, the just and unjust. Anyone who is not irritable is not a poet. It is his own defense, for he was highly irritable; several of his literary judgments are so biting as to be cruel. Baudelaire has another way of defending poetry and poets: "Rabble. By rabble I mean those who know nothing about poetry." (Letter to Jules Janin)

10

Edgar Poe deceives us less by the logical appearance of his deductions than by his assertive, absolute language; he has a way of taking hold of the reader with a tone of contemptuous domination against which one has no defense. So it is with the beginning, the first six pages of the "Manuscript Found in a Bottle," which are sober, strong, clear, exact, compelling, comminatory: having taken hold of us, he leads us like slaves to ironic annihilation in his conclusion, and we willingly disappear into the mythic abyss of the Ocean River.

11

Once, while reading *Prometheus Bound,* I had the same sensation as when reading a story by Poe, "The Fall of the House of Usher." No other poet since the Greeks has had the sense of fatality, of tragic necessity.

12

A situation like that of "The Pit and the Pendulum" combines the senseless and the complicated in a way that is stupefying. As an "inquisitorial" story, "The Torture by Hope" of Villiers de l'Isle-Adam moves and impresses very differently. Imagine Edgar Poe reading that story and being forced to recognize the superiority of idealistic over mechanistic fiction. I have never heard Villiers speak of Poe; he freely cites Swift, who also had a great influence on him.

13

Rue Morgue: Poe also overuses analytic devices, constructions like labyrinths, where he strolls insolently with an invisible thread in his hand. In such stories the deductive powers of the author are apparent; the carafe of M. Mace—any detective story —is really superior to the cold figuring of a Dupin. Yet the effect produced is very strong. Even when one finds the secret of such fantasies, he is again the dupe if he rereads the story. That is because in a story like "The Purloined Letter" the thesis is a sound psychological observation: truth does not always lies at the bottom of a well. Some secrets walk abroad and no one knows it. In order to see the surface of things, perhaps a special talent is necessary. Nevertheless, on the surface of the water one finds the scum, and everything that rises is swollen with the gas of putrefaction.

14

Even when impassioned and despairing, Edgar Poe's poetry has an ironic coldness. There is too much of the well chosen and willed (less than he tried to make us believe) in the expression of his anguish and his dreams. Besides, in spite of what Baudelaire said, he never achieved his poetic ideal, which was the oratorical line, freely moving, limpid, fiery—Tennyson's line; it is true that he says just the opposite elsewhere, and affirms that poetry should be the work of will and precision: although he repeated himself a great deal, Poe also contradicted himself a great deal.

15

It is difficult to accept the sincerity, even purely literary sincerity, of the strange sentiment expressed in the lines:
I stand amid the roar. . . .
The poet gathers a handful of sand and weeps at not being able to save even a grain of it from the wave's fury:
O God! Can I not save
One from the pitiless wave?
But that futile and ridiculous incident is the point of departure for an obscure and profound revery: it is the entire world that goes away with the devouring wave, with our joys, our lives, our dreams.

16

Poe is the most subjective of the subjective poets. He himself feels and suffers the terrors which he prides himself on creating coldly. Fear, and pain which engenders fear—these are almost the only themes of his poems, as well as of the stories that are finest and closest to his real genius. But only in the poems does he consent to reveal the feelings of deep tenderness that troubled and bewitched his life. He writes his stories for everyone; he writes his poetry for himself and some feminine hearts. The stories are only half of Edgar Poe, but the poems reveal him completely.

17

Some people have believed that the true Edgar Poe was the
Poe of hypnotism, phantasmagoria, perversity, mystification. I do
not think so. That man is the Poe who was resentful toward the
democratic masses, towards ignorant journalism, and who, instead of flying into a passion about it, derided it. But when
Edgar Poe mocks, he rises to such heights that his mockery
seems a charitable lesson; and the very people to whom he fruitlessly describes the absurd and the incomprehensible let themselves be mystified for the joy of taking part in masterful and
perfect games.

18

Of all his mystifications, the "Genesis of a Poem" is the one
that has been accepted most willingly and believed the longest.
Baudelaire, who miraculously entered Poe's mind and even
shared his manias, did not want to seem to question such positive statements. As for the ordinary reader, he was flattered to
learn, from the poet himself, that poetry is only a deliberate combination of sounds carefully selected beforehand like the little
squares of glass used by artists in mosaic. It is obvious that Poe
amused himself enormously in writing his paradox: that is
enough to make it legitimate. This paradox is in no way the
revelation of Poe's method of work. His method, like all others,
will remain forever unknown to us. We scarcely understand how
we ourselves work, how our ideas came to us, how we carry them
out; if we understood too well, we would no longer be able to
work at all. Those are questions that a writer ought to avoid
exploring. Besides, it is extremely dangerous to think too much
about one's acts or life: the *"Know Thyself"* is perhaps the most
harmful nonsense ever uttered.

19

Poe's system, in "The Raven," presupposes that a poet can
imagine successively and in a short period of time all possible
combinations of all the words that could be gathered around an
idea. That is to say that it presupposes the absurd, since the
principle of all verbal composition is the principle of association
of ideas, images, sounds—association and linking. Now, one
moves here in an infinite which is relative, to say the least; the

direction of the will can be exercised only on the immediate, the known—on the senses, the ideas and images that evolve in the order of consciousness. The will cannot evoke, and the consciousness cannot know, what moves outside the present activities of the intelligence. In composition, then, an immense part is played by the unexpected. If a poet imagined that he constructed a poem rationally and deliberately, he would be the dupe of a psychological illusion. In short, one can choose an image in his mind only if the image rises, like a star, over the horizon of consciousness. We know nothing of how it rose and how it has become visible; that takes place in the impenetrable night of the subconscious.

20

Baudelaire has some theories on versification that strongly resemble Poe's; they are his own, but the reading of the "Philosophy of Composition" and the "Rationale of Verse" influenced them later. "If it were necessary," he says somewhere, "I would have little difficulty in defending the kind of dogmatism I favor in versification." And he continues speaking of the mathematical laws of verse, saying: "the poetic phrase can imitate the horizontal line, the straight ascending line, the straight descending line; it can follow a spiral, describe a parabola or a zigzag making a series of superposed angles." With Baudelaire, one never knows where irony begins, and that exasperates common men. He had a great deal more ingenuity than is ordinarily believed. "He boasted more than once," says Charles Asselineau, "of holding a school of poetry and making any comer capable, in twenty-five lessons, of writing epic or lyric verse correctly. Moreover, he claimed that there are methods for becoming original and that genius is a matter of apprenticeship. These are errors of a superior mind that judges the world by its own power and imagines that what succeeds for him will succeed for everyone." That applies also to Edgar Poe.

21

What would Poe have thought of these sarcastic remarks of Baudelaire's: "You are a happy man. I pity you for being happy so easily. A man must fall far in order to believe himself happy!" (Letter to Jules Janin)

Poe would not have written that, but perhaps he would have understood—although with horror. It was in 1847, or perhaps 1846, that Baudelaire became acquainted with some of the tales of Poe, who was not to die until 1849. Now, in spite of the "strange disturbance" he experienced in reading them (letter to Armand Fraisse), he seems not to have thought of writing to the author. Nor does it appear that Poe was informed of Baudelaire's first translations, published in 1848.

22

Another aphorism that would have outraged Poe:
"Love is the taste for prostitution." (Fusées)
But that brutal defamatory word is transformed into a philosophic notion by Baudelaire's commentaries:
"There is not even a noble pleasure that cannot be traced to prostitution.
"At the theatre, at a ball, each person enjoys everyone.
"What is art? Prostitution."
And in *My Heart Laid Bare*:
"The most prostituted being is the being par excellence, God."
Baudelaire seems to connect this idea of prostitution with the "pleasure of being in crowds." Poe, in writing "The Man of the Crowd," has his point of departure in a totally different idea, less original, certainly, and less philosophic.

23

Villiers de l'Isle-Adam avidly followed all mechanical progress, as any of his tales, especially *The Future Eve,* will attest.
But progress did not befuddle him: he used it, and with a rather disrespectful irony. Edgar Poe's attitude was quite similar.
His way of mocking progress was to overreach it by his imagination. Likewise, Villiers in *The Future Eve*. Baudelaire, who was not interested in mechanics, says: "What more absurd than Progress, since man—as proved by daily events—is always like and equal to man—that is, always in the savage state! What are the perils of the forest and the plains when compared with the everyday shocks and conflicts of civilization? Whether man embraces his dupe on the street or downs his victim in unknown

forests is he not eternal man, that is to say, the most perfect beast of prey?" (Fusées)

Baudelaire, who has none of the talents of the novelist or the stage director, immediately gives his ideas a philosophic twist.

24

Baudelaire is evil, demoniac—knows it, enjoys it, is afraid of himself. Poe, weak, sad and ill, has horror of himself; but he also has pity.

25

Even more than Poe, Baudelaire has ideas one could write books on: "Superstition is the reservoir of all truths." (My Heart Laid Bare)

26

This maxim is from the Baudelaire of the last years; it would have made Poe shiver and one could cite it with impunity as Nietzsche's: "Before all else, to be a great man and a saint for oneself." (My Heart Laid Bare)

With so many resemblances, what a lot of differences between the author of "Ulalume" and the man who wrote, concerning the *Fleurs du mal:*

"Must one tell even you, who have not guessed any more than the others that in this atrocious book I put all my heart, all my tenderness, all my (travestied) religion, all my hate? It is true that I will write the contrary, I will swear that it is a book of pure art, full of antics and trickery; and I will lie like a puller of teeth." He says in a discarded preface for the *Fleurs du mal:* "This book was not written for my wives, my daughters or my sisters, nor for the wives, daughters or sisters of my neighbor. I leave that to those who have an interest in confusing good actions with fine language." Edgar Poe would not have confused "good actions with fine language," but he would have said that differently.

27

While Baudelaire improved by his oratorical taste the rather dry prose of Edgar Poe, he also muddled it. In his admirable translation there are some sentences in which the idea seems to have been betrayed for the sake of form. Is that bad? Perhaps, but poets do a good many other wrongs, and rime plays the tyrant more than the prose writer's cadence does. Sense of cadence in prose has nothing in common with the sense of music; it is a completely physiological sense. One unconsciously makes rhythm of his sensations, like cries of joy or pain prolonged. And thus everything gains nuance and suits itself to the thought better in prose than in verse. As a tool, prose is more complicated and at the same time more supple, but goes astray so easily!

29

Eureka is a sort of philosophic poem in prose in which strange, obscure, entirely personal pantheistic ideas are expressed: "What we call universe is merely the natural expansion of being." "Some day, after a thousand evolutions, our individual consciousness will become dimmed; our divine consciousness will increase; we will really feel our identity with Being, and an absolute One will be recreated from all the unified consciousnesses, a One disturbed from the beginning of the ages by the existence of individuals." The philosophy of the *Tales* is completely psychological. It is pessimistic; it admits original sin, the natural perversity of man: "The assurance of the wrong or error of any action is often the one unconquerable force that impels us to its prosecution." Such ideas attracted Baudelaire, who, stunned, refound himself in them. Poe's pessimism is the bitterest and the haughtiest. "If I were awake I should like to die. But now it is no matter. The mesmeric condition is so near to death as to content me." (Mesmeric Revelation)

Says Shakespeare in King John:

> Death! Death! O amiable lovely death!
> Thou odoriferous stench!

Poe also cherishes death:

> My love, she sleeps! O may her sleep,
> As it is lasting, so be deep!
> Soft may the worms about her creep!

30

In "The Case of M Bedloe," ["A Tale of the Ragged Mountains"] he almost defines what is now meant by suggestion—one will abolishing another, at least for one series of events, and only permitting the existence of an unconscious intelligence at the mercy of external influence.

31

The circumstances of Edgar Poe's death have never been clarified. His destiny was like Gerard de Nerval's in this sense, for no one has ever been able to do anything but guess about them. On this point, and on still another, they are alike, for weren't they both mad—mad with a marvelous and fertile madness, but mad? Poe, at least, was tainted by a strange mental malady, a paralysis of the will. He had a horror of alcohol, and he drank. He, who had called down the most terrible anathemas, he who had praised temperance, could no longer work except in a drunken hallucination: "One does not go at all too far," he writes in his Marginalia, "when one declares that the movement for temperance is the most important in the world. Indeed, temperance increases man's capacity for wholesome enjoyment. The temperate man has in himself under all circumstances the true, the only, condition of happiness." And he adds that man must be forced to it by physical fears, for hygienic reasons; moral concern is superfluous. As for himself, nothing stopped him, and, knowing Poe's high intelligence, one does not doubt for a moment that he foresaw the frightful consequences of his habit of drunkenness; he foresaw them and persisted. Nothing could better characterize a disorder of the will.

Edgar Poe, who had gone further into morbid psychology than any other writer of his time, was thoroughly acquainted with this weakening of will-power, or its deviations. He studies it under the name of *the spirit of perversity* when he shows us a man doing evil for the sake of evil, without pleasure, without self-interest and with terror, but dominated by a mysterious force. The story of "The Black Cat" is his own story, with only an identical denouement lacking. If he did not push the spirit of perversity as far as uselessly torturing another, was he not, in an even more refined perversity, the executioner of his own health, intelligence and genius?

33

Eugene Sue, Gaboriau, Dostoievsky in *Crime and Punishment,* have taken lessons from Edgar Poe. All these inventive policemen, these analytic prosecutors, are successors of Dupin.

34

A very aristocratic mind, only prizing certain superior faculties (his own—those that he possessed or thought he possessed to a high degree), Poe readily expressed his contempt for domestic humanity by means of mystification. "The Balloon Hoax," "The Case of M Valdemar," "The Adventures of Hans Pfaall" were simply prodigious practical jokes, *hoaxes,* as the Americans say. And how they succeeded, not only in ignorant America, but in Europe! In the article on Magnetism, in the *Dictionary of Popular Superstitions* by the Abbé Migne, one reads this: "We cannot leave this question of animal magnetism without making known to our readers an extraordinary, perhaps even incredible, occurrence about which the scholarly world has spoken a great deal." And he translates "The Case of M Valdemar."

35

In August, 1835, Poe had begun to publish the story of Hans Pfall in the *Southern Literary Messenger,* and it excited a great deal of curiosity; but the following month the New York *Sun* printed the famous Moon Hoax, whose notoriety halted the success of "Hans Pfall." It was the recital of the discoveries of the astronomer Herschel: the moon was inhabited. Ten years later, when no one was thinking about that "hoax," the same *Sun* published an article with this lead in big headlines:

Amazing News by Express Via Norfolk!

THE ATLANTIC CROSSED IN 3 DAYS!

Triumph of the Flying Machine of

Mr. Monck Mason!!!

Arrival on Sullivan's Island, near Charleston, S.C. of Mr. Mason, Mr. Robert Holland, Mr. Harrison Ainsworth, and 4 other persons debarked from the balloon *Victoria,* after a voyage of 65 hours from Europe to America.

It is Edgar Poe's story known as "The Balloon Hoax." This time the success was enormous. Poe himself has told of his amusement at seeing the fools snatch the newspaper that carried the news from one another. He had had his revenge. However, "Hans

Pfall" remains unfinished, for the author of the "Moon Hoax" gave his story the very ending that Poe had imagined. That writer who had the good luck to beat Edgar Poe once—not in the best genre, it's true—was named Richard Alton Locke and was a descendant of the famous philosopher.

*   *   *   *

The "Moon at One Meter" of the World Exposition of 1900 is a real moon hoax whose success with the credulous public at least had the result of permitting the construction of a telescope of unusual size. Edgar Poe would not willingly have participated in a utilitarian mystification. His hoaxes are entertainments and psychological experiments. However, one discovers in them traces of the peculiarly American taste for notoriety, billboards, barbarous publicity, extravagant journalism. Poe is a much more representative American than Emerson or Walt Whitman. His mind has some practical tendencies. Deprived of literature, he would have been an amazing businessman, or a promoter of the first order. One likes that in the author of "Ligeia," as one likes the paradoxical industrialist in the author of *Ursule Mirouet*. Baudelaire, who went on placing his faith in Edgar Poe, carefully disguised that part of his character.

36

I believe the best characterization of him would be this one: a great critical mind. Here, we are far from the judgment of a little popular dictionary: "American poet with a disordered imagination." That would be very appropriate for Baudelaire as well, and perhaps also for all the great writers, for a Chateaubriand as for a Goethe, for a Dante as for a Flaubert. Nothing is more absurd than to oppose the creative spirit to the critical spirit. Without the critical spirit, no creation is possible; there would simply be singing poets, as there are singing birds.

PAUL VALÉRY

"ON EUREKA"*

I was twenty years old and I believed in the power of
thought. I suffered strangely from being and not being. Sometimes I sensed infinite powers in myself; they collapsed in the
face of problems, and the feebleness of my real powers drove me
to desperation. I was somber, flighty, apparently pliant but hard
underneath, extreme in scorn, absolute in admiration, easy to
impress, impossible to convince. I had faith in a few ideas that
had come to me, mistaking their conformity with my being, which
had given them birth, for a sure sign of their universal value:
what presented itself so clearly to my mind seemed invincible;
what desire engenders is always clearest.

I protected these shadows of ideas like state secrets. I was
ashamed of their oddity. I was afraid they were absurd; I knew
that they were, and were not. They were futile in themselves but
potent because their singular strength gave me the confidence
I had. Vigilance of this frail mystery filled me with a certain vigor.

I had ceased writing poetry, and scarcely read any longer.
Novels and poetry seemed no more than the special, impure and
half-unconscious applications of some of the properties of those
great secrets I believed I had found one day through the single
unyielding assurance that they must necessarily exist. As for the
philosophers, I had cultivated them little and that little only

* Taken from *Variété* (Paris, 1924), pp. 123-145.

irritated me, for they never answered any of the questions that
tormented me. They gave me nothing but boredom—never the
feeling that they communicated an authentic power. And besides, it seemed useless to speculate on abstractions one had not
first defined. But is it possible to do otherwise? The only hope,
for a philosophy, is to become impersonal. We may expect that
great step at the end of the World.

I had dipped into some mysticism. It's impossible to speak
ill of that, since we find whatever we bring to it.

At this point I happened on *Eureka.*

My schooling, under dull and sorry masters, had made me
believe that science is not love; its fruits are useful, perhaps, but
its foliage is very thorny and its bark frightfully rough. Mathematics I reserved for distressingly precise minds, incompatible
with mine.

Literature, on the other hand, had often scandalized me by
its lack of rigor, sequence and inevitability in ideas. Its object is
often trivial. Our poetry is ignorant of everything epic and tragic
in the intellect, or else is afraid of it. The few times when our
poetry has ventured into the mind it became at once dull and
unbearable. Neither Lucretius nor Dante is French; we have no
epics of knowledge. Perhaps we have such a decided feeling
about the separation of genres, that is to say, the independence
of the various movements of the mind, that we cannot endure
works that combine them. We do not know how to make song
of stuff that can do without song. But for the past hundred years,
our poetry has shown such rich resources and such a rare power
of renewal that the future may soon give us a few of those works
in the grand style and of a noble austerity—works that have
power over the sensibility and the intellect.

In a few moments *Eureka* taught me Newton's law, Laplace's
name, the hypothesis he proposed and the very existence of investigation and speculation which people never mention to ado-
lescents for fear of their becoming interested, I suppose, instead
of measuring the astonishing length of the hour in dreams and
yawns. The things that most excite the mind's appetite were in
those days relegated to the arcana. That was a time when big
heavy books on physics did not breathe a word about gravitation, or the conservation of energy or Carnot's principle; they
were fond of three-way watertaps, Magdeburg's hemisphere and
the laborious and fragile reasoning inspired by the problem of
the siphon.

Yet, would it be a waste of their school days to give young minds some slight sense of the origin, the high destination and the living quality of the dry calculations and propositions inflicted on them in no order, in fact in quite remarkable incoherence? These frigidly taught sciences were founded and developed by men who gave them passionate attention. *Eureka* made me feel something of that passion.

I confess that the enormity of the author's pretensions and ambitions and the solemn tone of his preamble—the strange discussion on method that opens the book—only partly amazed and seduced me. Nevertheless, a master-idea was declared in those first pages, although wrapped in a mystery which suggested not only a certain impotence but also a will to hold back and the enthusiastic mind's distaste for exposing its most precious discovery. . . . And none of that was likely to displease me.

To attain what he calls *truth,* Poe invokes what he calls *consistency.* It is not easy to give an exact definition of that consistency; the author, who has everything necessary to give it, has not done so.

According to him, the *truth* that he seeks can be seized only by immediate acceptance of an intuition in which the mutual dependence of the parts and the properties of the system he examines are presented in actuality, as if tangible to the mind. This mutual dependence extends to successive phases of the system; causality is symmetrical. To a gaze that embraced the entire universe, a cause and its effect would be mistaken for one another and would exchange roles.

Two remarks here. I merely point out the premise which would take us far afield, the reader and I. Finalism has an important place in Poe's theory. That doctrine is no longer in style, and I have neither the ability nor the desire to defend it. But we must agree that the notions of cause and adaptation lead to it almost inevitably (and I do not mention the immense difficulties, and thus the temptations, presented by certain facts—the existence of instincts, etc.). The simplest solution is to dismiss the problem. It can be resolved only by means of pure imagination. Let others exercise it.

Now for the other remark. In Poe's system *consistency* is both the means of discovery and the discovery itself. It is an admirable scheme: pattern and practice of the reciprocity of appropriation. The universe is constructed according to a plan

whose profound symmetry is somehow present in the inner structure of our minds. The poetic instinct should therefore lead us
blindly to the truth.

Very frequently we find similar ideas in mathematicians. It
sometimes occurs to them to consider their discoveries not as the
"creations" of their powers of synthesis, but rather as their intellectual raid on a treasury of pre-existent and natural forms which
are accessible only through a rare conjunction of rigor, sensibility
and desire.

The consequences developed in *Eureka* are not always as
exactly deduced or as clearly drawn as one might wish. There
are shadows and lacunae. There are poorly explained interfer-
ences. There is a God.

Nothing is more fascinating to the lover of intellectual
dramas and comedies than the ingenuity, the insistence, the
sleight of hand, the anxiety of the inventor in the grip of his own
invention, whose vices he knows perfectly. Naturally, he wants
to display all its beauties, exploit all its advantages and conceal
its poverty. At all costs he wants to make it correspond to what
he wills. The merchant sets off his wares. Women are transformed
before the mirror. The priest, the philosopher, the politician and,
in general, everyone who is committed to proposing dubious
things to us, always mingle sincerity with silence (to put it
gently). They do not intend us to see what they do not like to
consider. . . .

Yet Poe's fundamental idea is profound and sovereign.

It would be no exaggeration of its reach to recognize the
theory of consistency as a very precise attempt to define the universe by its *intrinsic properties*. This proposition is found in the
eighth chapter of *Eureka: Each law of nature depends at every
point on all other laws*. If this is not a formula, it is at least the
expression of a will toward generalized relativity.

Its kinship with recent concepts is revealed when we discover in this *poem* the affirmation of *symmetrical* and reciprocal
relationships among matter, time, space, gravitation and light.
I have underlined the word *symmetrical; in fact, a formal symmetry is the essential characteristic of Einstein's representation
of the universe.* Symmetry gives it the beauty it has.

But Poe does not limit himself to the physical elements of
phenomena; he includes life and consciousness in his design. How
many things come to mind here! The time has passed when

people readily made distinctions between the material and the spiritual. The entire argument depended on final knowledge of "matter," which they thought they had dispossessed and, in short, on *appearance*.

The appearance of matter is of a dead substance with *potentiality* that passes into *action* only by an exterior intervention entirely foreign to its nature. In the past, people drew invincible conclusions from this definition, but matter now has another face. Experiment has made us conceive the opposite of what pure observation made us see. All of modern physics, which has in some way created *relays* for our senses, has persuaded us that our ancient definition had no absolute or speculative value. It teaches us that matter is strangely various and indefinitely surprising; that it is a mass or collection of transformations that graduate and are lost in smallness; that perpetual motion perhaps occurs. Bodies have an eternal fever.

At this moment we no longer know what a fragment of any body whatsoever can or cannot contain or produce in a moment or in a series of events. The very idea of matter is nearly indistinguishable from that of energy. Everything deepens in motion, in rotation, in exchange, in radiation. Our very eyes, our hands, our nerves are made of it. The first appearance of death or sleep that matter presents, its passivity, its abandon to external actions, is constructed in our senses, like the darkness which is made by certain superimpositions of light.

All this can be summarized by stating that the properties of matter seem to depend only on the scale on which we observe them. But then the classic qualities—continuity or homogeneity of texture—can no longer be absolutely opposed to the concepts of life, sensibility and thought, since these simple characteristics are purely superficial. On this side of the scale—crude observation—all the old definitions miss the mark. We know that unknown properties and forces function in the *infra-world,* for we have disclosed some properties that our senses were not constructed to perceive. But we cannot enumerate them nor even assign a finite number to the growing multiplicity of the chapters on physics. We do not even know whether or not our concepts are illusory when we take them into realms bordering upon our own. To speak of iron or hydrogen is to presuppose entities whose existence and permanence are proved to us only by our very restricted and brief experience. Moreover, there is no reason to .

think that our space, our time, our causality, have any meaning whatever out there where our bodies cannot exist. And, unquestionably, the man who tries to imagine essence can do no more than adapt the ordinary categories of his mind to it. The more he advances in his research, and the more he increases his powers of categorizing, the more he departs from what one might call the *optimum* of knowledge. Determinism becomes lost in hopelessly tangled systems with millions of variables in which the mind's eye can no longer follow laws and fix upon something that lasts. When discontinuity becomes the rule, imagination, which once strove to attain the truth that perception had suspected and reason had woven, must declare itself impotent. When *means* are the object of our judgments, we give up considering facts themselves. Our knowledge tends toward power and avoids a coordinated contemplation of things. Miracles of mathematical subtility are necessary in order to restore any unity. We no longer speak of first principles, for laws are no more than constantly perfectible tools. They no longer rule the world, but have put on the infirmity of our minds. We can no longer rest in their simplicity; like a persistent pinprick, there is always some unsatisfied decimal that calls us back to unease and to the sense of the inexhaustible.

We see, by these remarks, that Poe's intuitions about the composition of the total universe—physical, moral and metaphysical—are neither validated nor invalidated by the many important discoveries made since 1847. Some of his views can even be related, without much strain, to quite recent conceptions. When Edgar Poe measures the duration of his Cosmos by the time necessary for all of the possible combinations to be completed we think of the ideas of Boltzmann and his calculation of probability applied to the kinetic theory of gases. In *Eureka* there is a foreshadowing of Carnot's principle and of the representation of this principle by the mechanism of diffusion; the author seems to have anticipated the bold spirits who snatched the universe from its fated death by means of an infinitely brief passage through an infinitely improbable state.

Since a complete analysis of *Eureka* is not my present intent, I will pass quickly over the author's use of Laplace's hypothesis. The aim of Laplace was limited: he merely proposed to reconstruct the development of the solar system. He started with the fact that a gaseous mass in the process of cooling, with a core already highly condensed, rotated on an axis passing through its center of gravity. Laplace presupposed attraction and the invariability of the laws of mechanics, and he merely undertook the task of explaining the direction of rotation of the planets and their satellites, the slight eccentricity of their orbits and the minuteness of their inclinations. Under these conditions, submitted to cooling and centrifugal force, matter flows from the poles of the mass toward the equator and is laid out along the belt where gravity and centrifugal acceleration reach an equilibrium. Thus a cloudy ring forms but must soon shatter; the fragments of that ring finally mass together in a planet.

The reader of *Eureka* will see that Edgar Poe expanded the law of gravity just as he extended Laplace's hypothesis. On mathematical foundations he has constructed an abstract poem that is one of the rare modern specimens of a total explanation of material and spiritual nature—a *cosmogony*.

One of the most ancient genres that exists, cosmogony is a remarkably persistent and astonishingly various literary type. One might say that the world is scarcely older than the art of making the world. Through each Genesis—whether taken from India, China, or Chaldea, whether it belong to Greece, or to Moses, or to Mr. Svante Arrhenius—with a little more information and a lot more wit, we might be able to take some measure of the simplicity of the minds of each epoch. One would undoubtedly find that the naiveté of the design is unchanging, but we would have to admit that the art varies a great deal.

As tragedy impinges on history and psychology, so the literary form cosmogony touches on religion with which it is sometimes confused and on science, from which it differs, necessarily, because of the lack of verification. It includes sacred books, admirable poems, exceedingly strange tales full of beauty and nonsense, and physico-mathematical research sometimes profound enough to deserve a less significant subject than the universe. But man's glory is to be able to expend himself in the void; and it is more than his glory. Senseless search is akin to unexpected discovery. The role of the nonexistent exists. The function of the imaginary is real, and pure logic teaches us that *the false implies the true*. It seems, then, that the history of the mind can be summed up in these terms: *it is absurd in what it seeks; it is great in what it finds*.

The problem of the totality of things, and that of the source of totality, arise from the most ingenuous intention. We want to see what could have preceded light; or rather, we try to see whether a particular combination of facts could not precede all of the facts and could not engender the system that is their source (the world) and their authors (ourselves).

Then we may believe we hear an infinitely imperious Voice interrupt eternity, its first cry propagating extension, like a novel that is progressively more momentous as it flashes to the limits of creative will; we hear the Word open the way to essence, to life, to liberty, to the fatal contest of laws, of intelligence and of chance. Or we may find it a little easier (if we hesitate to cast ourselves from pure nothingness into any state imaginable) to consider the very first age of the world through the obscure idea of a mixture of matter and energy, making up a sort of substantial but neutral and impotent slime, which waited indefinitely for the act of a demiurge. Or, finally, better armed and more profound but no less troubled by marvels, we may struggle to reconstruct (by means of all the sciences) the most ancient possible form for the system that is the object of science. Yet an idea about the origin of things is never anything but a meditation on their present disposition, a way of degenerating the real, a variation on what is.

What must we have, in fact, in order to think about the origin?

If we must have the idea of a nothingness, the idea of nothingness is nothing, or rather, it is already some thing: it is a deception of the mind that plays a comedy for itself, a comedy of silence and perfect darkness in which I know I am hiding, ready to believe by merely loosening my attention. I know that I am there and have volition, and am indispensable in order to maintain, by a conscious act, the apparent nullity and the fragile absence of all images. But there is image and there is act: by a temporary convention, I call myself *nothingness*.

And if in the beginning I posit the idea of disorder pushed to extremity even in the smallest parts of what was, I perceive at once that this inconceivable chaos is arranged according to my conceptual design. I have jumbled the cards myself so that I can put them in order. Moreover, it would be a masterpiece of art and logic to define a disorder so subtle that no slight trace of order could be found, and then to substitute a more essential and refined chaos. A truly primal confusion must be infinite confu-

sion. But then we could no longer extract the world from it, and
the very perfection of the jumble would forbid us ever to avail
ourselves of it.

As for the idea of a beginning—I mean an absolute beginning—it is necessarily a myth. Every beginning is a coincidence;
here we would have to imagine some kind of contact between
everything and nothing. When we try to think of it, we find that
every beginning is a result—every beginning *completes* something.

But mainly we need the idea of this Totality we call *universe,*
which we want to see commencing. Even before the question of
its origin disquiets us, we must discover whether this concept,
which seems to force itself upon us simply and inevitably, will
not disintegrate under our scrutiny.

Vaguely, we think that the *All* is *some thing,* and, imagining
something, we call it the *All.* We believe that this All has begun
as all things begin, and that the beginning of the whole, which
must have been much stranger and more solemn than that of its
parts, must be infinitely more important to know. We make an
idol of the totality and its origin, and we cannot keep ourselves
from inferring the reality of a certain body of nature whose unity
corresponds to our own unity, which we feel sure of.

That is the primitive form, the childish form, of our idea of
the universe.

We must look more closely and ask whether this very natural—that is, very impure—notion can function in any reasoning
that is not illusory.

I will observe my own process of thought.

A universe is first presented to me by the mass of things
that I see. My eyes take my vision from place to place and find
impressions everywhere. My vision stimulates the mobility of my
eyes to expand it, broaden it, deepen it endlessly. No movement
of these eyes meets a region of invisibility; none fails to produce
colored effects. And by the grouping of these movements which
link and prolong one another, and absorb or echo one another, I
am imprisoned in my faculty of perception. All my diverse views
are composed in my impelling consciousness.

I acquire the general and constant impression of a sphere of
simultaneity that is attached to my presence. It moves with me,
its content is indefinitely variable, but it retains its plenitude
because of all the substitutions that it can undergo. I may change

place, or the objects surrounding me may alter, but the unity of
my entire representation, the property it has of enclosing me, is
not spoiled. In vain I run away or turn this way and that—I am
always enveloped by all the *seeing-movements* of my body, which
are transposed into one another and lead me relentlessly to the
same central situation.

Thus I see an *all*. I say that it is an All because in some
way it exhausts my capacity to see. I can see nothing except in
this single way and in the combination that surrounds me. All my
other sensations are referred to some place in that circle whose
center thinks and speaks.

That is my first Universe. The peculiar characteristics of
knowledge through the eyes seem to me so essential to *my own*
construction of a full and complete domain that I do not know
whether a man born blind could have as precise and immediate
an idea of the sum of all things. Sight somehow assumes the
function of simultaneity, that is, of unity as such.

But that unity is necessarily composed of what I can see in
an instant. I decipher the combination of mutual relationships of
forms or spots, and give them the qualities of depth, matter,
movement and occurrence; I study them and find what attracts
me and what disturbs me. And that unity gives me the first idea,
the model, the seed as it were, of the total universe that I think
exists around my sensations, masked and revealed by them. I un-
falteringly imagine that an immense hidden system supports, penetrates, nourishes and reabsorbs each actual, perceptible element
of my duration—the haste to be and to unriddle myself. I imagine
then that each moment is a knot of an infinity of roots descending
to unknown depths in an *implicit* extension—into the past—into
the secret structure of this thinking and plotting machine of ours,
which returns constantly to the *present*. The present, considered
as a permanent relationship among all the mutations that touch
me, makes me think of a solid to which my sensitive life is attached, like a sea-anemone to its shingle. On that rock, how am I
to build such a vast edifice that nothing could exist outside of it?
How am I to pass from my restricted, instantaneous universe to
the complete and absolute universe?

Now it is a question of a real seed conceiving a form that
will satisfy two essential requirements: one, to admit everything,
to be capable of everything and to form an image of everything;
the other, to be able to serve our intelligence, to lend ourselves

to our reasoning and to become more aware of our condition
and have more self-mastery.

But we have only to bring together these two requirements
for knowledge in order to suddenly awaken the insurmountable
difficulties inherent in the slightest attempt to give a usable definition of the Universe.

Universe, then, is only a mythological expression. The movements of our thought around that noun are perfectly irregular
and entirely independent. Scarcely out of the moment, scarcely
having tried to increase and extend our presence outside of the
self, we exhaust ourselves in our liberty. All the disorder of our
knowledge and our potentiality encircles us. Memory, the possible, the imaginable, the calculable—all the combinations of
our minds, in all degrees of probability, in all states of precision,
besiege us. How can one have a concept of that which resists
nothing, rejects nothing and resembles nothing? If it resembled
anything, it would not be everything. If it resembled nothing. . . .
And if that totality has the same power our minds have, our
minds have no hold over it. All the objections that arise against
the infinite in action, all the difficulties that one finds when he
wants to set multiplicity in order, become manifest. No proposition is big enough for this *subject* of such disorderly richness
unless the *predicate* fits it. As the universe escapes intuition, so
it transcends logic.

And as for its origin—IN THE BEGINNING WAS THE
MYTH. So it will always be.

BIOGRAPHICAL NOTES

Paul-Emile Daurand Forgues (1813–1883)

Although trained in law, Forgues abandoned law practice for journalism beginning in 1837, when he wrote for the *Journal du Commerce* under the pseudonym of Old Nick. He was editor of several periodicals, including the *Revue des Deux Mondes* and the *Revue Britannique*. Forgues published extensively on England and on English authors.

Charles Baudelaire (1821–1867)

A major poet of the mid-nineteenth century, whose reputation depends largely on the volume of poems entitled *Fleurs du mal,* published in 1857.

Armand-Augustin-Joseph-Marie Ferrard, comte de Pontmartin (1811–1890)

A student of law, Pontmartin contributed to royalist journals at the time of the revolution of 1830. Later, he was a contributor to the *Revue des Deux Mondes* and *l'Assemblée nationale;* his *Samedis littéraires,* on which his reputation was founded, were published in the *Gazette de France.*

Eugène Delacroix (1798–1863)

A leader of the French Romantic school of painting.

Jules-Amédée Barbey d'Aurevilly (1808–1889)

A prolific journalist, novelist and short story writer. *l'Encorcelée* (1854) has been considered his masterpiece; a collection of stories entitled *les Diaboliques* (1874) was at one time

popular. Articles printed in various journals were collected in
Oeuvres et les hommes, 4 volumes (1861–1865).

Charles-Louis-Stanislas, comte de Moüy (1834–1922)

de Moüy was a diplomat and a literary man, serving in
embassies in Germany and Greece, publishing largely historical
and anecdotal works.

Armand Renaud (1836–1897)

Administrator and writer. In the Hôtel de Ville of Paris he
became head of the fine arts department of the prefecture. He
published poetry and stories, as well as studies of English poets,
for the *Revue contemporaine.*

Arthur Arnould (1833–1895)

A politician who held several posts in the government of
Paris before becoming editor of *l'Opinion nationale* and who was
exiled after the rising of 1871 (he had been elected as one of the
communist minority of the National Assembly) only to return
in 1880. His published works include popular works of history
and politics, pop novels and plays.

Joris-Karl Huysmans (1848–1907)

Huysmans is primarily known as a Naturalist-Decadent
novelist *(Là-bas, A rebours)* although his later novels *(la Cathé-
drale, l'Oblat)* are works of Christian mysticism.

Albert-Victor Samain (1858–1900)

Of a Flemish family, Samain earned his living in Paris in
business, meanwhile publishing Symbolist poetry, largely in the
Mercure de France. In book form his poems are contained in
Au jardin de l'infante, Aux flancs du vase and *le Chariot d'or.*

Gustave Kahn (1859–1936)

A member of the Symbolist group of poets, Kahn was one
of its major theoreticians. With Adam and Moréas, he founded
la Vogue and *le Symboliste,* and justified free verse in the
preface to his poems, *Palais nomades* (1887).

Stéphane Mallarmé (1842–1898)

The leader of the Symbolist movement, Mallarmé earned
his living by teaching English in lycées.

Remy de Gourmont (1858–1915)

He was associated with the Symbolist group of poets as literary critic, and is considered to have been influential in the development of the "New Criticism" of the 1940s.

Paul Valéry (1871–1945)

Mathematician-poet, Valéry was a Symbolist in youth, then abandoned poetry, only to return to it and to achieve fame with the publication of *la Jeune Parque* in 1917. Valéry's published works include extensive literary criticism and philosophic essays.